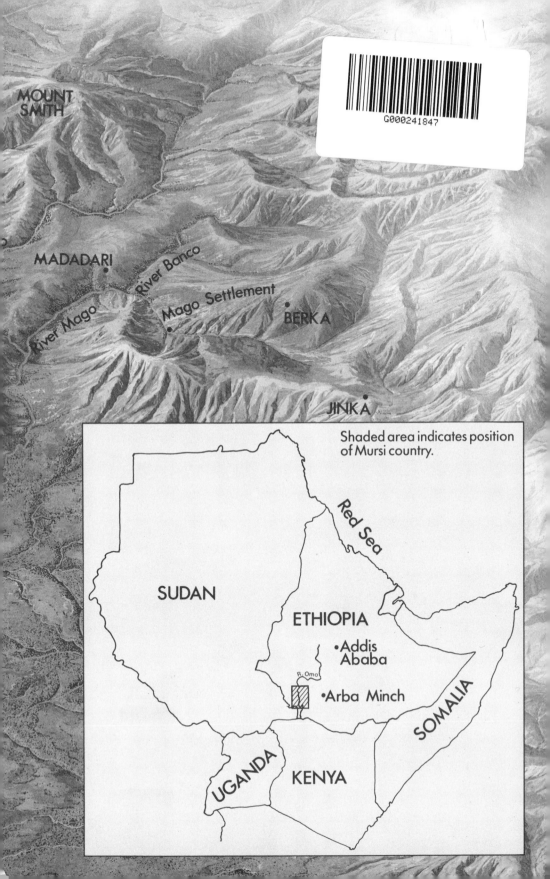

MOUNT
SMITH

MADADARI

River Banco

River Mago

Mago Settlement

BERKA

JINKA

G000241847

Shaded area indicates position
of Mursi country.

SUDAN

Red Sea

ETHIOPIA

•Addis
Ababa

R. Omo

•Arba Minch

SOMALIA

UGANDA

KENYA

A BOX FULL OF SPIRITS

A Box
Full of Spirits

ADVENTURES OF A
FILM-MAKER IN AFRICA

LESLIE WOODHEAD

HEINEMANN: LONDON

William Heinemann Ltd
10 Upper Grosvenor Street, London WIX 9PA
LONDON MELBOURNE
JOHANNESBURG AUCKLAND

First published 1987
Copyright © Leslie Woodhead 1987

British Library Cataloguing in Publication Data

Woodhead, Leslie
A box full of spirits
1. Mursi (African people)
I. Title
963'.004963   DT380.4.M8

ISBN 0-434-87788-3

Printed in Great Britain by
Butler & Tanner Ltd, Frome and London

For Yvonne who's heard it all before

ACKNOWLEDGEMENTS

Like the films it tells of, this book is anything but a solo effort. My thanks are due to a line of people as long as one of our processions of crews and porters in Mursi country.

I'd like to thank Granada Television for their support and indulgence over the decade of 'The Mursi Trilogy', and for permission to quote from the films here.

To David Turton goes my gratitude for the many hours of generous conversation over the years. The scale of my debt to his insights into the Mursi and their way of life will be obvious on every page. Any shortcomings in my understanding are of course all my own.

To the film crews and researchers who slogged every inch of the way with me go my thanks and admiration.

I'd also like to thank Andrew Robinson for his sustained encouragement, Keith Gage for the map and Tricia McKiernan, Margaret Syratt, Jane Wright and Valerie Pye for their help with the manuscript.

PROLOGUE

Going In

It had all seemed a lot simpler back in Manchester. Battering over the Plain of Death in a military helicopter, things look more confusing. Now, eyes screwed against the glare, I still can't spot the smoke signal. Dapper amid uproar, the Ethiopian captain tilts his Soviet M.I.8 over an unbroken wilderness of scorched bush. Zebras scatter in a sudden clearing.

As we level, it's there – a skein of smoke on a sky the colour of ash. We fumble the gear together and the crewman slams back the door. We're swamped with din and a blast of hot wind. The cameraman hangs in the opening, roped to a strut, filming with worrying space under him. I grab his belt, offering useless support to occupy my fright. Framed in the door, a rush of images: lurid green slopes, creased and empty; a twisting brown river; a scribble of ruined grey trees. Then, abruptly, three naked men standing in a stream. One waves.

We hover over a clearing, flattening grass and people. Shouts and frantic gesturing from the aircrew to clear a space under us. We go down gingerly on to uncertain ground. I'm back.

On 4 April 1985, I returned for a third time to the Mursi. For me, it was the climactic episode of a ten year adventure serial. In the summer of 1974, and again in early 1982, I came here to make documentary films for television.

Over the years, that simple statement has involved me in an encounter with an alternative universe. The extravagance of

I

oddities has included hundreds of miles of footslog across one of the world's more uncomfortable places, a cumulative weight loss of some five stones, blood for breakfast, crocodiles at bathtime and a vivid dose of malaria. Being with the Mursi has also become, I suppose, the most absorbing business of my life.

This is the story of those three encounters with the Mursi. It's also one addict's account of the inglorious but captivating trade of making television documentaries in strange locations, a rambling record of the barmy processes that somehow produce those seamless-seeming films that have given us all a nodding acquaintance with the Brazilian rain forest or the South Pole. Most of all, it's about the Mursi and about how, in a single decade, I've seen a people struggling to come to terms with a new world. Through those three visits, I've also seen how a complex way of life built over thousands of years, sustained by a sophisticated relationship with a harsh environment has begun to unravel under the impact of the 1980s.

The Mursi live in one of Africa's remotest places, on the far south-western edge of Ethiopia. This isn't the Ethiopia of the terrible news reports from the flayed, bare highlands. Mursi country lies in the greener lowlands, towards the borders with the Sudan and Kenya. There are around 5,000 of them, nomadic cattle-herders wandering between the mountains and the great river which, until the 1980s, held them in isolation from the outside world. The Lower Omo Valley which encloses the Mursi homelands has been claimed as the birthplace of human kind.

To this day, it remains one of the earth's few genuine wild regions. In huge spaces of arid bushland, lions and elephants and giraffes live and die unrecorded by tourist Nikons. And it's still a very tough place to get at.

Hence the helicopter. We'd chartered it at dizzying expense from the Ethiopian army in Addis Ababa. Now those hours in the shabby, friendly officers' mess, peering doubtfully at aerial photographs of the unmapped Lower Omo had come to a focus in a forest clearing a long way from anywhere.

Dazed by noise as the rotors slopped to rest, we tumbled out into a green valley. I was aware of fleshy grass, a wall of trees, steep wooded hillsides, an almost shocking extravagance of growing things. It was instantly clear why a quarter of the Mursi people had migrated from their traditional lands fifty miles away, driven by drought and hunger to a new home here in

2

the Mago valley, as they put it – 'in search of cool ground'.

Striding towards us through the grass were Mursi, tall and improbably slender. Still dislocated by the suddenness of being here, we were surrounded – naked Mursi bodies alongside our wilting new bush clothes, awkward handshakes, words and smiles and that remembered Mursi smell of smoke and earth. Unbelievably, somebody called my name and there was Komorakora, the Mursi priest and an acquaintance from 1974 and 1982. Even in this jumble, he preserved his stillness and the unwavering sense of connectedness with forces beyond the ordinary. Dozens of familiar faces pressed around and children giggled and gaped as we shifted boxes aimlessly, excited and overloaded.

Our arrival may have had the ingredients of a low budget science-fiction fantasy, but the Mursi were, as ever, effortlessly self-possessed. They remain, above all, warriors with the undented pride of a people who've never been colonised. They're arrogant and sceptical and scathingly funny. They pity us for our lack of cattle and hopeless feet. They're also ceaselessly demanding, as I recalled from earlier expeditions when we'd staggered back to Addis with little more than what we stood up in. Already, I noted as we began to unload the helicopter, claimants were eyeing up the prospects.

'I'd just about given you up for today.' Thank God, here was David Turton. For ten years, Turton had been our lifeline, the anthropologist whose obsession brought us here and who has guided and supported our little expeditions from the beginning. Turton has lived and worked with the Mursi since 1968, and though he'd never admit it, his story is an extraordinary adventure straight out of Victorian explorers' yarns. He learned the language a word at a time during a two year solitary exile, and to this day he's still the only outsider who speaks the Mursi language and has their trust. For Turton and the Mursi, the relationship remains breezily free of patronage or false sentiment. Conversations seem solidly founded in mutual abuse, shared laughter, and regular exasperation. I know that Turton cares profoundly about the Mursi. Never for a moment has he tried to own them.

It was good to see him here, in his element in shorts and canvas snake-gaiters, full of wiry competence amid the chaos of our arrival. Turton had trekked into the Mago Valley a week

3

earlier to make contact with the Mursi and to mark out a landing site for our helicopter.

After our delayed start in Addis Ababa that morning in what now felt like some previous existence, he'd almost written us off for today. Now, it was getting late, and the helicopter crew were anxious to be away, understandably edgy about the prospect of negotiating unknown mountains in the dark. 'OK, you'd better show us our base, David,' I said, as the Captain eyed his watch again. 'It's a bit of a trek I'm afraid,' was the ominous reply.

Turton led us, sweating, under the first boxes alongside the fierce little Mago river, over a dried-up stream and down a twisting track to our home for the next four weeks. The big bare clearing under a dome of trees was to become a haven at the end of unspeakable journeyings and our refuge against sun, wildlife and tempest. For now, I was mainly aware that it was a hell of a trudge from the helicopter and our imported 1,500 kilo burden of food, and tents, and film gear, and that endless list of things we thought we couldn't do without.

It was at least a crash course in learning the basic geography of the area. Half a dozen times, increasingly sweat-soaked and filthy, we hauled boxes and bags and bits between chopper and campsite. Each trip bombarded my overworked stills camera with yet more images of the helicopter squatting in the grass framed by naked Mursi leaning elegantly on duelling poles. Women stood apart, hands over mouths. Surprisingly mundane Mursi dogs snuffled around the immaculate Ethiopian aircrew, who looked very glad to be leaving.

As the light began to drain away we shouted our farewells to the outside world over the whining warm-up and then crouched in the grass with backs turned as the awesome uproar gathered towards lift-off. Mursi scattered around me, cloths flying in the dust clouds as the helicopter drilled over us. It spiralled back for one parting pass, and then was gone for a month. I registered a sharp pang of isolation as the electric uproar of the bush washed back.

On our campsite base – a vision of laughable disorder: boxes everywhere and 135 Mursi spectators. After a melting hour of wrestling with tents and trying to unscramble assembly instructions in gathering gloom, researcher David Wason and I escaped for a sluice in the Mago river. Still pallid and flabby, we tottered on the shingle to the guffaws of our Mursi audience already gathering in force to demand our soap. Hanging on to a half-submerged branch to avoid being swept away, I savoured the lukewarm brown jacuzzi and fretted distantly about crocodiles.

Back in camp, minus our first bar of soap, the darkness was beginning to hide the squalor. Vital equipment rescued from the rubble generated a cup of tea. I also managed to unearth a preposterously suburban picnic chair, its cheery blue and white stripes instantly spattered with Mago mud. It was a moment for the diary.

I'd never kept any kind of diary in my life until the first Mursi film eleven years before. I found during that extraordinary expedition the regular communion with the little black book became a precious therapy, a place of agonised confessional and private whimpering. The habit established then had blossomed into a location addiction and I now had a dozen of the tatty little volumes, the scribbled records of documentary wanderings from a Chinese commune to Hugh Hefner's games room. Amid the hopeless mess of our new home, I wrote:

'Gaga with exhaustion, slumped here as our chaotic site splutters into life. Lights crusted with mad insects, boxes everywhere in the gloom, a grotty dog nosing around. Mursi in every chair. Wason cooking, drenched with sweat, Turton making lemonade, Blakeley and Woods making bedframes, Mohammed burbling a radio, a hen I've been given fluttering on its stick and a huge haloed moon trapped in the trees. A pretty brown moth squats on our plastic table and my drying shirt seethes with insects. It all rushes back in all its absurd discomfort and joy. We can't find anything and the site rings with questions. For all the uproar, I like it here.'

There were six of us, four television castaways plus David Turton and our Ethiopian adviser, Mohammed Idris. Cameraman Mike Blakeley and sound recordist David Woods were what the union calls 'a short crew', working without their usual assistants because of the helicopter's limited payload. Blakeley had worked on our 1982 film in Mursi country and I had good reason to value his miraculous energies. I watched him now still hacking tables out of branches at the end of this huge day, then inventing a water-purifier and collapsing with Mursi visitors in gales of laughter over some shared obscenity. Woods was already doling out plasters and pills to tiny Mursi babies with worrying tropical ulcers, and fending off assorted hypochondriacs with good-humoured abuse. One tot fingered his beard with disbelief.

Researcher David Wason crouched over the smoking fire hoping to conjure something edible from one of our packets of freeze-dried dust which claimed to be 'Chicken Mexican'. I'd worked with David for years in odd places, but this was something else. He dripped into the fire and puffed hugely on his pipe to repel the squadrons of attentive flying things.

Mohammed Idris from the Ethiopian Ministry of Information and National Guidance had been with us in 1982. He was unfailingly helpful and supportive and keen to learn all he could about film. Mohammed's energy had been decisive in negotiating the vital helicopter and in steering us through the maze of permits and official sensitivity in the capital. But as he pressed his ear against our radio to try and catch the Ethiopian news in his neat leisure shirt and slacks it was clear he felt a long way from his home in Addis. A devoted Muslim, he spent the evening constructing a mosque in our storage tent and disappeared early with the prospect of dawn prayers.

A muddy Mursi dog sniffed suspiciously at the remnants of a Hilton hotel packed lunch, the last hint of that other world 300 miles away. The dog wasn't impressed and wandered off after departing Mursi. Lightning flickered noiselessly behind the trees like a warning of battle.

It was time to face the tents. I crawled into the sweltering dome in the dark to head off an invasion of insects, hastily zipping up the door and sluicing the walls with throat-clogging repellent. Wason followed and, after ejecting a huge spider, we wriggled into our sweaty sacks. By torchlight, I confided in the diary:

'11.10 p.m. – Hilarious bedtime under a dazzling high moon. Uniquely late first night chatting round the picnic table, Scotch and insects. Talking with Turton, strong film themes are hinted and possibilities emerge. It all sounds like a lot of horrifically tough walking. So here we are again in the ghastly tent, Hilton vanished over the horizon. It's hot as ever and the night boils with noise. Hopefully Mogadon will provide.'

Three and a half weeks, 150 miles of walking and 20,000 feet of film later, an odd little procession trailed through the forest alongside the clearing where our helicopter had set us down so long ago. Behind David Turton came Mike Blakeley with an object new to Mursi country on his shoulder. Arriving in a pretty glade sheltered from the glare of the afternoon sun, the column came to a halt and began to unload its novelties. On a platform of branches constructed with casual skill by a party of Mursi, Blakeley placed his burden. The television set brought to the forest clearing something of the surreal dislocation of a Magritte painting. As curious Mursi gathered to take a look at the white men's latest useless import, the rustic platform also received a video player and a bright blue car battery. The baffling ritual items were arranged on the temporary altar as more people wandered into the semicircle, propped on duelling poles or sitting on the carpet of leaves. One man sat happily in a picnic chair he seemed to have claimed. Soon, around 200 people had gathered to see television for the first time.

For a society entirely innocent of the merest notion of television, it was an occasion full of uncertainties. It was made potentially disturbing by the fact that television's newest audience were going to see themselves on the screen in the films we'd made with them on our earlier visits.

Turton had alerted us to a problem. He advised that the image of people now dead, seen to be walking and talking in our films, might be genuinely troubling for their relatives who would perhaps conclude that we had somehow made contact with the spirit world. For all the frailty of life here, the Mursi are profoundly distressed by the death of close relatives and some have to be restrained from trying to commit suicide in the nearest river. Forewarned by Turton, some people had chosen to stay away now, and we'd already lost a swaggering young warrior who felt unable to face his dead father on the screen.

For anyone who might have missed the warnings, a Mursi called Ulichagi rose to make an introduction. 'When the white man comes,' he said, 'he asks where's so and so, where's so and so? Now,' he explained pointing at the set, 'we're all in this thing, some of your dead fathers and dead children are here. You may shed tears. Do you want to see it or not?'

Murmurs of acceptance went through the audience. I pressed the 'play' button on the video and we began to retrace the Mursi's story through an extraordinary decade.

Watching those people begin that journey through their past, I was flooded with remembrance of how it had been for me. It began in the early summer of 1974.

THE FIRST EXPEDITION

June–July 1974

I

'You're breaking my plane.'

The captain's patience was beginning to fray as the morning heated up. I could see his point. For an hour now, we'd been trying to cram a protesting old Volkswagen jeep through the doorway of an even older Dakota. The fork-lift truck driver aimed his load at the opening once again, and another dent was printed on the flaking fuselage. In the black shadow under the wing, the captain fumed. Marooned on the tarmac, I had a sudden conviction that the whole venture was both crazy and doomed.

We'd been up and away before dawn, a single star blazing in the hotel window as I fumbled myself into action and worried foggily about the day. Driving out through the ramshackle suburbs of Addis Ababa, a warm wind in my face heavy with unfamiliar smells, biblical images of laden donkeys and sheeted figures plodding around us in the bronze half-light, I had a moment to take in what was happening.

It was 15 June 1974, the day when the months of talk and planning had finally become real. I'd never quite believed it, I suppose. Even after ten years of wandering the planet as a current affairs producer, filling my passport with the routine exotica of the documentary vagrant, this was something – as they used to say on television – 'completely different'. Those years of sampling strange places via the indulgence of Granada Television and the 'World in Action' series had found me waking up in some uncomfortable locations. But none of it – a Peruvian earthquake, guerrilla wars from Laos to Rhodesia, policemen in South Africa and torturers in Brazil – had prepared me for the Mursi.

The chance to become involved with something new had come at a welcome moment. The years of pursuing guilty men in Swiss blizzards or student revolutionaries in American ghettos had been vastly enjoyable, but I wasn't sure I had anything to add. I knew the style and the routines too well, and I couldn't quite bear to listen to myself going through it any more. 'Disappearing World' was something else.

In the early 1970s, my Granada colleague Brian Moser had pioneered a new kind of television documentary. His first films for 'Disappearing World' brought some of the remotest people on earth into contact with a mass television audience with an immediacy that was novel and startling. I can still remember the shock of being addressed directly by a South American Indian, disturbing in feathers and paint, talking with casual authority about his daily life in the depths of the Amazonian rain forest. It was a sudden and utterly unsentimental revelation of a different way of being alive, at the same moment unimaginably exotic and mundanely identifiable. It was difficult to watch without being forced to look again at comfortable assumptions. The chance to make that kind of film with a people in an almost uncontacted area of East Africa was for me, jaded with journalism, the offer I couldn't refuse. It felt as though it might just be one of those rare moments that usually pass before you can identify them where a swerve of life could be available. It also sounded like fun.

I wasn't the first choice for the Mursi film. A colleague had turned it down, because he discovered he'd be completely out of contact for five weeks without even a radio to summon assistance from the world. He wanted a unit doctor to join the crew. He went and did something else and I, less sensible and more restless, inherited a film about democratic decision-making amongst a remote tribe of East African cattle herders.

Stranded now at the airstrip with the obstinate jeep, the piles of survival gear, and the furious captain, all my long-suppressed doubts blossomed in the heat. Here I was, a man who'd never spent a night in a tent or walked further than the car park, blundering on the edge of five weeks in a wilderness. For the moment, however, my alarm seemed premature. It looked as though the film might never even get off the ground. I'd have to slouch back to Manchester and concede that we'd wasted thousands of pounds in discovering that we couldn't fit a jeep into a plane.

'Let's take bits off it.' The radical suggestion came from André Singer, the researcher. His blond moustache looked unusually droopy. André had hired the wretched jeep in an Addis backstreet and properly felt some responsibility. 'Why not?' I agreed, blithe with desperation. Chris Wangler said something less neutral and attacked the jeep with reassuring conviction. Christian was our sound recordist, a non-stop Canadian who grew up on a Saskatchewan farm and knew about things like tying complicated knots and dealing with troublesome jeeps. I had limitless confidence in his survival skills if we ever managed to test them. As Chris and André wrenched the mudguards off the jeep the Ethiopian aircrew watched without enthusiasm.

Pat Turton was another witness of the agony on the airstrip. While her husband David had flown ahead with our cameraman in the hope of grabbing some aerial shots of Mursi country from a light plane, Pat was stuck with us and the jeep. Having only met Pat and David for the first time the day before in our dash through an Addis hotel, I was already impressed by Pat's unstoppability. She faced the prospect of our hazardous flight and the weeks in Mursi country seven months pregnant. As an experienced nurse and veteran of Mursi discomforts, I presumed she knew what she was in for. 'David will have decided we're not coming,' she said with the resignation of the old hand.

Sitting impassively in the deepest shadow under the wing was Ulichagi. Ulichagi was a Mursi, a very long way from home. He'd been in Addis for the past month with David Turton helping with translation work. He was one of the only Mursi ever to visit the outside world, and he'd had his fill of it over the last few weeks. The unimaginable uproar of Addis, cars and buildings and crowds had been absorbed with massive aplomb. A John Wayne western had interested Ulichagi only when the cattle were on the screen. Just once he'd been impressed, when Turton took him to a cattle research station and he saw a cow which gave twenty times more milk than any of his back in Mursi country. Uneasy in a jacket and trousers borrowed from Turton, he watched our comedy with the jeep, his feelings unguessable.

I looked at my watch through a haze of sweat. Two hours

already consumed and no progress of any kind towards Mursi country. 'Whose idea was this bloody jeep anyway?' Chris muttered as he hauled the doors off their hinges. It had seemed like a good idea weeks ago in Manchester. Peering at maps and photographs of the Ethiopian bush, the jeep looked like a useful import. Matured in naivety and far-away offices, the plan was to fly the jeep in a chartered Dakota to a speck on the map called Hana, 300 miles south-west of Addis. From there we would drive forty miles through the trackless bush into Mursi country. We'd spent hours tracing through *Jane's Aircraft* to try and calculate the size of cargo doors in World War Two transport planes. Faced now with the stripped down skeleton of the jeep, still unloaded, I wondered uneasily about the quality of our logistics and about much else.

Another despairing heave, and with a jolt that registered on the captain's face, the jeep was crammed into the belly of the plane. We piled in our mountains of equipment around it at a scramble while the flight-crew lashed the thing to the floor with dodgy-looking straps. Huddling waist-deep in boxes while the jeep strained at its moorings, poised to mow down a massive fuel drum, we waited for lift off.

The 30-year-old Dakota bellowed wearily down the runway. For a very long time we remained utterly earthbound. 'Maybe we're going by road,' I offered. People smiled tightly in the gloom. Finally, with heart-stopping reluctance the protesting plane dragged itself off the tarmac. We crossed the end of the runway only feet off the ground and crawled out over scorched grasslands without gaining height. Nobody said anything and the faces across the plane matched the way I felt. Only Ulichagi seemed unconcerned by the latest evidence of our lunacy. The jeep looked gigantic now. With the piles of stuff around us, it was an alarming reminder of a cameo on the tarmac when we'd weighed everything on a rusty old scale and had been pronounced hundreds of kilos over the limit. The captain had ordered drastic surgery and then relented under a hail of important government names from André. As we wallowed along now, still only feet from the ground, engines screaming, it had the quality of a slow motion nightmare.

I'd always been fatalistic about planes, surprisingly for someone who suffers from vertigo standing on a chair. Even my worst aviation horror – bouncing across a burning landscape after the routine B52 pounding of central Laos, in a light aircraft piloted by a drunken CIA man while the headphones crackled warnings about MIG 21s in the vicinity – even that seemed cosy alongside this extended agony. I watched the patterns of brown fields and cracked river-beds unravel under us and recalled André's stories of how the Ethiopian fleet of Dakotas, cast-offs from Iran's airforce, were a dying breed, worn out by decades of slog.

With infinite effort, we began at last to gain height. The metal cooker we shared with the jeep cooled as the Ethiopian highlands opened up below us, burnt yellow and grey to the horizon. Ravenous after our reprieve, we unclenched and hunted down the dainty white picnic boxes the hotel had provided in the dawn. With the gaiety of relief, we attacked hard-boiled eggs and shouted brave jokes. 'Nobody lives in Ethiopia,' yelled André, 'they simply fail to leave. I read it some-where.' We giggled and gnawed sandwiches. His face lit by a splash of sun, Ulichagi gazed out of a window.

We moved over a vast lake, milky and unhealthy-looking. A cloud of impossibly pink flamingos scattered as our tiny shadow crossed them. Stunned by heat and noise, I drowsed and jolted awake to a prospect of green mountains, crumpled and weary. 'We must be getting close by now,' said André. 'I don't recog-nise anything,' Pat said. They both looked worried and I knew why. A couple of weeks earlier André and David Turton had survived a hair-raising hour in this area when they'd flown down in a light plane for diplomatic preparations with the regional governor. Their pilot had become totally lost over the moun-tains, scraping an emergency landing with the last drops of fuel. Now our Dakota was lumbering in a slow circle, clearly hunting for a hint of our landing strip in the featureless bush. We banked and the jeep shifted a sickening inch. Suddenly, Ulichagi smiled and pointed. 'Hana,' he said.

Bracing myself on the fraying canvas seat, I waited for the shock of landing and tried not to think about the jeep. Then we were down with hardly a jolt, taxiing in thick grass. I spotted our cameraman through a window, filming us in the dust gale of our arrival. A crewman struggled around the jeep and banged open the door. Enveloping heat and the dangerous smell of Africa rushed in on us. I slid down from the cargo door into a crowd of pretty, tattered kids, big-eyed with the novelty of it all. Greetings to David Turton and cameraman Mike Dodds and then David made a vital introduction.

'Leslie, this is Captain Cherkole. Captain, Leslie Woodhead.'

'Welcome to Hana,' the Captain growled. 'Doctor David has told me about the filming.' As we shook hands, I was aware of his barely concealed anger and prominent revolver. The complexities of this remote place, elusive as yet but tangible, soaked in with the heat. Hana has to pass for the capital of this region, the last whimper of government before the wilderness. It's a scatter of weary straw huts set on scabs of red earth, a muddy river and a handful of sullen resentful policemen longing to be somewhere else. Now they slumped in Hana, highlanders banished to the stifling lowlands among people they considered savages, incarcerated with heat and disease, barely provisioned or paid, waiting for a reprieve. The current ruler of this sad place was Captain Cherkole, big and powerful in stetson and T-shirt, his bulky chromium watch winking tetchily in the punishing afternoon sun. And, for the Captain, our arrival was just one more headache.

Hana is in the territory of the Bodi, the Mursi's closest neighbours and, like them, cattle-herding nomads. As we began to lug our huge load out of the plane, I had my first glimpse of Bodi, standing apart on the edges of the thronging kids and bewildered policemen, very tall and almost unnaturally thin. Naked except for occasional cloths thrown over a shoulder, they carried a disturbing and exciting sense of that other life we'd come to explore. I could see they also carried rifles slung across their shoulders, and through the chaos of our unloading Turton told me worrying news.

'Things have really turned nasty between the Bodi and the Mursi,' he said. 'A Mursi came up here the other day and shot a Bodi boy and now it looks like war. It's going to make filming very tricky.' 'It's a bit late to turn back,' I said, damping my alarm in hauling a box of freeze-dried mince. We'd known that relations between the Mursi and their neighbours were edgy, but this was a stunning development to be greeted with. Ulichagi had obviously heard the news too. He kept as close as possible to us as we unloaded, tense and sombre at finding himself isolated, a solitary Mursi in the heart of enemy territory. No wonder Captain Cherkole was less than welcoming. Added to his chronic uncertainties as revolution toppled Emperor Haile

Selassie back in Addis, the Captain now had a bunch of meddlesome Englishmen blundering into the middle of a shootout on his patch.

Meanwhile, there was the jeep. With the rest of our refuse scattered around in the long grass, there was no avoiding the problem we'd been worrying about for months – how to transfer the jeep the awkward four feet from the Dakota doorway to the ground with the nearest fork-lift truck 300 miles away. We did have a plan in the form of two long planks. André had located the planks with immense difficulty in Addis and we'd transported them in the plane. Faced now with the reality, it looked absurd.

The rough new planks bit into the earth, the other ends propped uncertainly on the metal sill. Sticky with effort, Chris and André and assorted policemen shoved the jeep into the doorway. Armed with a shiny new shovel from our imported toolkit, one of the aircrew dug into the bush to try and make some kind of foundation for the shaky structure. It was clearly going to be a memorable few minutes and Mike settled the camera on his shoulder. I still have that piece of film. Running it now, the scene looks even messier than I remember, bodies everywhere fumbling with the jeep, sweating faces, close-ups of straining hands hauling the front wheels on to the planks. There's no soundtrack, but the pictures are clamorous with gestures and conflicting orders. At the end of the sequence, André sits in the driving seat, peering anxiously over the bonnet at the tottering ramp and then, hair falling over his eyes, looks down to check the clearance through the doorway. Mike zooms in and the close-up reveals a leeway of about half an inch. The aircrew stand in the grass, hands on hips in disbelief. The film flashes and runs out before the climax. But in my memory, the soundtrack returns with a sickening snap – the sound of a strap breaking which was supposed to lower the jeep cautiously down the ramp. Freed of its restraint, the jeep slammed down the planks to arrive at last in Hana with a jolt that must have tested the weary suspension to its limits. Scattering policemen and children, André slewed to a stop almost lost in the grass. We greeted it with a tired cheer.

As we started to pile our stuff into the jeep and a big police lorry, the Dakota was already roaring beside us. I yelled at a crewman about coming back for us in a month and stuck a bottle of Scotch in his hand. In moments, the plane was charging away from us and lifting steeply over the scrub, freed of its awful burden.

'I have given you a good place at the river,' said Captain Cherkole and barked at his men to finish loading the lorry. The police truck looked surprisingly and reassuringly healthy, a good deal more so than our jeep which appeared disturbingly vulnerable now, dumped in the bush. So it was comforting to hear from Turton that he hoped to persuade the Captain to help ferry our load on the long trek south to the edge of Mursi country – if we provided the fuel. Ploughing through the head-high grass on the short journey to our first campsite, the punishing realities of attempting to drive through the bush were already becoming clear. I sat in the bucking cab of the lorry, focused on a purple and white butterfly fluttering inside the windscreen, while André inched ahead of us with the Captain in the jeep, almost lost to view in the undergrowth. Over the competent chug of the lorry, I could hear the jeep's engine whining in protest as it struggled to survive its first encounter with the bush.

We jolted through a tangle of trees and suddenly we were alongside a little river. Ahead of us, André stopped and we pulled in, disgorging policemen and boxes. I got down and registered wearily that we seemed to have arrived somewhere. It was harder to accept that we were ending up in a Hollywood caricature of the Dark Continent. 'It's like a set for a Tarzan film,' I said to André. The sunlit scenario of tree, creeper and river seemed to have been arranged with a production designer's relish. The river, of course, looked fittingly crocodile-infested. To complete the cliché, there was a spasm in the trees above us and a big black and white monkey swung away chattering furiously.

Back in the real world, Chris Wangler was attacking the long grass with a machete, apparently refreshed by his exertions with the jeep. Mike Dodds was beginning his first tussle with tent building. I'd worked with Mike and Chris from time to time over the past half dozen years in some unlikely spots, but we'd managed to avoid tents until now. They were a freelance film crew, one of the very best of the crop who'd flourished in the late 1960s, recording the heady days of rock n' roll and revolutionary flirtations, while finding new ways of extending the possibilities of the recently developed lightweight filming gear. They'd both done their share of documentary swashbuckling. Mike had been shot at in West Africa in '67. Chris had done a documentary stretch in Vietnam as well as recording feature films like *If*. The last time we'd been together was on Richard Nixon's back lawn with 100,000 angry students and Jane Fonda protesting about Vietnam and Cambodia. I'd left them to rush back with the film, jogging through the sweltering streets of Washington for a rendezvous with a taxi at a place I'd never heard of called The Watergate Complex. Now Mike and I pondered the assembly of a camp-bed like a Meccano puzzle. He was telling me about a recent job shooting a car battery commercial at the North Pole. Meanwhile, the Turtons, veterans of all this were doing sensible productive things with nets and sleeping-bags. All around was the litter which had seemed so essential and now represented such a burden – the eccentric boy scout inventory of windproof matches, Marmite, insect sprays and a troubling little snakebite kit all jumbled up with the hundreds of packets of freeze-dried food. Ulichagi stood amid the scattered boxes, tense and watchful, staying close to David's rather antique shotgun which was propped against a tree. Suddenly his eyes shifted in alarm. Almost soundlessly, a Bodi had arrived on our campsite, his rifle slung over his shoulder.

Registering Ulichagi's tension, David moved quickly to talk to the Bodi. The man spoke softly, composed and eloquent, moving his hands expressively. The menace subsided as I noticed he had a cigarette stuck in the barrel of his rifle. It was my first experience of a frustration that was to become a daily fact. While Turton was clearly fluent and easy in conversation, I was inevitably shut out from the flow of events until David had a moment to interpret. It was a new and dislocating experience to try and make documentary through a filter, but it was obviously inescapable. As he talked to the Bodi, I quietly confirmed with David that it might be worth filming the conversation and we slipped into our first sequence without drama. Drifting around our half-built campsite, we shot a few minutes of murmured talk about the rumours of a Mursi–Bodi war. The Bodi seemed encouragingly uninterested in our antics with camera and tape-recorder, a bonus of the certainty that he was the first person I'd ever filmed who had no notion of what we were doing or why. As we identified the shot and slammed the clapperboard, I could see David wince. His discomfort was aggravated when I asked him to get the Bodi to walk away to provide us with a continuity shot. It was a crass intrusion of unnecessary film grammar, and Turton sighed with exasperation. Leaving us to our squabble, the Bodi drifted away as quietly as he'd arrived. 'Christ!' David exploded, 'Does it have to be as artifical as that?' 'It depends whether you want a film,' I blustered. We returned to the chaos of our arrival, sour with the unresolved dispute.

From the start, the relationship with the anthropologists had been fundamental to the 'Disappearing World' films. Their passions and commitments and insights have always been the basic fuel of the series, the crucial ingredient which moves the programmes beyond the travelogue. Quite apart from a knowledge of the local language, the special understandings of anthropologists, who've often been working for years with the people we plan to film, have to be indispensable. The best of the films hold that elusive balance between the priorities of academic anthropology and peak-time television for a mass audience. But I'd heard of some memorable rows, and I could already see it wasn't going to be easy.

As the day rusted away into a spectacular African sunset, even upstaging the Hollywood set, we wallowed in the river. Hanging in the warm muddy bath, Turton and I talked through our tiff and swapped some frustrations. It was obvious we were both going to have to learn on the job. And I could see I'd have to change the habits of a professional lifetime if we weren't to end up with a useless stalemate. Then there was the war.

For now, there were more urgent priorities. Water-purifying was already established as a far more pressing activity than filmmaking, involving an endless succession of staggers to the river to dredge up buckets of brown water as offerings to a magical plastic bottle we'd imported. Minutes of pumping through the carbon filter were rewarded with an agonising thin dribble of water, but at least it looked reasonably clean. Ulichagi had a fire blazing in moments and we broke into the first of the huge stock of freeze-dried food. 'Vegetable Stew with Rice', it said on the packet. It looked like sawdust with mouse droppings, but we were too weary to care. Soon we were fighting the flies for it.

With the light almost gone, Mike cajoled the hurricane-lamps into life. We sprawled in the gloom, battered by the absurdities of the day. André raided the emergency Scotch bottle, just in time to be caught red-handed by a visiting delegation of Captain Cherkole and some of his ragged police. Having drained the bottle, they huddled round the fire while the Captain talked about the harshness of life in Hana. 'Our government knows nothing of our hardships here,' he said. 'We have no medicines and only the food we can grow. I haven't seen my wife and my children for nine months.' His tattered subordinates gazed mournfully into the fire as the Captain enquired if we had any copies of *Time* magazine with us. *Time*-less, they trudged off into the darkness, the Captain's scarlet socks and white plimsolls glowing in the last of our firelight.

It was impossible to postpone my first encounter with a tent. I crawled into the sticky blackness with André and groped for the little book I'd bought in a Manchester stationer's. Maybe I just had the energy to start some sort of diary. Balancing a torch in my boot, I began, 'Saturday 15 June, Hana. After the months, it all really happened . . .'

I scribbled a fragmented account of the interminable day, and then peered through the mosquito net stretched across the doorway at the darkened campsite. 'Ulichagi lies quiet and watching, caged in net. Joni Mitchell cassette from the crew's tent merges with the uproar of insects.' God knows about tomorrow, I thought distantly. But at least, warmed by our Scotch tonight, the Captain promised his sturdy lorry for the long journey south to Mursi country in the morning.

His shadow shrivelled by a towering sun, the Captain dipped his finger into our jerry-can. He looked up angrily. 'I said benzine. Where's the fuel for my lorry?' I wasn't dreaming. It was horribly real. The police lorry stood alongside the Captain's shabby straw hut, sagging under the load of our lives for the next month.

But we weren't going anywhere. Our cans of petrol, transported with such agony from Addis were useless. The Captain's lorry ran on diesel. We were stranded before we'd really begun.

2

I looked at my watch for the tenth time in as many minutes and decided it was time to worry. I fretted to the diary: 'Noon. Waiting. Worried.' From a tree just behind the scruffy campsite, two vultures watched us stoically. 'One each,' I said to Mike as he glanced up from his paperback. He looked baffled, and I explained I was taking a vulture's eye view of us rather than suggesting an exotic lunch. Eric Clapton ran out on the cassette and the noise of Africa rushed in. The sky was a bruise, throbbing heat.

'12.55 p.m.' I wrote. 'Waiting. More worried. Something has obviously happened to the jeep.' It was two days since the crisis over the fuel for the Captain's lorry and I'd advanced about 400 yards towards Mursi country. Now Mike and I were marooned on a new site just outside Hana, worrying. Somewhere over the smudgy horizon, the rest of our expedition was scattered, and somewhere between them and us were André and the jeep. He should have been back before dark last night. Now we read distractedly, ears straining for a different note in the African din. My book was a novel by Nadine Gordimer about violence and death in a newly independent African country. A good man had just been killed on a remote track. I wanted to be away from here.

It had been a ridiculous forty-eight hours. I'd already lost count of the schemes that had blossomed and died as we thrashed around for a way to transport our cumbersome caravan down to Mursi country. For an hour on the first morning, we'd fed off the fantasy of rescue in the shape of a visitation of immaculate Swedes. They'd landed suddenly at the Hana strip in the midst of our nightmare mix-up over the fuel. The arrival of Count Von Rosen on the way to some estimable Scandinavian relief mission seemed calculated to tip our lives even further towards the surreal. David said the Count had pioneered the air-dropping of relief grain, and he was an impressive figure as he strolled from his natty little plane, cool and ordered in his stylish green fatigues. He reviewed our shabby tableau and agreed to ask after diesel fuel at the Mui airstrip on the other side of the Omo. Soon he was back, wobbling his wings in a dismissive shrug over Hana as he roared off to do good somewhere else. Sadly, he was to be killed soon afterwards on another relief flight.

Back at our river site, we'd agonised about what to do.

'How about mules?' I asked hopelessly.

'Honestly, they're even more trouble than the jeep — if we could get some — which we can't,' David said. 'Surely there's lots of this stuff we could leave here,' he suggested, scanning our burden of film boxes. 'Then we could think about porters.'

I thought about forty miles of walking and pleaded: 'The jeep might make it in relays. If we leave some of the food here and shift stuff down in stages, the jeep should be able to cope.'

Well, it had worked for an hour or two. André had packed the jeep's boot with socks and dried soup and then bumped away with Turton. Before we could get down to worrying, the police lorry roared into camp with a note from David saying the jeep had only just survived the Hana river so we should move camp to the other bank to spare it further crossings. The Captain had lent his lorry for the evacuation, desperate to see us gone and we rushed down the almost vertical bank into the river with such abandon that Pat had to indicate pregnancy to calm the driver down.

The new site was tatty and open, surrounded by sinister-looking holes. 'It looks like wild boar,' Pat diagnosed. 'They're dangerous.' But at least she didn't have long to think about it. By early afternoon, there was evidence of André. Audible for minutes, he was lost in the bush until he crashed through the wall of grass and into the site. It was an entry worthy of panto-mime, farcical and obscurely alarming, flooding the domestic campsite with a dangerous whiff of the wild places he'd come from. André sat in the jeep for a moment, dazed and smothered in a froth of foliage and insects while the machine simmered, scalding to the touch with its exertions.

'We've found a site at the river Gura,' André said at last. 'It's a mad drive, but we made it. You just have to aim at the bush and hope there's nothing animal or mineral hidden in the grass.' He crammed down a plateful of instant chicken and pasta, piled in more boxes and then spluttered off into the wilderness with Pat and Ulichagi. That had been almost twenty-four hours ago and we hadn't seen him since.

Suddenly alone with Mike, the raw sense of place hit me. I wandered away from the camp, returning soon, edgy with a new awareness of where I was. I retreated to the diary: 'A dangerous feel on a walk to the river. Snake-gaiters seem all too vulnerable in this martian grass. Clouds of yellow and white butterflies at the river. A big brown eagle-like bird swoops in and lands, watching me. A sudden realisation, without drama, that it's one of those rare moments when you do have to keep yourself alive. The crammed profusion of life – every leaf bitten to a lacework. The country sings like a kettle, permanently on the boil.'

After dark, the Captain had arrived in chatty mood. In his brown leather stetson and fraying grey sweater, he sat by our fire and told us his radio had just reported an Irish bomb in the House of Commons. It felt like a rumour from a distant planet. As always, the Captain's big watch said 7.30, and he wasn't in a hurry. In the end, Mike surrendered and excavated the brandy from the tent. Of course the Captain hadn't forgotten that funnel we'd used to pour fuel into the jeep – the one we'd made from an ornate box with *Remy Martin* embossed on its side. And yes thanks, he would mix some lemonade powder with his brandy. Blending with his relief that Ulichagi was off his patch, his second mug found him mellowing. 'The vultures think you're white goats,' he chuckled. As the bottle got lighter, the Captain returned to his favourite theme. 'This place is not good. I hate it. I sent a letter to the chief of all police in Addis. I asked him to come here to Hana to see how we live. In two months maybe I'll get posted somewhere else. I don't look at my children's photos. I miss them too bad.' He said he was 36, the same age as me.

At last he went, trailed by a scatter of men, all munching our

24

liquorice bonbons. In the tight circle of our hurricane-lamp, Mike and I chewed on a freeze-dried dinner. The air was syrupy and still, the bush pulsed like a power station. I was very glad I wasn't on my own. We were thinking, without enthusiasm, about the tent when four policemen came out of the darkness. Mike reached resignedly for the brandy, but they went on into the gloom and began to haul down trees. Sluicing our paraffin on the pile, they lit a huge bonfire. 'Lion,' a policemen said. We laughed out loud. 'Lion near,' the man insisted. They heaved a whole tree on to the fire and went away. The sparks flew to the stars, and I traded nonchalance with Mike about the lion. Then we crawled into the tent and Mike unsheathed a big knife. Just in case.

Now we had sagged all morning under a sullen sky, nattering at our watches and wondering about the jeep. Worry shaded towards alarm. Around three in the afternoon, as I brewed yet another mug of tea, André walked into camp. He looked shattered and he had a tale of complex catastrophe. On the drive back to Gura yesterday, the starter motor had packed up in a dry river-bed. They toiled for ever, but nothing happened. Pat decided to trek on through the bush with a Bodi the two and half hours to David at Gura, leaving André and Ulichagi to camp alongside the useless jeep.

André was still mildly hysterical about their night. 'It was wild,' he spluttered between gulps of tea. 'Ulichagi was nervous as hell, sitting up all night with the gun waiting for Bodi attackers. Then Chris arrived back from Gura and we shoved at the jeep with three passing Bodi. The bloody thing still wouldn't start, so I decided to walk back here.' It had taken him three punishing hours. I shared my frustration with the diary: 'So now we have people strung along this impossible track at three points and no way of moving them. It would be funny if it wasn't so worrying – as well as useless in terms of the film we came to make which seems almost incidental at the moment. Our only answer is with the luckless Captain.'

'Dr David is always making trouble.' The Captain was not pleased. 'Always he brings big problems for me when he comes here.'

'Well it's not really his fault this time,' I said lamely. 'It's us who brought the jeep for the filming.'

'Always trouble from Dr David.' The Captain wasn't to be side-tracked.

André and I stood like erring schoolboys in the Head's study. The setting didn't make the dressing-down any more comfortable. As the Captain raged on about 'Dr David's' sins, I took in the flimsy hut. The sun sliced through the weary latticework walls, jabbing a faded photograph of Emperor Haile Selassie and a torn poster proclaiming 'Fly jet to East Africa'. A bent wire coat-hanger hung from a nail.

The Captain paused in his tirade and André bravely offered a sketch-map to locate our scattered colleagues. Finally, there was no avoiding it. 'So if you could possibly let us have the use of your lorry to transport us and our equipment as far as Gura where we can hire porters I'd be hugely grateful,' I gushed. 'And of course I'll go on to Jinka afterwards and explain how helpful you've been and get some replacement fuel for you,' André added.

A lengthy silence gathered in the hut.

The burst bag of paraffin-soaked flour jolted in my lap as we bucked on another sickening dip. Alongside the open window, a grinning Bodi youth leaped and yelled, his sheet flying around him. A herd of zebra scattered in the grass. At last, we were really on our way towards the Mursi. I felt a rush of raw excitement. The Captain had made us wait for our reprieve, arriving at our camp after dark to claim the remains of Mike's brandy.

After the second top-up, he agreed that his lorry would come in the morning and take us as far as Gura, sweeping up the fragments of our scattered expedition as it went. 'But after Gura, no more,' the Captain growled ominously. He asked me to send him a dictionary when I got back to England.

Soon after seven we'd loaded up and ploughed away into the bush. Immediately we were outside the limits of my world.

Ten years on the road in pursuit of Television had dragged me across some strange landscapes. Some places still snag on the memory. I remember Cairo on the verge of war in 1967, endless and awful. The teeming slum canyons and a terrible graveyard that is also home for thousands of the living were my first encounter with a version of life outside the tidy certainties of

Europe. I remember the lovely mountains of northern Laos, the setting for a squalid and murderous guerrilla war where I interviewed a 10-year-old boy equipped, with combat fatigues, grenades and a small but deadly rifle, by the CIA. I remember the desolate spaces of the Kalahari desert where South Africa had dumped thousands of its black citizens. I remember a ruined valley in the high Andes where a colossal statue of Christ watched over a sea of mud which had engulfed a town of 20,000 people after an earthquake.

But this was something wilder and stranger. A scalding wind buffeted around the cab, raw with the stink of earth and vegetation and unknown things. Beyond this lorry, I felt cut adrift from all the familiar markers of the century I lived in. We ploughed along through head-high grass at a walking pace, the sweating police driver juggling ceaselessly with the gears. A wildebeest bounced away on springs. Then in the middle of a tangle of bushes, we were almost in a head-on collision with the jeep. Chris gaped at us across the bonnet, up to his waist in grass and debris. 'I got it started,' he yelled and led off back through the curtains of grass. At once, he was swallowed and we tumbled on, alone again.

After a long time, we tipped into a stomach-churning dive and broke through into an open river-bed. Marooned amongst socks and boxes and spilled food packets, Mike and Ulichagi sat surrounded by a dozen armed Bodi. Mike and Ulichagi looked very glad to see us, the Bodi scattered as I raised my camera. We slung supplies and people into the back of the lorry and headed on south.

Now the going was rougher than ever, the ground littered with huge stones that flung us around the cab, mimicking the varied pleasures of an assault course and a particularly sadistic fairground ride. More Bodi youths bounded alongside the lorry, like outriders at a state procession, effortless and naked. The driver prodded me and pointed, urging me to take pictures. Grinning faces bounced in the viewfinder and the eyepiece jabbed my cheek. I gave up, reproved for the tourist spasm.

Suddenly, there was the jeep again, with André under it. The metal sheet protecting the undersides had been ripped off. We threw it in the back of the lorry and set off again in convoy. And then alongside another brown river, we found the Turtons.

'There's a good place to camp on the other side,' David shouted, 'but I wouldn't risk driving the jeep across. It's deep and the bottom's really rough.'

The lorry surged across the river Gura to an open space beyond the other bank. Dumping the load, I walked back to the river with Mike to face the jeep problem. We waded across to David, almost waist-deep in places, stumbling on the stones hidden under the thick brown water.

'I don't fancy the jeep in that,' I panted as I sluiced up the bank, spurting soup out of my laceholes.

'No chance,' said Chris with the benefit of some jeep experience. 'The only hope is to get a tow from the lorry,'

'They'll be delighted, I'm sure,' I said and sloshed back across the river to try it out on the long-suffering driver.

Soothed by cups of insectful coffee, the policemen watched our preparations. Chris heated up the twisted undershield over a fire and attempted to bash it flat with a rock. The rest of us lurched around in the river, feeling for stones and trying to clear some kind of underwater track for the jeep. Bodi sat on the bank, giggling and enjoying the show. After an hour, we'd done all we could.

The lorry screamed and strained at our nylon rope as the jeep nuzzled into the river with André at the wheel. For an agonising moment I was sure the rope would snap. Then with a menacing twang, the jeep shot out of the water, skidded crazily on the muddy bank and slewed to a stop. I reported to the diary: 'We've made it – and it puts us further still from help. A farewell to the police with a pleading note to the Captain to pick us up on the 15th and money for his fuel. Now back to our new site for a vast, short-tempered sort-out. Tempers edgy in the noon heat, drowning in gear and food. It seems the rear suspension on the bloody jeep is badly bent after its adventures. Buddhist calm the only way.'

By day's end, some kind of order had been improvised and even a glimmer of optimism could be detected around the campfire. After all, tomorrow might contain the chance of actual filming with a delegation of Bodi elders rumoured to be coming to talk about prospects for peace. André and Chris had an improbable scheme to rebuild the jeep's suspension, and David seemed hopeful of porters. Even Ulichagi was beginning to relax as he got closer to home ground. He hunched in our circle round the fire as talk turned mellow. Lying back to take in the huge sky that seemed more star-heavy each night, Mike spotted the bright blip of Skylab arching overhead. Ulichagi had seen it too and talked quietly to David. After a brief exchange, David laughed and Ulichagi shook his head. 'What did he say, David' I asked. 'Oh, it reminded him of a car crash he saw in Addis. He said we white people are crazy, always trying to make death for ourselves in iron boxes.' Then Ulichagi asked me if I'd been to the moon.

They came out of the bush in a ragged procession, unhurried but bringing with them a sense of occasion. The Bodi elders of Gura were coming to talk. There were eight of them, and as they approached I relished the random eccentricity of their appearance. One man was naked except for a white cloth draped with fine dash over a shoulder. Big metal rings bounced in his ears. Behind him, another man sported a battered straw trilby, a shirt as blue and patched as a French peasant's door, and nothing else. A small man with a knowing face balanced on his head a huge circular beret which might once have been black. Another walked with authority in lime-green shorts and a louche felt hat. One of the delegation carried at his shoulder, with the poise of a waiter conveying a tray of champagne glasses, a neat wooden jar sealed with bright leaves.

Almost all the men carried big, old-fashioned rifles. It seemed these people lived at some tideline of the world's cast-offs; but I knew the rifles had a more precise and sinister origin. They'd been left behind by Italian armies thirty years before when Ethiopia was Mussolini's fascist colony of Abyssinia, filtering through to the Bodi and the Mursi in the lower Omo via unimaginable networks. It was, I suppose, shabbily inevitable that these ugly but effective weapons should be just about the only imports from the outside world apart from the ragbag of old clothes. Now, David told us, the fat bullets were an important item of currency in these parts, regularly traded as a key inducement in purchasing a bride.

But for the moment, the rifles and the bullets were being put to more conventional use in the war between the Bodi and the Mursi. Dozens had been killed recently, and for both sides the penalties of war were becoming intolerable. David had heard from Bodi at Hana how the collapse of ordinary life was creating hardship and hunger. Worst of all, the opening up of a warring no man's land between the normally neighbourly Bodi and Mursi had meant the loss of land vital for cattle and agriculture. It all focused, it seemed, on the ownership of a place called Mara, still miles to the south of us at the northern boundary of Mursi country. There was plenty for the elders to talk about.

Under mucky grey skies, we were filming as they arrived on the hillside behind our camp. One man gravely shook the crew's hands as they continued to shoot. Soon, they settled down in the long grass with David and a tense-looking Ulichagi. The talking began. We filmed from a discreet distance for a while and then moved in quietly, Mike kneeling in the grass with the camera on his shoulder.

At first it was mainly David and the Bodi in the felt hat. The Bodi have their own language, but they're bilingual in Mursi and they knew David well enough from his journeys to earlier field trips. But it was Ulichagi they really wanted to speak with. As a chance ambassador for the enemy, he might be a way to help end the war. The reluctant go-between sat and listened as the Bodi spokesman, a man called Goloinminta – the man in the felt hat – made the most of his opportunity, his rifle propped against his knees. His drift was clear enough and I caught the word 'Mara' regularly.

Weeks later, David's translation filled in the details. 'If your cow eats my grain,' Goloinminta said, 'then we become enemies. Let us keep apart. Go and say that. Mara belongs to us. You Mursi should move south. Then we can end this war. Go and say that if you want peace.'

Ulichagi buried his head in his hands for a moment and then looked up. 'I'll tell them that. We Mursi will debate these things at Mara. I'll tell them that.'

The little conference broke up and the Bodi drifted down to our camp. David caught up with me. 'It doesn't look good,' he said. 'The Mursi are never going to take that. They've been at Mara for twenty years and it's one of their best cultivation sites. They're hardly likely to move back now. Still, Ulichagi's got to report all this in a debate when we get down there.'

'So much for objective documentary,' I said. 'It looks like we're part of the peace process, and it looks like you're stuck with your Dr Kissinger role.' David chuckled unhappily.

As we exchanged gifts, the elegant Bodi jar proved to contain soured milk. It put a severe strain on our politeness as hosts. The elders wandered round the campsite retrieving our cast-off food packets and plastic film containers in a brief but chastening lesson about our casual wastefulness. Then they walked away into the bush.

There was a splutter of rain. Ulichagi waved a burning stick and clapped his hands. 'He's trying to stop the rain,' David explained. The rain stopped. It had been a productive morning and at last we had some useful film, though our expedition seemed bound up in the developing themes of peace in a way that felt utterly removed from our tidy Manchester proposals for a film about debating amongst East African cattle-herders. And after an interminable week, with our time leaking away we were still a long way from the nearest Mursi and we still had a wounded jeep.

By early afternoon André had worked his miracle. Cannibalising bolts and improvising boldly, he'd rebuilt the warped rear suspension. In my relief, I tried not to think about our discovery that the spare wheel didn't fit. With a rashness fuelled by desperation, we decided to risk another push south with the jeep. David and André loaded up, and I walked a few hundred yards into the bush with the crew to record their departure.

The film still has a ghoulish fascination. In a single shot, the hopeless naiveties are perfectly captured. First, there's an empty patch of bush. On the soundtrack, the lugubrious descending notes of a bird are challenged by the approaching whine of an engine. Then the jeep lurches into view looking ludicrously vulnerable, piloted by two men in floppy hats. Right in front of the camera, they stop at a yawning ditch. David gets out to direct André round the hazard, and then we pan them away, smashing down small trees as they disappear. I say 'Cut' and they vanish for twenty-seven hours.

The diary followed the graph of my concern:

'Still no jeep. I watch the ants scurrying on our tent hem and wonder how we're ever going to get there . . .'

'A fractured night, dreams of sea-journeys ill-prepared and my son's face in tears. Another grey morning, overlaid with quiet depression about the jeep. Ulichagi says hyenas on site during the night . . .'

31

'Where the hell are they . . .'

'Becalmed. Chris, Ulichagi and I just back from a fifty-minute walk to see what we could see. "Nothing," says Ulichagi mimicking our hopelessness. Nothing is mountains in the distance, a flat plain, tall grass and white heat. I carry the gun, for decoration it feels like. Ulichagi finds edible seeds in a wild boar scuffle. I feel myself out in the growing certainty there's going to be a lot more walking like this. Back in camp, Pat is edging towards real worry now.'

Around three in the afternoon, André and David strolled into camp looking remarkably unruffled. They had a wretched tale to tell. The jeep was broken in the bush yet again, prospects of porters were dodgy with the war flaring around us. It was the worst yet. Through the afternoon we cast around for options once again in touchy swirling conversations. We were still swapping endless permutations involving hypothetical donkeys and gigantic tottering loads as we lay in the blessed river for our evening absolution.

But in the dark with Albinoni spiralling to the stars from the cassette and Ulichagi shouting at a fingernail of full moon some sort of prospects had begun to clarify. David had returned from a recruiting drive through nearby Bodi settlements and seemed more hopeful of porters.

Now that we'd at last made the awful commitment to the long march, I could hope some end to our shambling uncertainties might be possible. I wrote: 'Tomorrow is clearly going to be a make-or-break day. Thank God for a cool crew. Morale still amazingly good I think.'

Cowering in a dry ditch trying to hide from the sun somewhere in the furnace of that day, Chris Wangler told me a joke that seemed at the time to say it all. At least I think it was a joke.

'A scorpion came to the edge of a great African river and wanted to get across,' Chris began. 'He shouted to a passing crocodile: "Hey, crocodile, carry me over the river on your back." "Not a chance," the crocodile said. "You'll only sting me to death when we get across." "No I won't," said the scorpion. "Trust me. I wouldn't do anything so mean after you helped me." The crocodile looked doubtful, but he was a decent sort. Finally, he agreed to carry the scorpion across the river.

The current was fierce, and the river wide, but the crocodile swam skilfully, keeping the scorpion safe on its back. At last, they reached the other bank. As the crocodile crawled out of the water, without warning the scorpion plunged its sting into the rescuer's neck. "I ferried you across the river and you promised not to hurt me," gasped the dying crocodile. "Why did you do that?" "Why?" the scorpion replied, "this is Africa." '

Although it hurt to move at all, I shook with laughter until the Bodi porters began to look at me uneasily. I suppose I must have been mildly deranged, but it had been a day the scorpion would have understood.

It started promisingly enough. We sat on our packed boxes in clean morning sunshine as Bodi began to arrive. First there was the old man in the blue shirt, then a group of laughing young men. Soon, dozens of potential porters were wandering around the stripped campsite, checking out our inducements. Turton unfurled the bales of creamy cloth we'd bought in Addis and people fingered the stuff approvingly. Then there were the beads. I'd gagged with disbelief when David urged us to bring the bags of little white beads. For some reason, they were made in Czechoslovakia. It didn't help to lessen my unease at the prospect of actually offering beads to natives which felt like a descent into a 1930s comic strip parody of an Africa where cooking pots are full of missionaries. The Bodi seemed delighted with the beads. Some more practical folk preferred money, rolling up the grimy Ethiopian notes and inserting them into pierced ears.

Turton allocated the loads, keeping a careful record of who was carrying what in a little notebook. The Bodi were equally watchful, suspiciously lifting bundles and rucksacks and miming horror at the weight of silver boxes. Further negotiations ensued while Pat Turton coped briskly with a parade of porters hungry for aspirins. For a long time I was sure our huge black box full of vital film stock would never find a taker. At last, a willowy young man slung it effortlessly on to his head. As the sun got down to business, we were ready to go.

I retreated into the bush to take a photograph as the file moved away. Once again, I had blundered into a Hollywood set, only this time the movie was *Sanders of the River*. André led off looking suitably intrepid in a raffish stetson. Behind him stretched a line of twenty-seven Bodi porters moving easily under their assorted loads, shouting and laughing. Some of them were actually running. One man carried somebody's black leather briefcase; a naked youth had a shiny hurricane-lamp over one shoulder, my sensible green suitcase on his head.

I shambled into the procession. In two minutes I was drenched with sweat, in four cursing the weight of my little camera bag while the Bodi with the massive stock box dashed past me. Before I could hit a rhythm, I was stopped by a man whose load had collapsed, an early casualty of my lousy knot-tying. My lack of boy-scouting was already costing dear.

We moved out on to a burnt plain through head-high, bone-coloured grass. It was hotter than I'd ever imagined possible. The thing was, I told myself, not to stop. I tried to let the rhythms of just keeping going possess me. For some reason, my footsteps insisted on lodging inside my head in patterns of four. One-two-three-four took me over entirely and there was nothing else in the world.

We walked on forever. I gulped recklessly at my water bottle – one-two-three-four – and scrambled up a hill of baking stones. For a long time, parched bushes hemmed us in, denying any sense of shape or order in the landscape. Then there was a stopped group ahead of me. Mike and Chris were sweating over a reconstruction of another of my wobbly loads with its Bodi porter. I juddered unwillingly to a halt and joined in. Too soon, we were walking on into the burning middle of the day, me slogging along behind Mike and Chris. I thought I could just about manage a photo. 'Where's my bloody camera?' I croaked.

For a dismal half hour we hunted around through acres of identical grass but it was hopeless. I'd left it at the last repacking place, but where was that? Feeling close to hallucination, I tramped on, cracked, thirsty, mechanical. For the first time I could sense the edge of my stamina, but guilt kept me in motion.

I was uncertain of its reality when the jeep suddenly swished towards me with André and Mike on board. It was true though. They'd revived it yet again and were headed back to Gura to collect stuff the porters hadn't been able to carry. It didn't seem to matter much. I walked, my entire being concentrated on 'where do we stop?'

Just at the point where I was doubting whether guilt or memories of the scorpion joke could keep me on my feet, I saw a patch of blue shirt ahead. Chris and the Turtons and the Bodi and our burdens seemed to have stopped. Journey's end was a stunted tree, bristling with murderous thorns. I collapsed on a box. Instantly, the tree speared me but I was too spent to care. Looking indecently sprightly, David began to pay out the porters. He chatted as though he'd just enjoyed a Sunday afternoon stroll round the park. I sat on my box incapable of speech, bleeding steadily from my thorn gash. After a while, I joined Chris in doing things with the beads, scratching for an illusion of self-possession. Amid the litter of yet another camp-site, the day slowly untangled. David escorted the nervous Bodi some way back into the bush by way of reassurance about Mursi snipers; the jeep returned; we had a testy discussion about tomorrow. I began to revive a little.

At the end of a glorious afternoon, I told the diary about a spot of adventure: 'Sitting in the jeep in the middle of Africa – me, Mike, and all the insects in the universe. A stick-insect four inches long wobbles up the doorpost, followed by a hairy green spider. We've just driven David and Ulichagi on into the bush to try and find porters for tomorrow. My first jeep trip was literally mind-boggling, like the Star Gate at the end of *2001*. A tunnel of grass rushes at us. It feels like 1,000 m.p.h. Just hang on and pray. Alongside me, Mike smiles at the absurdity of the risk.'

Back in camp, I slapped calamine lotion on Chris's bum and we counted 700 bites. Fireflies fizzed past as Ulichagi crooned a quiet song. 'I want my camera and a cold beer,' I wrote. 'Tomorrow, please God, Mara.'

Not yet though. Somewhere in the dark I found the diary: 'Awful night of deluging rain, thunder, and lightning flashing on my watch of 2.15 a.m. David joins us in the tent as the downpour begins, and we're all awake till it ends at 4 a.m. Now lions roar in the distance.'

But the morning was alive with brilliant drippings.

And then the Mursi came.

3

On Saturday 23 November 1968, David Turton arrived at the river Omo for the first time. It had been a long way to come in pursuit of a footnote. It began with a tantalising reference in a book by a German anthropologist to an uncontacted group of hunter-gatherers who were said to live alongside the lower reaches of the Omo in the remotest region of southern Ethiopia. As a newly graduated anthropologist, Turton was on the lookout for a people who could offer the basis for his first fieldwork. And that intriguing footnote had another attraction. It coincided with a sudden opening up of Ethiopia, after decades of isolation, in the late 1960s. Emperor Haile Selassie had given permission for Louis and Richard Leakey to excavate for the earliest evidence of the human race in the Lower Omo Valley and the door was open at last. For the young Turton, it all looked very promising. But at the end of the long trek down to the Omo from the mountains to the West, he found disappointment.

The handful of Kwegu he could locate simply didn't match up with the textbook requirements for hunter-gatherers. They cultivated crops and, worse still, instead of the bows and arrows promised in the footnote, they carried large rifles. On top of all that, there seemed to be too few of them for a sustained study. Disillusioned, Turton trekked south down the west bank of the Omo. In the first week of December 1968, he found himself looking across the river into Mursi country for the first time.

Listening six years later to David's quietly matter-of-fact account of that initial encounter, it was hard to believe it wasn't an episode from a nineteenth-century explorer's tale. Even with the filter of academic understatement it was an extraordinary story. Turton persuaded a Mursi youth to take him across the river, well-stocked with crocodiles, in a hollowed log canoe to a small settlement on the other side. Entirely alone with the suspicious Mursi, not knowing a word of their language, he struggled to make contact. For three weeks, the Mursi sent him back across the river every night refusing all suggestions that he might camp in their settlement. But by now Turton had made a decision. 'I decided to try and do my fieldwork with the Mursi instead of the Kwegu. I suppose it was basically a romantic thing. They were simply the most uncontacted group of people in the most inaccessible place.'

On 1 January 1969, Turton was at last allowed to pitch his tent in Mursi country. It seemed that rivalry for his supplies of cloth and medicine had led to an offer of hospitality from a nearby settlement. Unwilling to lose their stake in the well-stocked white man, Turton's suspicious hosts relented and his life with the Mursi began.

For the next two years, the young English anthropologist who had once studied for the priesthood in Rome survived and lived alongside a shifting group of nomadic cattle herders. While the rest of the world watched men walking on the moon, Turton ran with the Mursi in a nighttime escape from enemy cattle-raiders. He sweated through a dose of malaria. Supplementing his meagre supplies with soured milk and cows' blood, he was often hungry and weary from ceaseless treks alongside the Mursi as they pursued their subsistence across an unforgiving homeland. With the changing pressures of the seasons, he followed the movements from grassland to river and back again.

Slowly, with the help of Mursi who showed a special patience, he began to learn the language. First, it was a word at a time, painstakingly transcribed as it sounded into a notebook. Then under the weeks and months of solitary immersion, the shapes and rhythms of the talk around him seeped into meaning as they do for a child. Turton began to know people like Ulichagi, and he began to be known as 'Lusi Golonyi' – Red Boy, after his sun-scorched face. A favourite campsite became 'London' for the Mursi. And they asked him constantly about his world. Was it true that white men were cannibals? How long would it take to walk to his country? Did white people die, or did they grow new skins like snakes?

As the hard, absorbing months piled up, Turton also discovered a focus for his work. He became fascinated by those gatherings of men under a shade tree that meant another Mursi debate. Witnessing a succession of debates and finding himself increasingly intrigued by the oratory and spontaneous order through which the scattered, leaderless Mursi tackled the problems of their society, Turton wanted to know more. When he went home at last in January 1971, he was determined to return.

By November 1973, David was married to Pat and had become Dr Turton with a post at the University of Manchester. And the Turtons were back in Mursi country. They found a people emerging from crisis, struggling to cope with the worst drought and famine in living memory.

On his first field trip, Turton had been told that though they were often hungry, no one ever died of starvation. As a speaker put it during a debate: 'Hunger is something you just have to put up with. You just bind your stomach tightly and wait till it passes.' Now he found that almost a fifth of the married men he'd surveyed in 1970 were dead. There were terrible stories of desperate people committing suicide by walking into the river to be devoured by crocodiles, of abandoned old people and widespread infant mortality. A man accidentally trapped by his head in rocks while searching for honey had been left to die by his starving brothers. Pat Turton, a qualified nurse found evidence everywhere of severe malnutrition.

The reason for the tragic decline in Mursi fortunes was simple and devastating. The rains had failed for three successive years and the Omo floodings vital for seasonal crops hadn't materialised. Now, as we had discovered seven months later, the war with the Bodi inflamed by hunger and resulting pressure on land was compounding the crisis. We were approaching Mursi country in unhappy and difficult times.

It was the women I saw first. They walked towards us out of the bush, and for a moment I found it hard to look at my first Mursi. David's photographs and descriptions hadn't prepared

38

me for the fearful reality of the cut lips. Slashed through to the gum under the lower lip, the stretched skin dangled below the chins of some women revealing an alarming void where bottom teeth had been removed.

I knew the Mursi valued the lip-cutting as a special mark of Mursiness but it seemed at this first contact the most repellent and unaccountable of human decorations. None of the women had inserted a circular clay plate into the dangling lips and it seemed to make the mutilation even harder to accept. The women looked back at us with equal astonishment and, as far as I could see, unqualified distaste. The metal rings fringing their goatskin skirts jingled as they moved watchfully around our campsite. Then they began to haggle cheerfully with David about portering rates for the final lap of our journey to the border of Mursi country. We turned yet again to the business of putting our lives into bundles, but I was flooded with relief that after all the farce and confusion we'd actually met up with some Mursi.

By the end of the day, the diary lavished punctuation marks on an even bigger relief. 'Mara at last!!! We've reached the infinitely awaited Mara. It's like the last chapter of *Lord of the Rings* and we haven't even started the film.'

Mara was of course just another campsite at the end of another day's trudging, a clearing under a generous shade tree alongside a little river. But this was Mursi country and all around us, sitting on our boxes and staring at the unimaginable white men and their unaccountable doings were scores of Mursi.

I groped to imagine how it must have been for Turton arriving alone amongst these people six years before. A naked man cradling a rifle fingered my hair, and I was very glad I could share the moment with a ribald film crew.

It wasn't menace I felt, surrounded by these tall smiling men, just a swamping sense of having arrived in their place, a very long way from any of my old certainties.

I sat on a box and tried to register a few details. Some men had sheets thrown over a shoulder like Roman senators; others furled a skimpy cloth round the waist like a miniskirt. Many were naked except for metal rings wound tight round their biceps or a thin strand of colourful beads round their necks. Almost everyone sported bold earrings in drooping pierced ears, big hoops like curtain rings or bits of metal from God knows where. One man had somehow stumbled on what looked like a bunch of keys for a suitcase and hung them from his ears. Another had come across a beer-can pull on some expedition to a highland village and now wore it proudly.

Our scorched pink skins looked comically out of place alongside these spare bodies, black with an absolute mattness that seemed to suck in and neutralise the sunlight. In the shadows, faces glowed indigo.

The man with the rifle was still peering at my hair, and it was plain that our weird thatching was a source of wonder and revulsion. Mursi hair seemed to be an endlessly inventive variation on a minimal theme. The mossy little outcrops on the shaved heads had been trained into furrows and whorls, tonsures and skullcaps. The tousled excess of our early 70s mops was apparently as unappetising for them as a cut and gaping lip seemed to us.

There was a lot of spitting. The chorus of rasping throats, mingling ceaselessly with a fusillade of gobbing was to become the familiar background to many of our soundtracks over the coming weeks. Turton reported that the Mursi found our habit of swallowing our saliva utterly bewildering.

Nine men sat in and on our weary jeep and shouted at David for trips into the bush. Ulichagi looked very happy to be on home ground. Bold women and spidery giggling children peered in wonder at our unimaginable hoard of things. I was suddenly aware that we must be by far the biggest invasion from the outside world these people had ever experienced. Instead of the single tent and few sacks of David's previous visits, six white people were scattering heaps of strange novelties from scores of silver boxes and orange nylon rucksacks. I tried to see it through the eyes of the young warrior who sat alongside me watching intently as I fiddled with our plastic water-purifier and loaded a bright yellow film cassette into André's camera. It was impossible to conceive what he might make of it all.

Some of our imports were clearly less baffling and a lot more interesting. Knives, buckets, hammers, ropes, containers of any kind provoked murmurs of approval. It was immediately obvious that the Mursi weren't bashful. The tug on my green towel accompanied by an unambiguous jerk of the thumb towards the claimant's chest revealed that communication wouldn't always need David's assistance.

Chris dug out a tape from somewhere and a song by Crosby, Stills and Nash billowed round the campsite, scattering a couple of inquisitive monkeys from the branches overhead. Mursi gathered round the recorder looking puzzled as David Crosby agonised about whether to cut his hair or let his 'freak flag fly'.

Slowly, a kind of order began to emerge. The light faded and the Mursi drifted away into the bush. After dinner, we sat round the fire in the noisy darkness and David talked about debating. 'Decisions are being made under those shade trees,' he said, 'but it's not as simple as that. One of the things that's going on is that news is being passed on. The debates are also a way of handing down information about how problems were dealt with in the past for people who don't have any written records.' 'But presumably they're more than a bush newspaper,' André said. 'Oh yes,' David continued. 'The debates are about getting people to do something together. But it's not really a matter of thrashing out the best plan on a cost-benefit basis from a whole range of possibilities. For the Mursi, there are almost never new problems and a pretty limited set of solutions. The real business of the debates is to rally the maximum public support for one line of action – and it's always a line that connects with traditional values that everybody accepts.' 'Sounds fine doesn't it?' Pat obviously had her reservations. 'Don't forget to mention that this splendid democratic debating is for men only.' 'Not all of them either,' David said, smacking a fly on his arm. 'You have to be past your mid 20s before you're allowed to speak. No of course it's not what we understand as democratic, but you have to remember what debating means for the Mursi. It's not something you do only when you have a problem. It's something that should be going on all the time. For them, a community that debates together stays together.' He unfolded a plastic sheet to cover our food boxes against the inevitable nightly downpour. 'Anyway, I hope you can see for yourself tomorrow. People reckon there's going to be a debate here to talk about Ulichagi's news from the Bodi.'

I dreamed of being recruited as a secret agent for the South African police and woke at first light to thunder and rain drumming on the tent, thinking that I hadn't seen my face for days. The morning passed in a slow turmoil of rationalising the messy campsite while I helped Pat to take blood samples from Mursi spectators for a medical research programme. The warriors winced and grimaced as their thumbs were pricked, but we were impressed by their trust and forbearance in submitting to what must have felt like an unprovoked assault. Moving along the lines of men in soaking noon heat, I indulged a passing fantasy in the role of Albert Schweitzer.

The alert to scramble for the debate came suddenly in the early afternoon. I grabbed the tripod and some film cans and we panted after David across the river Mara and up a steep bank on the other side.

And there it was, the scene we'd come so far to find, a Mursi debate under a shade tree. It was just as I'd first encountered it months before in some of Turton's black and white photographs. Three dozen men sat quietly in deep shade against the tree; a man with a spear was beginning to pace up and down in the long grass. Then I saw it was Ulichagi and there was no more time for sightseeing.

Somehow, we were filming as Ulichagi began to speak. He walked slowly, crossing and recrossing the little arena. His words came in gusts, emphasised with the long spear, separated by reflective pacing with only the sound of his feet in the dry grass. The audience listened, motionless and attentive.

Just visible fifty yards away, almost lost in dense greenery, sat a little group of women. Close to me, a man with an alarming mud-striped face and bloodshot eyes fingered his rifle. Another man in a battered green cap looked tense and angry. Even without access to the language, it was obvious that the message Ulichagi had brought from the Bodi – that the Mursi should leave Mara to them – was getting a hostile reception.

Shirtless and dripping in breathless heat, I crouched with Mike and Chris in the grass trying not to break the spell as we filmed. It was soon clear we needn't worry. People were much too concerned with the debate to pay any attention to the meaningless antics of the white men. Even Chris's unavoidable intrusion, panning the speaker to and fro with the long-distance rifle microphone didn't seem to register. I knew I was looking in on something remarkable.

After about five minutes, Ulichagi walked into the audience and the man in the green hat stood up and took his place. As he paced up and down carrying his rifle, there was no doubt about his feelings. He spoke rapidly and with anger, repeatedly stabbing his arm northwards towards Bodi country. Weeks later, Turton's detailed translation confirmed the message:

'The Bodi, the Bodi, the Bodi – they steal our cattle and kill our people, sneaking up at night. Those miserable liars! Let them come and wipe us out. I won't leave Mara – ever!'

He finished with a shout and a dismissive sweep of the arm.

We juggled with hot film cans and melting tapes as speaker followed speaker. The torrent of talk quickly swallowed up all our ten-minute magazines of film and I had to take over on camera as Mike frantically reloaded. Our confusions seemed to emphasise the effortless order of the debate. Without the intervention of a chairman or any apparent discussion, man after man said his piece and then made way for another. Everyone was heard in attentive silence. Then it was the turn of Rabithella.

Rabithella was a Jalabai, an influential man, and David had told us something about him. It seemed he was one of a handful of older men with a special skill in oratory who are always listened to with special attention. Rabithella wasn't especially rich in cattle or fierce in war, but when he spoke in debates people said: 'His words stick.' For a society which placed such value on talk Rabithella was an important man. He certainly looked the part now, as he stalked through the grass rifle in hand, with the face of a hawk and eyes bright with disdain. Round his sulphur yellow shirt he wore a bullet belt and a weathered floppy hat was jammed on his head. He moved with urgency and authority and there was no guessing his age. Measuring his pauses with the skill of years, he rapped out his bitter rejection of Ulichagi's news from the Bodi.

'This river we call Mara – it's a river of my ancestors. It's the boundary between Mursi and Bodi, between our cattle. Are there any Bodi graves here? They're lying. Do they intend to cultivate here? Isn't it enough to take our cows and slaughter our people? When they've killed us all, then they can take our land. What can they be dreaming of?'

Rabithella had finished. He strode into the audience murmuring, 'Now let's hear from someone else.' But after an hour and seven speakers it was almost over. A spare, muscular young man got up. He spoke only briefly and then, without drama, the debate was done. People moved away chattering into the

43

blaring heat of the afternoon. Then David gave me the bad news.

'I'm afraid what they've agreed on means a lot more walking.'

'Tell me the worst,' I groaned.

'Well the last speaker spelled it out. They're going to have another debate about twenty miles south of here at a place called Moizoi.'

'Jesus' was all I could manage as I heaved the tripod on to my shoulder. Mike and Chris looked resigned.

There was clearly no choice. We had to follow the peace theme and the debates, but it was stunning to discover we had to move on so soon after crawling into Mara. The mirage that it might be the base for the rest of our filming was snuffed out.

Back in camp we discovered that beads, cups and knives had mysteriously disappeared. Scores of suspects sat around the tents enjoying the show. At bathtime in the river, we hung on vindictively to our shrinking bars of soap, deaf to all laughing appeals and blind to the many extended palms of the usual gallery of spectators.

After dinner, we walked out of camp into the uproarious darkness. I had a notion that it might be interesting to have an ongoing narrative commentary from Turton, reflecting on the things we'd filmed each day. My hope was to use David's recorded comments as part of the soundtrack for the completed film to help solve the daunting problem of trying to explain the ways of this exotic place to a British television audience.

We sat in the dark and Chris switched on the tape recorder. 'Let's talk first about how the debates actually work,' I began. 'I couldn't see how any conclusion could come out of this afternoon's talking.' I was just aware of David's silhouette against the piled-up stars as he started, hunting as usual for the exact words.

'There's no voting because they have time to go on talking until some consensus – some sense of the meeting emerges. They have time to go on talking so they can avoid the split which inevitably takes place when you ask people to vote.' Chris snapped off the recorder and yanked away his headphones. 'Sorry, the bloody frogs are swamping David.'

It was an extraordinary noise, like an orchestra of tubular

bells chiming out from the river. Mike and André groped their way off towards the source of the recital and there was a big splash. 'Got 'em,' I heard Mike shout. The froggy bells stopped abruptly. Chris switched on and David continued.

'What I think is happening is that a number of men speak, a sense of the meeting emerges, and then towards the end of the meeting, one or two acknowledged Jalabai speak in a way that sums up the sense of the meeting and most important of all connects it with ultimate Mursi values. And that puts the lid on it. The result is the Jalabai who've spoken towards the end tend to get credited with actually having made the decision, where in fact what they've done is – they've summed up the sense of the meeting and they've given it the stamp of their authority.'

By now the frog chorus had recovered from Mike's boulder and were bonging away like Westminster Abbey on Coronation Day. Further rocks were shrugged off without a hint of variation in the cacophony. Defeated, we walked back to camp as it began to rain.

In the morning, I had a troubling decision to make. It was obvious that this was the end of the line for the jeep. There was no chance that it could survive a crossing of the fast flowing River Mara just beyond our camp. But I'd had it with the wretched jeep anyway. We'd learned some painful lessons about the albatross potential of the thing, and its tendency to turn us into full-time mechanics was threatening to sink any prospect of getting out with a film.

It had to stay at Mara – along with the bulk of our supplies and equipment if we were to move quickly enough to follow unpredictable events. Given the ever-mounting seepage of more or less anything from the site at Mara, someone clearly had to stay behind and guard the stuff.

To his great credit, André took it more or less like a Victorian hero, cursing with surprising restraint. I tried to reassure myself with the fact that André was himself a graduate anthropologist, though I was unsure how an Iranian specalist might be equipped to cope with what could be weeks alone with the Mursi in the front line of a tribal war. With a selflessness worthy of Captain Oates, he turned his energies to filling three sacks with food for our long journey south. I began to wonder whether he wasn't relieved at being spared the awful hikes to come.

Meanwhile, the Mursi had spotted a marketing opportunity. A group of women arrived in camp and made it plain they were offering lip plates for sale. Chris, a passionate critic of capitalism, colonialism and all their works, was tempted. 'They'd make great ash trays,' he suggested, mainly I thought to make David wince. He succeeded. The plates were simply but beautifully fashioned from red clay with a groove round the edge to accept the stretched lip. I held one and found it surprisingly heavy. As our relationship with these people grew more relaxed, the lip cutting seemed even harder to fathom.

I watched a couple of tiny Mursi boys decorating their arms and legs with bandages of cast-off film stock and retreated to my diary:

'Nothing we throw away won't make a decoration or even a utensil. A fantastic lesson in recycling, this trip. I now feel drowned in the experience of this film – like military service half-way through, I can't properly recall the time before it began or imagine a time when it will be ended.'

At Rabithella's cultivation site, the air seemed to scorch my lungs. We sheltered under a rickety bird-scaring platform while a sullen girl stared down at us, her lip-plate jutting defiance. The girl's skin glistened silver against a sky burnished blue black. It was too hot to think.

We'd come to try and gather some domestic material before we went south, but it was gruelling work on this airless afternoon. The women were nervy and uncooperative, scuttling away to hide whenever they spotted the camera. His frustration made Mike fractious. 'This is hopeless,' he grumbled as another girl ducked into the shelter of the giant sorghum stalks.

But gradually, the women began to be bored of hiding, and we began to get glimpses of life on a hot afternoon in a Mursi settlement. We filmed a girl whirling a slingshot on the platform, winding up like a discus thrower to send a stone hurtling over the sorghum to scatter birds with a crack like a rifle shot. As the settlement lost interest in our intrusion, it became clear how the normal patterns of life had been warped by war and crisis.

Even in good times, the Mursi live constantly with what Turton calls 'subsistence anxiety'. Their entire existence is shaped by the struggle to worry a livelihood from their tough homeland which offers them no more than 35 miles by 17 between the rivers that enclose them. They have been able to survive in their isolated and marginal territory only by evolving a variety of subsistence activities. And the remorseless culling of people and animals by natural checks has always remained a crucial ingredient in maintaining the Mursi way of life.

Although they think of themselves above all as cattle-herding people, the constant battle with tsetse fly and rinderpest added to a basic shortage of water and grazing means that the Mursi never have more than a quarter of the animals they would need to survive entirely on a diet of milk, blood and meat. Three quarters of their food has to come from the cultivation of sorghum, which is crucially dependent on a brief rainy season and the flooding of small areas along the river Omo.

For the Mursi the result of their interlocking priorities is a necessity for constant movement, scattering people in temporary settlements between the grasslands and the Omo in response to changing seasonal pressures. In the dry season from October to March, the men follow the cattle into the eastern grasslands in search of grazing and water while the women cultivate sorghum at the Omo. Between April and September, when water is usually available from holes dug in the beds of Omo tributaries, cattle settlements can be established within reach of cultivation areas on the edge of the grasslands.

The hard realities of their environment mean that the two worlds of the Mursi – the world of the Omo and cultivation and women, and the world of grasslands and cattle and men – are only able to come together briefly. June, when we had arrived, should have been the high season of that coming together, a time of eating well and dancing and relaxation.

But Rabithella's settlement had a desolate feel. The temporary brushwood compound with its handful of conical straw huts was almost deserted. A scatter of tiny children grizzled quietly, a woman stood beside her hut, fiddling abstractedly with a lip plate. A young man with a twig in his mouth tinkered with his rifle.

'The war's really hit them,' David said looking round the compound. 'There should be cattle close to here now it's harvest time, but it seems the boys have taken the herds miles away down south to keep them away from Bodi raiders. People are scattered all over the place.'

One central image of Mursi life seemed unaffected that afternoon. Under a shade tree alongside a dried-up river-bed, Rabithella sat talking quietly with a group of men. In my three visits to Mursi country it was to become a scene that gave rise to endless bitchy speculation amongst our film crews. I suppose the fundamental question that exercised us as we plodded past yet another group of lounging men on our way to yet another uncomfortable and distant location was: 'How do they get away with it?'

While the women toiled ceaselessly with children, cultivation, grinding, cooking, housebuilding, birdscaring and a score of other exhausting labours, the men seemed to sit for days on end under those trees, chattering, laughing, spitting, sleeping. Towards evening, their young sons would return from a gruelling day of following the cattle and the men would rouse themselves to return to their settlements for a meal of sorghum porridge prepared by the women. It wasn't to be until our third film ten years later that I really began to understand how the spirited Mursi women see their situation and we found a way to film the marvellously ironic view they had of our liberal sympathisings.

On this fiery afternoon, the talk was of war and of how peace might be made. Rabithella gnawed on a stick of sugar cane and told us how the last war had been resolved twenty years before. 'We Mursi and Bodi – when we're at war and we're exhausted and ready for peace – we have no holy place for making peace. When the Bodi peacemakers come, we simply kill a cow.' Rabithella slammed his palm onto his closed fist, miming the act of felling the animal with a big stone. 'We cut the peritoneum into strips and tie them round our necks. Then we make coffee. We tell the Bodi: "Go home and sleep four nights." We go to their settlements. Then they kill a cow. Again we tie the peritoneum round our necks. Enough, the war is ended.' He spat decisively.

We started walking away from André and Mara at 10.30 the next morning.

In the confusions of negotiating our way out of a strike by porters who suddenly demanded a hundred percent increase in their fees, we hardly had time to say goodbye to our researcher who was probably about to become the most isolated Englishman in Africa. It was of course a regulation flawless day, merciless as we scrambled up slopes of hot shale and out into a wilderness of grass. At least, I kept telling myself, David has said it's not more than three hours to Moizoi.

Five hours later, we cowered under a bush while Mike fantasised a banquet of iced lager, chilled Chablis and tingling gin and tonic. Our water bottles were long empty, and I'd ceased to believe in David's encouraging predictions that Moizoi was just over the next ridge. Even the Mursi looked shrivelled. For lack of anything else, I passed round handfuls of lemonade powder, shaking the yellow crystals into a dozen suspicious Mursi palms. I lugged my diary from a sweat-soaked shirt pocket and scrawled: 'We sit under a tree in Africa with the Mursi, all licking "Rise n' Shine" from our hands.'

We went on numbly through tangled mazes of greenery where I kept losing the Mursi just ahead of me. The light began to mellow towards evening. Then, without warning, we broke through into a vision of something like paradise. All three of us, Mike, Chris and I, actually shouted 'paradise' as we ran towards the mirage.

A delicious little river, clear and sparkling ran through a pretty green valley. To my joy and disbelief, David confirmed the mirage was real and it was called Moizoi. I teetered over stepping stones, dumped clothes and everything and fell into the generosity of water.

It was almost worth the torments of the day to hang in the cool river. I shut off and stayed there for a long time. I could only recall one such blissful reprieve. In 1970, after days of dehydration, exhaustion and fear, filming with a group of ZAPU guerrillas and hiding in a ditch close to the Zambezi river, I crawled back into Lusaka and a comfortable hotel. I lay ecstatic in a shining bath with glasses of lager and ice cubes lined up along the rim. But on that occasion it had been all over and I was going home. This time there was no lager and no end in sight.

With the sky glowing copper behind trees standing like tuning-forks along the river, we slashed at the grass to start one more campsite. The porters were already gone, incredibly re-tracing that endless path back to Mara. Soon the tents were up and a freeze-dried dinner was melting on the fire. I confided in the diary:

'Some lessons – we can't go on with treks like this. We can't afford the time, the cloths or the energy. We certainly can't carry on hopping up and down this exhausting land. Now three locals have arrived. They greeted me in a whisper by the river. Pat's shocked by their thinness. They talked of Bodi raids right down here in the "stomach" of Mursi country. Colossal din of life alongside the river here – frogs rev up like speedway bikes above the general uproar.'

Over the days that followed, we established new routines at the river campsite, shooting occasionally at settlements in the area while Turton scouted tirelessly for news of the war and of debates. The river subsided to a trickle after days without rain.

The diary insisted improbably that this was only our third week and ticked over with cameos of the meandering days:

'We come upon the Priest's mother who looks like the oldest woman in the world and was here when Italian explorers passed along the Omo in 1896 . . . David has retrieved his radio from a tent he left here months ago. The World Service news reveals we're all a quarter of an hour adrift. Nothing new – Nixon in Moscow, rain at Wimbledon . . . Ulichagi's homecoming after two and a half months in Addis. His wife said to David "You've come". To Ulichagi himself, she said not a word . . . Awful night of heat and tossing and bites . . . Chris entertains some kids and tells them "fascist" while he taps a picture of John Wayne. A pretty teenager fancies Chris, but not his hair . . . Feel shattered, my back flayed to sun-tatters.'

The hypnotic sequence of days was broken at last by a sudden debate near the river. It was a stilted little occasion with only three speakers, but its consequences for us made a dismal diary entry:

'Now the problems really bite and the decisions press – where to go, what to do as the time begins to drain away. The debate decided David should go all the way back to Gura(!!) and fetch the Bodi for peace talks. Agony in the afternoon. We perm possibilities and even look up phases of the moon. The Mursi say peace must be made before the moon wanes if at all. It's a really difficult decision – do we go south to meet up with the cattle and hope to snatch the beginnings of peace talks on the way, or rush north now?'

Within an hour, of course, everything was overturned. I saw David murmuring with a worried-looking Ulichagi and then he flopped beside me to report: 'It's crazy. Ulichagi's just told me that while we were on the way down here to Moizoi, a Mursi raiding party went up into Bodi country and they've been in a shoot-out. So there's no point in us dashing up north for peace talks now.'

I wandered down to the river and envied the order of a squadron of 2-inch blue dragonflies. I wrote: 'Planning has just become impossible in this swamp. Numbing sense of starting all over again.'

The next morning, we saw our first evidence of the war. In a settlement about half an hour from the river, we filmed with a boy who'd been injured during an incident with the Bodi. He crawled out through the doorway of his hut, clearly in great pain, his wounded arm supported by a girl. His right elbow was shattered, a livid pink mess hopelessly patched with grass. In a hoarse whisper, he told David how it had happened. Three weeks ago he was one of a group chasing a Bodi raiding party which was trying to snatch cattle from the far south of Mursi country twenty miles away. He was shot, and the others fled. With his uninjured arm, he traced the height of the sun above the horizon. 'When the sun was low, the Bodi stopped looking for me, and I found my way home in the dark.'

Pat bandaged his wound expertly and dosed him with antibiotics. His immaculate new dressing looked impossibly optimistic in the tatty, dispiriting settlement, and it was hard to conceive what the boy's life would be like now with a damaged arm.

The war followed us in the afternoon to Ulichagi's settlement. He led us from our campsite, climbing up after almost an hour onto a ridge at a place called Ma'do. It was a welcome liberation of handsome spaces after the days of being hemmed in by the dense bush. As our little procession moved along the ridge, we could see a map of Mursi country laid out below us. Almost ten miles away, the River Omo showed like silver stitching on the dark green band of impenetrable bushbelt that surrounds it. Wobbling in heat haze along the horizon was a frieze of mountains.

At first, I couldn't see a sign of Ulichagi's settlement. David located it for me, directing my eyes to an inconspicuous dent in the edge of the bushbelt. With the assistance of Mike's zoom lens it resolved into a trim little compound circled by a brushwood fence. As I zoomed out, the settlement merged and melted again into the huge landscape.

Inside Ulichagi's compound, his family were busy with the ceaseless round of tasks which I now recognised as daily life for people who have to work at survival. But it seemed a relaxed and pleasant place as we moved round the edges of the neat compound, trying to be as unobtrusive as our fantastic invasion would allow.

A woman knelt over a curved stone, dipping and rising with the effort of grinding sorghum into flour. On a stiff animal skin, a pretty girl winnowed grain, letting it fall in torrents through her hands and blowing away the chaff. Another woman snapped branches to fuel the fire. The usual scatter of kids and babies played in the dust. Sitting quietly near his hut, Ulichagi watched his toiling family. He looked glad to be home after his weeks in that madhouse of Addis Ababa with Turton.

He caught my eye and said, 'A-chali?' The Mursi word for 'good' had been one of my earliest gleanings. 'A-chali hang,' I answered, and on this glorious afternoon Ulichagi's domestic idyll did look pretty good. Certainly it must have compared well with the frightening squalor he'd have witnessed in the teeming slums of Addis.

David had talked about Ulichagi's family, and it was instructive about some harsher realities. Ulichagi had two wives, one inherited from a dead brother. A short time ago, his 4-year-old daughter had died after being bitten by a poisonous spider. Now Turton was also able to point out other evidence that things weren't as relaxed as they seemed.

'You see where those grain storage platforms are?' He gestured towards the corner of the compound. 'Well a couple of months ago, there were three huts standing over there. They must really be worried about the war.'

One of Ulichagi's wives showed us what had happened to the huts. We followed her with the camera along a twisting, almost invisible path that led off into the dense bushbelt behind the compound. After a few minutes, we broke into a little clearing. The three huts were hidden away here, dismantled and rebuilt in the hope of staying undetected by any future Bodi raiders. It was an understandable precaution after recent attacks in the area had killed and wounded a number of Mursi. I had a momentary snapshot of recollection from my childhood – an air raid shelter in the back garden of a Glasgow suburb, nights smelling of earth with the noise of bombs in the darkness.

We walked back over the ridge towards our camp. It was a sublime afternoon, like a warm bath, with the colossal perspectives of the Lower Omo valley spread around us in tawny evening sunlight. Slimmed down to a semblence of fitness by our exertions, I found I could even enjoy the walking. For a moment at least, I could feel why David loved this place.

4

'Seven a.m. Lying in bed with madly itching, peeling back, the tiresome unsatisfactory routines of the morning ahead, then a trek to a place called Waren. Fed up with feeling tatty, longing for order and home.'

The diary had become vital therapy, a necessary fix to start the day by imposing some illusion of order on the unpredictable mess I felt I'd inhabited for as long as I could remember. We crawled out of the tents and went into the motions of yet another pack, dismantling mud-spattered tents, clanking bed frames, cramming damp rucksacks. This morning though, the routine had a new ingredient.

A shout and a sudden spasm of activity around the Turtons' collapsed tent jolted us out of our lethargy. I saw Galai, a Mursi boy thrashing the tent with a stick. In the folds of a sleeping bag, a brown snake was writhing towards death, its white belly livid against the blue nylon.

'God, that looks nasty David. How long d'you reckon it's been there?' I asked, fascinated and alarmed as the Mursi bashed the snake to stillness.

'It must have been asleep in the tent lining all night,' David said.

'Probably harmless anyway,' Mike said dismissively.

'I'm afraid that was one of the deadly ones,' David said mildly, wandering off to retrieve washing from the line, soggy with overnight rain.

The Mursi youth tossed the dead snake into the bushes. I

turned to the routines of the morning, light-headed with too many exotic assumptions too early in the day.

As we huddled round the smoky fire grubbing for breakfast, there was another interruption. An unremarkable brown bird flapped over us and the Mursi boy dropped his sooty porridge spoon. Plunging into the river, his eyes fixed on the bird, he vanished into the bush.

'Honey bird,' said David and we scrambled wearily for the film gear. Turton had told us a couple of days earlier how the Mursi trail the honey birds in the hope of being led to a bees' nest and a source of much-prized honey. We floundered across the river and into the dense bush on the other side, half-dressed and panting in pursuit of a sequence. Lumbered with camera, tape recorder and spare film we were instantly left far behind by the teasing bird and the bushwise Mursi.

Lost in the wet undergrowth, I wondered distractedly if this was how David Attenborough went about those immaculate wildlife films. After a few hopeless minutes when we were just about to call it off in favour of breakfast, we blundered into a clearing and found the Mursi gazing up at the honey bird which was perching unconcernedly in a tree. Mike started filming as the Mursi looked at the bird and the bird looked down at its assembled pursuers. Chris poked the microphone at the tree to catch the odd quizzical tweet. Nothing happened for a while. Then the Mursi turned and walked away. It seemed the honey bird's mission, like ours, had been abortive. No honey, no sequence, and still no breakfast. We trudged back across the river.

As the sun slammed through, we completed our pack and made thin jokes about the walking to come. Mursi straggled into the campsite and David slowly began to recruit porters. Our supply of cloth to pay the porters was shrinking alarmingly after the long trek in, and we'd tried to trim our loads to the absolute minimum. We were also trying to budget for a long walk south to make contact with the Mursi cattle, a vital sequence in the developing story of the film.

'We really are going to have to watch it or we'll have nothing to barter our way back to the plane,' said David, anxiously scanning our skimpy bale of coarse white cloth.

'Maybe we could rip up our bedsheets,' I suggested half-jokingly.

'It may well come to that,' said David grimly.

At last we were ready to move. David assigned loads to the porters and we filled our water bottles. Then everything changed.

Striding easily towards us across the river were some men I recognised. They were the group we'd hired the day before as messengers to André, still exiled alone with the jeep and our stores twenty-five endless miles to the north. They were back with the equipment we'd asked for, but they were also carrying other things. The tallest of the party ambled up to me with a grin, betraying no trace of his fifty-mile round trip. Dangling from one hand, he carried what looked like a natty handbag. As he came closer, I realised it was a tortoise, a grass thong laced through its shell as a handle. In his other hand he had a stick – a cleft stick. In the cleft was a silver foil bag that had held lemonade powder. In the bag was a letter from André.

Headed 'Saturday – I think . . .', it contained stunning news. 'Our dear Captain Cherkole descended with his lorry late last night. He made two things clear. "Tell Dr David to do all he can to make peace with the Mursi and I will do the same for the Bodi. If not, they will get big trouble from us." He seemed pretty determined to stamp on anything, and since yesterday he says the army clamped down on Addis again, arresting more and stressing military control, our beloved Captain might want to shine on one battlefield or other. His second problematic statement was that he would collect us all and our gear in a week's time from today.'

As I reached that part of my public reading of André's letter, there was a chorus of disbelieving obscenities from my colleagues. Via the cleft stick, we were delivered the impossibility of trying to complete the film in days. I don't know how many of the others shared the dazed relief that collided in me with the dismay. I returned to André's letter feeling numb. He had a new worry it seemed.

'It's all about monkeys. One noble savage yesterday dumped a sick monkey on me as a present for David. Whilst feeding the wretched thing with milk, it tried unsuccessfully to nip me. No teeth however pierced any skin, but a minute quantity of saliva may have got on my finger. A beautiful finger I hasten to add, but one covered with scratches and sores, etc. The real question, you may have guessed, is whether there is any threat at all of rabies. Otherwise there is nothing else to report from this thriving, throbbing metropolis.'

'What do you think, Pat?'

Marshalling the practicality of the trained nurse, Pat delivered her prescription. 'If he's still alive by the time he gets our reply, he'll be fine.'

As I scribbled my best effort at a comforting reply, addressed to 'André and monkey', we tried to rebuild our plans. It was clear we had to make the rendezvous with the Captain and his lorry in a week's time. That meant there was no chance of the long walk further south we'd planned to meet up with the all-important Mursi cattle. For all the confusion and the loss of film prospects, what I mostly felt was a guilty relief. At last there was some limit to the physical slog. Best of all was the merciful suggestion of a lift back to Hana. My faith in the comforting fantasy spoke volumes for the resilience of my battered optimism. I finished my reply to André and Mike added a cheerful postscript: 'Be prepared to greet four very thin people in a week's time.'

Meanwhile, there was still today's walk. We braced ourselves for a trek that was now driven into the blazing centre of the day. There was to be yet another last minute reprieve. It arrived in the impressive form of the Priest, Komorakora. We slumped gratefully on our packs as David began a consultation.

I was intrigued to have a sight of Komorakora at last. David had talked about the man and his critical importance for the Mursi and I'd been fascinated. The Priest was, as David described it, a kind of lightning conductor between the supernatural world and the Mursi, and a vital guarantee of the survival of Mursi-ness. But for all his importance, his secular authority was non-existent. Among the leaderless Mursi, the Priest had no more wealth or power to demand obedience than anyone else. He had however the potential for danger through his access to power for good and evil via his other-worldly connections.

Seeing him now at close quarters, I could understand why David had said that being with Komorakora always made him feel unworthy and earthbound, like being in audience with the Archbishop of Canterbury. He spoke so quietly I could hardly hear him a few feet away. His elegant hands moved in small feathery gestures, a massive ivory bangle at his wrist. But his stillness came off him like an odour, and the eyes in his delicate chiselled face seemed to be narrowed to contemplate something we couldn't see.

As quietly as he'd come, the Priest left. David gave us a report of the conversation, and I recorded the results:

'Our options solidify. A debate here tomorrow seems a strong prospect. So we wait here another day. But anything's possible now. We lie in the shade, not able to face an afternoon un-packing what we spent all morning packing. David chases off hordes of women and kids who've moved in over the past hour.'

But of course, the afternoon was another thing. It began with shouts and a horn blast on the far side of the river. 'It sounds like another Bodi raid,' David said as he dashed away. We shambled after him, in time only to glimpse a scatter of young men running into the bush. We trailed back to our stripped campsite just as the horn echoed again along the river. 'It's a debate,' David yelled, and we grabbed for the film gear.

After the confusions of the morning, it was a powerful and memorable occasion. Approaching along the river bank, a man was blowing repeatedly into a stubby horn, the strident barks bouncing off the rocks. Grave and unhurried, men gathered from every direction, arrogant young warriors with nonchalant rifles, dignified old men carrying carved stools. One man flaunted a curling feather in his headband, others displayed fierce daubs of grey or yellow mud on their faces. As they assembled in a grassy clearing alongside the river, their silence invested the occasion with a sense of crisis. Most men waited in the shade; a few stood, leaning on duelling poles, their outlines echoing the tall palms that fringed the river. Without formality or introduc-tion, a man rose to begin the debate.

For the next hour, we shifted around in the undergrowth trying to make a film record of the debate. Although we couldn't understand a word, it was clearly a grave occasion. A succession of speakers strode through the grass, their voices rising in passion as they agonised about war and crisis. We'd witnessed something of it in that first debate we filmed a week ago. But this time there was a new sense of urgency and concern. These were very worried people. They received the speeches with sombre attention. I was struck more forcibly than ever before by the demonstration of complexity and sophistication in a way of life that had seemed at first encounter trapped at the level of subsistence. We changed to our last loaded film magazine as Turton crouched beside me and whispered disturbing news.

'It seems some Bodi passed right through here last night and went down south to the Mursi cattle. They killed a couple of herd boys and got away. They're debating about what to do now. Some people want to move down to the cattle. But they might decide to move the cows up here to guard them.'

'God, that would be great for us,' I said with the self-obsession of the film-maker, as Mike and Chris quietly identified another film roll and began to follow a new speaker.

It was a testing business for the crew. With the debaters pacing up and down ceaselessly between fierce sunlight and deep shadow, Mike had to concentrate intently on focus and exposure. I tried to whisper directions into his ear and then realised I was wasting my time. His free ear, the one not nuzzling the camera, was the deaf one, forfeited to a Ugandan border guard's boot during another documentary assignment five years earlier. Mike continued filming, happily oblivious of my directions. For Chris, the restless patterns of the debate demanded that he follow every movement of the speakers with the directional gun microphone. Meanwhile the flood of talk was consuming our last loaded film.

I panted back along the river bank to our campsite and dug into the crew's tent for film cans. Struggling to recall Mike's lessons, I fumbled in the black, cloth changing-bag, my hands slippery with sweat, and prayed I was reloading the magazine properly. It was a curious job for a director, but conventional demarcations and vanities had melted early under the assaults of the lower Omo.

'How's it going?' Pat said, doubtfully observing my contortions.

'It's going,' I said and loped off to the debate. I arrived back just in time to retrieve another completed magazine and run for the campsite and another reload. As I thumped along, I reflected hazily that it was an odd way to direct a film.

'It'll be over soon,' Pat offered sympathetically as I rummaged in the bag again.

Back at the debate, things did seem to be resolving. As Mike slammed on the new magazine, David whispered that the Priest was summing up the consensus of the debate.

'It seems they've decided to bring the cows up here and build a defensive compound,' he said. If the Priest hadn't looked as dignified and unworldly as ever, I could have rushed up and kissed him. Back in camp. I discovered that Galai, our helper, had vanished with my watch.

We collapsed into the tents soon after dark. I could only squeeze out a few weary words for the diary: 'The end of a ridiculous day. An exhausted calm is all I can manage. We've all had enough. We can only wait here now and hope the film comes up north to us.'

With time draining away, the next twenty-four hours drifted by, uneventful and frustrating. The almost total absence of Mursi visitors felt distinctly strange. David went off to look for cows or news of cows, and returned to report hearing rifle shots and yet another Bodi raid. A Mursi had told him about a wounded herd boy. 'Only his eyes live,' the Mursi said. David had also been told that the boy who took my watch had been fired on by the Bodi. It seemed they'd missed.

At the day's end, David returned weary from another news hunt, arriving in camp backed by a ravishing yellow sky stencilled with sinuous black palm trees. We were absurdly thrilled by his message. The cows were already on their way north to us. I confessed to the diary:

'None of us dare admit our relief at the possible return of the cows. After so many reverses, even hope is dangerous. But if only they come I feel we can have a really strong film.'

Round the fire after dinner, I tried to explain to David why the return of the cattle seemed so important for the film. I was sure that their arrival as predicted in the debate would give vital narrative coherence to a film that could otherwise appear a shapeless ramble. David had also told us how the cattle would give back meaning to the entire Mursi society and I felt that if they came before we had to leave, we would have an excellent chance to gather the kind of material we'd been denied by the disruptions of the war.

'But why are you so keen about that kind of narrative tidiness,' David asked. 'It seems to me you're in danger of imposing a phoney story on the real mess of events.'

'Whether we like it or not, we're partly in the storytelling business,' I insisted. But we were both too tired to mount our own favourite debate. In the tent, before crunching the nightly Mogadon, I wrote: 'I never wanted to see cows so much in my life.'

By 4 a.m. Chris was crawling into the tent to join Mike and me for the second time. His bold plan to sleep out in the open seemed less attractive as the rain hammered on the tent. I fell asleep and dreamed I was going bald. As a sullen grey light thickened on the tent wall, the crew drowsed on while I read a paperback about the Scottish clearances and fantasised about a family holiday in Venice that was somehow supposed to happen in a few days time. For a second morning, we were becalmed on the bedraggled site, starved of news. Around 11 a.m., as a thin drizzle faded out, a party of men sloshed across the river towards us. We filmed them as they sprawled exhausted on the rocks. His rifle propped against a tree, one warrior arranged another's hair.

David chatted quietly to some of the men. They had grim news of the war. Yesterday afternoon, it seemed, there'd been a shootout near André at Mara. One Bodi had been killed, two injured. A Mursi was dead. André must have heard the firing. We could only wonder about his alarm so far from any support. David had also picked up other news of special interest to film-hungry television people.

'It seems the Bodi was killed by a young Mursi boy. It's his first killing, so there'll be a big celebration when the raiding party get back here. We'd better hang on to see what happens.'

'The cows will have to wait for us,' I agreed.

It began with the sound of distant singing, fierce and emo-tional, away in the bush beyond the river. We ran for the film gear and Mike was shooting as we spotted a file of men coming in from the north. Agonisingly, Chris was having problems with a faulty mike cable. Panting alongside me, he changed cables on the run. Thumbs up, and we were rolling just as the returning raiders exploded in celebration. A single rifle shot ricocheted along the river and then a voice sang out a triumphal phrase, echoed by an affirming chant down the line. Now we could see a score of them, filing along the far bank, rifles across shoulders.

They crossed in the shallows, and men were coming in from every direction. Soon, there was a spontaneous procession, moving together through the bush, song and counter melody re-echoing, shrill exultant whistles cutting into the harmonies. Their progression was like a force of nature, heady with shared feeling. As it all spilled out around us, it was as though we were invisible. Tripping and stumbling as we filmed, I felt clumsy and intrusive. But we were merely irrelevant. The procession surged on, utterly regardless of us, heading for some important place.

'Out of film,' Mike yelled, snapping a completed magazine off the camera and slamming the last loaded one in place. It was time for my delivery service again. As the men headed off into the bush pursued by Mike and Chris, I pelted back along the narrow twisting track towards the campsite and another frantic film-loading session. Minutes later, I was crashing along the track again in search of the action and the crew. Almost immediately, I was totally lost. Sweat-soaked and filthy, I lurched along colliding with thorn bushes and getting tangled with everything. I was just about to give up when I almost collided with a rangy young Mursi. We stood on the path staring at one another, locked in different lives. Feeling oafish, I struggled to find some way of asking for help. Suddenly I remembered the name the Mursi had given David. 'Lusi Golonyi,' I stammered. Without a word, the Mursi led me into the bush.

We came upon them in a clearing, just finishing an impromptu debate. In moments, it was all over. People wandered away, the charged emotions abruptly dissipated. Dripping but exultant, Mike and Chris switched off. They enthused about what I'd missed, a vivid sequence of wild song and celebration, laced with rifle shots.

'Terrific stuff,' Mike said. 'Pity you missed it. We didn't need the other magazine.' We strolled back to the camp in a blessing of late afternoon sunlight.

In the dark, we gathered round the tape recorder and replayed the day's excitements. The songs and gunfire drowned out the uproar of the bush, even swamping the chorus of river frogs which had revved through our nights at Moizoi. We sipped precious brandy and found more to laugh about than for days. As the fire faded, we talked about the film. The diary held the mellow feel:

'A long conversation about how to reconcile the anthropology with the showbiz, me with David. We do get on and I can only hope we can work it out. Of course I agree with him about the importance of a permanent record. I think he accepts a necessary degree of filmic style. We shall see, months and thousands of miles away in a quiet cutting room – seems an inconceivable distance away.'

As we moved towards the tents, a Mursi messenger arrived with another overturning note from André. Captain Cherkole had a problem. He wouldn't be picking us up with the lorry after all. Our return journey was as problematic as ever. With revolution flaring in Addis, André reckoned our rescue plane was dodgy. We could be living in Hana for ever. To make the most of our chances of escape, we had three days to finish the film.

Those three days were to provide some of the most extraordinary and memorable hours of my life, teeming with images of haunting power that brought me at last into some kind of contact in feeling with a different way of being alive. The desperate last possible days of shooting transformed the film. They also shifted some old certainties and assumptions in me.

It all began unpromisingly enough, trapped in the tents yet again while unseasonal rain thrashed down on us, then trudging through mud under leaden skies to the ridge overlooking the eternities of bushbelt along the river Omo. We arrived, dirty and dispirited to witness what looked for a moment like a small miracle. Whole trees were moving through the bush in a crazy parody of *Macbeth*'s Birnam Wood. As my eyes struggled for meaning in the vistas of merging greenery, I registered that gangs of naked young men were slashing through the bush, dragging trees and foliage into a huge, almost undiscernible circle, green on more green. They had to be making the defensive compound that had been agreed in the debate. We filmed as the compound took shape to the accompaniment of a fine, swirling worksong. Perched on a rock with half a dozen laughing boys, we tried to record more singing. Time and again, songs collapsed in giggles. Then suddenly it all came into focus in a perfectly-shaped little cattle song. A plaintive solo voice was answered and reshaped in a descant of other voices, in grave and exquisite harmony. Closing my eyes as the song wound on, I was flooded by a rush of unexpected feeling. For the first time I knew Turton was right. It wasn't a journey back in time coming here and these people weren't living an earlier, simpler version of my

63

life. Their song might be trapped in our stainless steel tape recorder, but they knew some things we didn't.

We played back the song to the boys, gathered in astonishment round the tape recorder. They might be innocent of technology or of the world beyond their horizon. But David had talked about how he'd never seen emotional illness here, and the cattle song, like the debates seemed to contain something of that sanity.

As the song cut out, I caught another sound in the ongoing uproar of the bush, something I hadn't heard before. Faint bells, dottily reminiscent of trim alpine meadows, signalled the approach of the longed-for cattle.

And here they were, massively matter-of-fact after all our fantasies, pouring down the ridge towards the compound. We filmed blissfully as hundreds of the big humped beasts shouldered their way through the grass to a celebratory soundtrack of bells and bellowing. A scatter of insect-thin herd boys moved through the throng, I could also see the Priest and Ulichagi with dozens of other familiar Mursi, relishing the flow of animals. I felt that for the first time I was seeing the shape of Mursi society, freed for a moment from the dislocations of war.

David had often talked about the crucial significance of the cattle for the Mursi. From marriage to aesthetics, cattle define the way the Mursi organise their lives and the way they see themselves. Impressed by the piles of equipment we'd brought with us, Ulichagi had asked David how many cattle I had at home in England. Since getting the reply, he'd looked at me with pity. The Mursi sense of who they are is largely invested in their cattle. Although they're too precious to be killed for meat and are little more than famine insurance for people who survive through cultivation, the cattle are wealth. A man cannot marry without handing over cattle to his bride's father – 'in the twenties these days is a good bride price,' David had said – and that central fact of Mursi life has its reverberations everywhere.

We followed the herds streaming into the new compounds, slithering around on the carpet of cow dung as we filmed. All around us, I could see confirmation of the Mursi obsession with their cattle. Horns were elaborately trained into handsome curves, bulls wore heavy, decorated collars. A splendid brown cow, shiny with health, boasted a trellised head-collar more complex than anything I'd seen in Mursi country. Turton had told us how young men were expected to be fanatical about cattle. Those who weren't were regarded as drop-outs. Men should sit around at the end of the day, discussing the markings and colours of their favourite animals. It seemed the entire creative energies of a people were centred in the cattle. For me, it was contained in a couple of images. A strapping young man sat on the ground under a cow, drinking directly from its udder. He sucked noisily, entirely oblivious and absorbed as we filmed. Nearby, another man stroked a cow's neck and sang quietly.

A dismal slog back to camp, boots weighted with mud couldn't quite obliterate the glow of the day's shooting. The hopeful mood even survived the discovery of my latest blisters and a puddle of paraffin all over the floor of our chaotic tent. Before the Mogadon, I confided to the diary desperate hopes for the last available forty-eight hours of filming down here in the heart of Mursi country: 'An early start tomorrow in the hope of ceremony and grand-slam debate. If only it happens, we'll have cracked it. God preserve my insane optimism.'

The next morning delivered the inevitable reproof. Another night of wakefulness and bucketing rain left the track to the ridge a gluey obstacle course. I whimpered to the diary: 'Swinish trudge through the bush, me portering the bloody tripod. Absolutely soaked with sweat and rainy leaves, boots loaded with mud which has to be shrugged off every few steps. Wretched hard work.' But almost immediately, there was no time for scribbling. Events began to explode around us, bizarre and unpredictable.

A black goat, bleating with terror was dragged past us and down into the compound. We plunged after the action, arriving just as the goat's throat was slashed open, spilling its blood over an impassive white ox. For all the raw force of the ritual, it was an oddly casual occasion, the men performing the sacrifice expressionless and matter-of-fact. The wet scream of the dying goat tipped my stomach, but mercifully we had a distraction. 'The sodding viewfinder's steamed up with condensation,' Mike said, scrubbing in exasperation with my grubby handkerchief. As we fussed with the camera, a young black ox skittered past, pursued by a gang of excited boys, whistling and laughing. Trying to follow them, we almost fell over a circle of men studying the intestines of a goat.

A friend who saw the scene in the completed film could de-scribe it back to me in lurid detail ten years later. It wasn't easy to forget. On a skin, the intestines were laid out, coiled and glistening. Round them, rapt and troubled were a dozen men, including Ulichagi and the Priest. But the important figure was Biobume, a stately old man who wore his sheet round his head like a turban. Biobume was clearly an expert in reading the future from entrails, and he didn't look happy. Pointing at the details which bothered him, he delivered his predictions in a fractured whisper. As the second set of entrails were set before Biobume, David explained that they were laid out like a map of Mursi country. From the position of bloodspots in the entrails, experts could foretell dangers like the approach of Bodi raiders. Months later in a Manchester editing room as we untangled the sequence, David confirmed the bad news written on the watching faces. It seemed an elder brother of the priest was going to fall ill. On the soundtrack, Turton also heard a couple of spectators discussing our filming antics. 'I don't mind the one with the ear,' the man said of Chris's microphone, 'but the one with the eye drives me crazy.'

The exasperated little exchange was a useful corrective footnote to our mood that day after the rush of blood and guts we'd been recording. David had discovered that the goat sacrifice had been to purify the cattle after the death of a herdboy in the Bodi raids, but I still felt oppressed by the things we'd witnessed that morning. It all seemed to throw into relief the darkest and least accessible areas of Mursi life, the territories of the spirit hardest to share. David wandered off with Ulichagi in search of news about a possible debate and we sprawled on the ridge to wait, sticky under a lid of low cloud. Glutted by the events of the morning and the three-week accumulation of exhaustion and discomfort, I waited out a tetchy hour with Mike and Chris and a circle of curious Mursi.

Only twenty-four hours after our joyful encounter with the returning cattle and my new sense of contact with Mursiness, I grumbled sourly to the diary: 'Stretched out on the hillside, ringed by irritating Mursi spectators fingering gaiters, hair, watch, soul. We grow to dislike them, so devoid of dimension and style. Apart from debating, their life seems perilously short of the things that make humanity interesting. And the remorseless intrusion becomes hard to bear. We feel ambushed by Mursi, cows and flies. Much talk of going home.'

It was an ill-humoured and unworthy little outburst, particularly given the scale of our own uninvited intrusions on these people. But it was some indication of the strain of preserving liberal agendas under the assaults of some uncomfortable realities.

I saw yet another pushy young warrior tap Mike on the arm and mime puffing a cigarette. For some reason it was Mike's last straw after weeks of seemingly inexhaustible good humour. The Mursi tapped him again. 'Why don't you go away and invent the wheel or something,' Mike said. I knew how he felt.

I remember Pat Turton's bitterness about the Mursi way of death. More than once, Pat had talked with angry bewilderment about the Mursi practice of abandoning old or sick relatives in the bush to be killed by wild animals. David quietly insisted there was no other way for a people who lived always on the verge of survival. He also reported many experiences of individual Mursi devastated by bereavement. As we walked back from the ridge, the circling ambiguities went with me, unresolved.

I saw our site carpeted with food packets, elastoplasts, Pat's blood-sample cards, toilet paper and the littered evidence of the squalor we'd brought with us. Most of my clothes seemed to have disappeared, but it didn't matter any more. Pat and Chris bickered on about the PLO and far-away nightmares. A tatty Mursi dog sniffed round our tent. He was wasting his time with our food almost gone. Although we were still two weeks away from Hana and our rescue plane the air felt full of endings. And tomorrow was our last possible day of filming before the long walk out of Mursi country.

It was hard to remember there was still a world of television studios and editing rooms. But the possibility compelled me to review some hard truths. There was no avoiding it. Even after the strong material we'd managed to gather over the last two days, at the end of all the miles and the effort, I wasn't sure we had enough for a film.

The diary glowed with the miracle of that final day: 'Breakthrough – we have a film. Stunning day on the ridge, thirteen magazines of what we came for, non-stop sweat, but thrilling. Its suddenly over. We all smile and feel good. Swirling mare's tail clouds for celebration.' It was an absurd cavalry-to-the-rescue way to end, but it felt like a childhood Christmas morning.

It all began to happen as soon as we arrived that last day, a gust of excitement wafting down from high on the ridge in a confusion of wild singing, horns and whistles. We scrambled up the stony hillside towards the din. At the top, an extraordinary procession was gathering. Scores of men, daubed and decorated, stood under a huge sky overlooking the new compounds and the marvellous spaces of the Omo Valley. Ecstatic and edgy, they sang and chanted a fierce plainsong. At the head of the column, a pair of men pranced with the stiffened legs of excited cats, arms flung upwards like bulls' horns, rifles thrust at the sky. In the main group I spotted a startling figure, his naked body stippled with a dozen white handprints.

We filmed, working fluidly with the flow of things. Turton broke away from a conversation with a strangely skittish Ulichagi. 'The Priest is going to hold a purification ceremony,' he reported. 'What's that all about?' I asked, shoving the tripod out of Mike's way as he moved down the line of men, camera on shoulder. 'Well, it's to cleanse the Mursi of their enemies and give them new strength for the fight. People are going to be coming here from miles around. There should even be men from up near André at Mara. It's a big thing.'

I slammed an identifying clapper-board with a grateful flourish. 'Any idea what we should look out for?' I asked. 'I think they're going to perform a ritual attack on the Priest's compound. Then they'll act out killing him.'

Stalking down the hillside, all rifles and menace, the four-man ceremonial death squad had a terrible conviction. Mike and Chris shadowed them, like an extension of the murderous dance. A shot rang out as the men passed through the brushwood opening into the Priest's compound. Inside, the raiding party began a hypnotic circling of a smoking fire, their feet smacking rhythmically in the mud. Gravity gathered around the isolated figure of the Priest, standing remote, casting his sheet over a shoulder. In moments, a vortex of men enclosed the Priest, spiralling round him in a whirlpool of possession and commitment. They bound their spell with a fierce humming chant, louder and louder in an irresistible pulse of feeling.

It was an occasion of quite overwhelming power, sweeping away in an instant my glib judgements of the day before. The sense of something remarkable swept us all. Mike and Chris recorded the sequence in a single astonishing take, the film catching the irresistible *élan* of the events. Even the sudden prospect of Chris falling flat at one point in the mire of cowmuck failed to break the spell.

But though we filmed, we couldn't enter. I'd felt compelled to keep the crew outside the circle and our exclusion underscored the ultimate impossibility of capturing the dimensions of the ritual on film. And soon a second wave was swelling as the men of Mara flowed into the compound and joined the great circle. As the movement at last exhausted itself, the Priest stood silent, almost detached. He took up a wooden bowl, brimming with water and bright green leaves.

Moving round the circle of men, he began the final act of the purification. Around us, men shivered in anticipation, emitting strange stifled trills of ecstasy. There was a sound like a hissing cat and I shifted to see the Priest spraying water from his mouth into the faces of the men. One man hopped and gibbered as the Priest murmured some words. Then he drank from the bowl and moved on to spray another group. Alongside me, a man with a disturbing yellow-daubed face burst into a brief, joyous song. Again the quiet words from the Priest.

Armed with David's translations, I understood the force of those seemingly casual blessings. 'Let your foreheads be powerful,' the Priest said. 'Let the stones split under your feet. Our rifles will flame like theirs. Our bullets will go round trees and find the Bodi in the long grass.' In a few unforgettable minutes we'd witnessed the dimensions of the Priest's power – so powerful that his danger had to be neutralised by the ritual attack, powerful now in binding and strengthening the Mursi for their war.

And then quite suddenly it was over, mild groups wandering out on to the sunny hillside as though nothing had happened. We swapped inadequate words, hoarding a unique half-hour in our lives. 'Let's go – there's a debate,' David said.

Out on the ridge it was hot now. The men squatted in a big half-circle, conjuring shelter from low scrubby bushes. We filmed the debate, scorched and tired and high on the sense of breakthrough and ending. Our mood was, I suppose, tuned to the epic as we watched the sequence of men orating against the majestic backdrop of mountains beyond the Omo, streaked now with cloud.

But sitting weeks later in an English garden reading David's translations of that debate, I confirmed that the epic quality hadn't merely been an illusion of our excitement and relief.

The very first sentence of the first speaker began: 'Death followed me and followed me to the very limits of our land. Death hemmed me in down there.' Mike gulped at a water bottle and I took over briefly on the camera. Framed through the viewfinder, I saw an epic again. It was almost too much – tall back-lit figures in flowing togas, spears catching the sun. It was easy to filter the spectacle as Greek drama recycled by Hollywood. Viewed raw again, it was an occasion of painful authenticity. The passion of the speeches stung through the language barrier and Turton's translation confirmed the harsh realities. Speaker after speaker chastised the men of Mara for staying with their crops in the north of Mursi country instead of protecting their cattle in the southern refuge. 'You hung on to your cow with no legs,' accused one speaker in scathing reference to the sorghum crop. 'Why are the Bodi not weeping? Are we to weep alone?'

Biobume, the expert in reading the future, tore into the young men for their cowardice. Jabbing northwards with his spear, he repeatedly scorned the Bodi threat. 'There they are, a little cloud in the distance. Don't they have backsides to sit on and shade trees to sit under? If you had eaten meat off the same leaves with us, and drunk as we did with our elders, you would have learned from us how to behave. You're useless!' Biobume thundered. Humiliated and roused, a young brave in a yellow shirt leaped up, exploding into his personal cattle song as an act of defiance. Confronting Biobume, the man cradled his rifle menacingly on the old man's shoulder. It was an electrifying moment, defused with marvellous disdain. 'Sit down,' Biobume murmured, turning away, 'sit down.'

Then there was Mitatu. He'd visited our camp, a grizzled witty old man, painfully thin, sardonic and impressive. David had called him 'the tallest Jalabai for miles around,' like Rabithella, a man of influence, a debater of great skill and authority, who was always listened to with special attention. Now he stalked on the ridge, wiry and sarcastic. 'What's wrong with our people?' he asked. 'If you'd gone scouting, wouldn't you have seen the Bodi tracks? Won't you leave their ghosts among the cattle? How did you allow the Bodi to pass through here? Did they fly?'

As Mitatu continued, Mike and I toiled up the hill for a wide shot. Near the summit of the ridge, we looked back on the debate. Tiny figures moved on the vast stage of bush and sky.

Looking down now on the grand panorama of Mursi country laid out in receding perspectives of bushbelt, river, grassland and mountain, I was struck again by something Turton had said on our long trek south. While we slumped under a tree for a precious few minutes, he talked about how this country which looked to the casual eye like a wilderness, bore in reality the indelible imprint of human intervention. The patterns of growth and erosion, the shapes of forest and bush, were moulded by thousands of years of passage and survival by people like the Mursi. I dumped the camera tripod on the ground and fumbled for some connections. Powerful expressions of ritual and community weren't easy to take on board for an unshakeable atheist like me, a solitary only child who'd never even joined the scouts. I felt overexposed to sun and paradox. Perhaps it was enough that the things we'd witnessed that day had complicated my feelings about the Mursi and put some real figures in the landscape.

We scrambled back down the hillside. Picking up a spear, the Priest walked out to speak. He paced and turned for a long time before beginning. His voice was strained, and very quiet. 'Boys have died down south. If we had stayed together, it might have been all right. As it is we're scattered and the Bodi slip through unnoticed. Calm down. Don't split your heart. Calm down Mitatu. Don't point your finger so much. They have done wrong. But leave off now.'

I had my back turned, loading another magazine, as the uproar began. The sudden cacophony of horns and whistles spun me round. Dozens of men were on their feet, massing around the Priest. They circled again in a final demonstration of Mursi solidarity. Then with a chatter of rifle bolts, the drama was over. The intense focus of shared purpose dissolved in moments and people drifted away. Feeling drained and happy we loaded the day, preserved in thirteen silver tins, into our rucksacks and headed for home.

Back in camp, we found that our entire stock of necklaces, carefully hoarded to pay for our porterage back to Hana, had been stolen. Pat had been asleep and the intruders must have been well-informed. I retreated to the diary: 'The last three days have transformed our prospects and we feel the effort has at last paid off. Just for a moment now, fulfilment and a wallow in a beautiful evening sky. Now, of course, a new set of problems begin, heralded by the loss of the necklaces. How to get out?'

5

For some reason, I was plodding round my Cheshire living room in flippers and a complete frogman's outfit. I swam to the surface of the dream to find the rain drumming on the tent. I registered the slum of decaying socks, tangled film gear and mud, and ached for home. This was supposed to be the day we began the long trek for Hana and England, but an exploratory unzipping of the tent door revealed the worst morning yet – leaden skies, sluicing rain, Mike's towel sinking in a big brown puddle. A strange animal wind prowled around the site as I zipped out the desolate prospect.

'How about a sing-song?' Chris suggested. It was two hours later, and we were still trapped in the tents. None of us had the heart for a chorus of 'Land of Hope and Glory', and Chris consoled himself by studying the roof of the tent while pondering the mystical properties of the pyramid. Mike tried to anaesthetise himself with a book. I dubbined my boots hopefully and recalled my farewell to Ulichagi the afternoon before. I gave him my sheath-knife, and he looked very happy. 'He says he'll have it when he's an old man, and his grandchildren will remember you,' Turton translated. My righteous glow received an instant dampener. Uligachi had something to add. It was, it seemed, a classic Mursi thank you and David passed on the message with the resigned chortle of the man who's been there before. 'He says he'd like your empty petrol can as well.'

The rain drummed on and I sought refuge in the diary. 'I begin to feel like Captain Scott, trapped with his diary. An inch-long jumping insect and a green thing with legs shelter inside our tent wall. Presumably we will get out sometime.'

The next diary entry told a happier story. '5.15 p.m. MARA! Sitting shagged in the sun in André's immaculate campsite, one third of the way home.' The dismal morning was forgiven and even the hours of ghastly plod were beginning to fade. There had been moments in the day when I regretted that the frogman outfit was only a dream as we waded slowly northwards through the drowned bush, soaked and mud-spattered.

There were frequent nervy halts as the Mursi refused to go on until an escorting gun-party caught up, and the final two hours seemed endless under ferocious sun.

But at last around four in the afternoon we broke through a maze of greenery to find ourselves at the river Mara. It was almost shockingly swollen from the muddy trickle of our outward journey, and Mike and I clawed along the bank hoping for a shallower spot to make the crossing. Soon we gave up and committed ourselves to a final date with discomfort, sloshing across almost up to our waists. On the other side, fuelled by a mad burst of relief we raced each other in squelching boots towards André and the campsite where he'd been marooned for two alarming weeks.

It was a remarkable spectacle. Cordoned inside roped rectangles of neurotic tidiness, were neat tents and a burnished jeep. Squatting obediently outside the perimeter like spectators at a Lord's Test match were scores of Mursi.

'I'm very glad to see you,' André said with painful sincerity.

'How's it been, Robinson?' I asked him. 'Don't ask,' he said, and then told us for a long time. It sounded awful, a rare mix of terror and farce. As we hauled off our dribbling boots and gulped tea, he poured out an account of his life while we'd been away hunting a film. 'I had to wait 'til it got dark before I could venture out for a crap,' he reminisced.

'Rifles were going off all round me in the bush and the locals were really jumpy.' Somehow, amid all the alarms and distractions, he'd got the jeep firing again. I looked round and counted fourteen Mursi braves sitting in the spotless vehicle.

After dark, with the World Cup burbling on the radio we sat round the fire luxuriating in the prospect of heading home. Turton talked about the Mursi. 'For them the passing of time doesn't seem to have the overtones of sadness it does for us. They live in a kind of perpetual present.' But when conversation turned to the Mursi picture of the Universe, it was plain that the lack of interest in the future didn't imply a limited curiosity. Turton had found that they had a complex understanding of planets and constellations, using the seasonal drift of the stars to regulate crop-planting. 'But they're flat-earthers,' he said, 'and of course Mursi country is seen as lying at the very centre of things.' It seemed that Mursi confidence in their superiority might have taken something of a knock as a consequence of our arrival from somewhere over the horizon with our inexhaustible supply of technical miracles.

'I must admit we've all had unworthy moments when we've wondered why they haven't got round to the wheel yet,' I confessed. If David winced, it was too dark to see. 'It just seems there are different priorities for them,' he said. 'It's as though they've poured all their energies into social engineering like the debates rather than into technology like us.'

I was awakened next morning by a message from the imported technology. On the radio a woman with a voice like the Queen was telling the world about 'English working-class writers of the nineteenth century'.

A Mursi studied my empty boot polish tin. As I struggled out of the tent, a bird shat on my shoulder with depressing accuracy. It was the start of a trying day.

Now that they had an orderly base for the first time in weeks, the film crew were anxious to catch up on some paperwork. They emerged from an hour of trying to match up their records of film cans and tape boxes with some worrying news. Several rolls of film seemed to be unaccounted for. I slopped muddy shirts in the slightly less muddy river and tried not to think about the possibilities. After its exile with André, my suitcase had offered me a wardrobe glowing with green mould and it seemed reluctant to dissolve in the gritty brown river. I traipsed back to the camp with a bucket of sludge for purifying to find three of our bedsacks had been stolen from the bushes where they were airing. It was the loss of potential portering inducements that concerned us most but before we could mount a search, we were driven into the tents by a sudden downpour. We emerged ten minutes later to find that everything on the clothes line, including just about everything André still possessed, had vanished. I recorded the losses with resignation. 'I accept David's studious point that we're getting more out of them than they are from us, but the thieving is really becoming serious now. David clears the site in a quiet fury. The loss-rate is almost laughable now. We'll be lucky to hang on to the jeep at this rate.' In response to our weary protests. Rabithella organised a vague sort of search, but it was clearly hopeless. We consoled ourselves with a silly charade.

I was looking at the photograph just the other day. It still conveys a quality of mild but unmistakable lunacy. Three of us, Mike, Chris and myself, march in single file, arms swinging, along a tract of flattened grass. Behind us, nailed to a tree is a crude sign 'Dodds Lane'. The parody of the Beatles 'Abbey Road' album cover may be a bit elusive, but the daftness was curiously soothing at the time. I suppose it had something to do with calling up a tiny hint of the familiar in a place where we were far more likely to encounter a zebra than a zebra crossing.

The moment was abruptly punctured by a spindly youth walking out of the undergrowth. Wrapped round his arms and torso, he wore half a magazine of our exposed negative. The hunt for our missing rolls of film was over.

It was hardly surprising the afternoon should have ended with a flare-up. We arrived back in camp to find Pat Turton slopping the cherished remains of our Scotch into a basin of prunes. 'For Christ's sake Pat,' Chris exploded. 'I was only trying to brighten up your dinner,' Pat said. It was a petty business, but revealing about the fraying tolerances of tired people a long way from home.

As so often before, the day ended with some kind of healing. Silhouetted against an improbable orange and black sky, a young Mursi called Ulikoro blew music from a hollow branch flute. We filmed him, and it was at once corny and oddly moving. The range of notes was absurdly limited, but something rich and poised spiralled out over the bush. I remembered what Turton had said about the Mursi's different priorities. Lightning veined a horizon that was staining black like spilled ink.

The blast of David Turton's shotgun provided some relief at last. The crowds of scavengers scattered into the bush, shouting and laughing, and at last we had some space to organise our departure.

Getting out of Mara was proving a messy business. On a campsite reduced to a mud-wrestling arena after yet another overnight downpour, we bundled up grimy loads for the long march north. The Mursi began to arrive early. For miles around, the word had clearly gone out that the circus was leaving, and this was the last chance of a souvenir. Soon hundreds of bargain-hunters were crowding round us surveying the prospects. David slung up roped enclosures, but within minutes we were swamped again. Newspaper fragments from a plant press were grabbed and rejected by scores of hands, and the area round the camp quickly began to look like a municipal rubbish dump. The shotgun was a dramatic gesture, but it seemed to have worked for a moment.

As we scrambled in the mud, I tried to hold on to Turton's analysis. He had to be right, but it was hard to see past the press of bodies and the grabbing hands. David had reminded us that our arrival represented the most massive bonanza of material goods these people had ever imagined. Spilling rope and saws and buckets and bowls, we were a Mursi consumer's dream. Inevitably, they couldn't imagine how we could need it all and of course they were right. The casual purchase of a knife in a Manchester camping shop could change the life of a man in this environment who had no knife. We'd also seen enough of the Mursi's patterns of sharing and obligation to know what they would expect of us. I'd watched how a single glucose tablet handed to a child would in seconds be divided into fragments and be melting in half a dozen mouths.

In a place where survival was so marginal, it was hardly surprising that one relative's claim on another would be a basic moral principle. You might well need to claim the same life-saving help next week that you offered today.

Our problem was that our own immediate future was not without its uncertainties. With the neurotic jeep and war-threatened porters, we had no idea how long it would take to get to Hana. And when we arrived, the doubts surrounding our rescue plane were something I preferred not to think about. We had to try and hang on to enough supplies to insure ourselves against an obstacle course of possibilities. The lessons of the past few weeks had destroyed any illusions about a cosy ending.

Struggling for some kind of equity, we gave away all we could risk. Happy people made off into the bush with orange plastic bowls, kitchen knives, cardboard boxes, threadbare shirts and ragged underpants. At last, as the sun steepled towards noon, we were ready to move. I watched the reborn jeep bounce out of camp with Mike and Pat and piles of equipment. André must have seen my expression. 'It'll be fine,' he said.

'Where the hell are they?' I could hardly take it in. We crouched under the same murderous thorn bush I'd met up with three weeks before and speculated yet again about the vanished jeep. Standing around us were twenty very nervous Mursi porters, jumpily aware of being on the southern edge of Bodi country and anxious to be away. I felt more exposed than ever before and more aware of the big rifles. I tried to look busy with my diary: 'Absurd turn of events – the jeep's not here at the rendezvous. Two possibilities: either they missed the site, or they decided to go on. Both are equally infuriating for us. They have the cloth on board so we can't even pay off the nervy porters. Now Chris and André have headed on up the track to see what's happened. Meanwhile David and I are left alone with the porters and their loads and their rifles.'

It had been a surprisingly tolerable hike. After a whispered tip-off from Ulikoro that some of the porters were considering making away with their loads, we stationed ourselves along the line and tried to police the convoy. It was pretty futile in the dense bush, but at least it helped take my mind off the walking.

We did have one potential bust-up when Chris suddenly spotted that the man ahead of him was wearing some unusual ear-rings. Mike had been lamenting the loss of the graduated slides from his light meter for days. It was arguable that Chris's sense of solidarity with his colleague, when he discovered the slides hanging from Mursi ears, caused him to over-react. Yanking the things out of the chap's lobes with a yell of 'you thieving bastard' was hardly calculated to cement our relations with the porters.

Nevertheless we'd arrived under the thorn bush in good time and with all loads intact. Now we had jeep trouble again. As David and I waited for news, I was aware that the porters were getting increasingly restless. Anxious be off, some had agreed to

77

take money rather than wait for the cloth and our roll of grimy Ethiopian dollars was all too conspicuous. In the circumstances, I was impressed by the Mursi restraint. But after two hours, things were looking decidedly edgy. One man noisily threatened to take our film-stock back to Mara, and it took all of David's impressive diplomatic skills to head off a fight.

Around 4.30 in the afternoon André and Chris plodded back carrying the cloth and wretched news. They'd finally come upon the jeep about an hour to the north. It was, of course, broken again. Mike and Pat had simply missed our rendezvous point.

'What the bloody hell were they doing? How in God's name could they possibly have missed it? They must be blind or dense!' The absurd rerun of our cock-ups on the journey south made me crack into real anger for the first time. Chris and André, who had more reason for fury after their long hot recce began resignedly to put up the single tent they'd retrieved from the jeep. 'Yes, it's maddening,' David conceded, but he was already loading up for his walk to join the jeep party. In a triumph of diplomacy, he even managed to persuade some of the Mursi porters to go with him. My useless spat exhausted, I began to help build our seventeenth campsite.

The following afternoon, I registered a fatality: '4.50 p.m.: The end of the line for the jeep. What we'd all expected from the start has finally happened at the edge of a stream in the middle of nowhere called Chingith. After 10 solid hours of trying everything, we can do no more. The usual long whine, bangs, more bangs, but nothing. We reckon the problem must either be a cylinder head gasket or even piston rings or valves welded solid by heat. But whatever the reason, we've come to the end of our invention. I feel nothing. It's just a fact. Now we walk, RIP, VW Jeep, Chingith.'

It was to be two days before we were able to walk away from the dead jeep for the last time. Marooned and incongruous in the long grass, it looked like a stranded whale. I wondered how long it would be before the weather and the Bodi would pick it to the bones. The problems of the disbelieving hire company in Addis seemed too remote to be real.

For a while it seemed a sweet liberation to be free of the thing. But we were already paying the penalty in the logistical convolutions which had slowed our progress towards Hana to a cumbersome crawl. Since the decease of the jeep, Turton had scouted up and down the bush as far as Gura, hunting for Bodi porters who might help to shift us to the next camp on the Everest of our return journey.

With the war still festering, it wasn't an easy job. It soon became clear that the only way to keep moving was to fragment the expedition, sending on advance parties whenever David managed to return with a few porters. With painful slowness and endless tensions about money, weary people seeped north. I even began to relax a little about keeping our date with that plane in faraway Hana.

Finally, only Chris and I were left to keep wake with the jeep. It felt like a kind of reprieve to be out of the front line for a few hours, slimmed-down to basic survival equipment and with space to contemplate the possibility of going home. We resurrected our wobbling blue plastic table with a shoe lace and pulled up the two remaining film boxes. Dripping into mugs of tea as a purple sky boiled up behind the rattling palms, we wallowed in reminiscence. Chris talked about his family and growing up on a Canadian farm. For some reason, he insisted on showing me how to tie a hangman's noose. A sudden rain squall drove us into the tent. I closed my eyes and was flooded with an intense longing for home, focussed in the image of my son's face.

We talked on until the light was gone. I risked some mellow reflections: 'Staggering stars piled over us. We gape and talk about black holes and John Donne and Wilfred Owen and film-making and going home.'

I can only plead fatigue for the foolish rush of optimism. The Lower Omo wasn't finished with us yet.

Fording the river Gura holding a porter's rifle above my head provided Mike with another home-movie sequence, but the heroic guerrilla fantasy was seriously undercut by the slime oozing out of my laceholes as I staggered up the bank.

I arrived at the Gura camp to find Chris already sawing up one of our broken hurricane lamps to make jewellery for a circle of interested Bodi. Throbbing with weariness after the walk, I croaked: 'Jesus, Chris, how can you possibly feel like doing that?' He bashed a curve with a rock. 'No problem Leslie. It might be good public relations for getting porters to Hana.' Another ankle bracelet jingled off the production line.

But Turton advised it was going to take more than recycled trinkets to get us moving again. We would be becalmed while the recruiting of porters went on for the final lap to Hana. Meanwhile, there was the increasingly unfamiliar prospect of some filming.

The strange conical hill never seemed to get any closer as we tramped across a plain littered with big stones. It was a leached, barren place like one of those airless landscapes beamed back by space probes from the surface of Mars. At last, towards the end of a fiery afternoon our little group passed through a brushwood gateway and into the Bodi defensive compound.

Immediately, I felt the watchful tension of the settlement. Ranged along a massive wall of red boulders were dozens of young Bodi men. Rifles poked through gaps in the rocks. The hillside climbed steeply behind the defences, dense with hostile thorn bushes.

We set up quietly and filmed a sombre interview with a group of men, filled with suppressed anger and defiance. As we wrapped up the gear, a man walked towards us from one of the nearby huts. In his hands, he held my long-lost camera.

It was nice to be reunited. I could barely conceive how the thing had passed the weeks since we'd gone our separate ways, but it looked healthy and unruffled. I scrambled up the hillside behind the Bodi settlement with Mike to celebrate with some pictures. We looked out on a panorama worthy of the moment.

In the smoky evening light, a huge plain receded below us towards a band of violet mountains. A couple of water-holes glinted orange in the middle distance, holding the last of a giant old sun. From out in the plain, long skeins of cattle trailed towards the settlement, their bells drifting up to us like a hint of fragrance. I snapped as Mike filmed, relishing the marvellous scale of it all. From up here the peace and order of the land gave no hint of the bitterness we'd witnessed as we struggled over it.

Suddenly, it was almost dark. David was anxious to be away. We walked out into the plain, picking our way by the afterglow of a lovely orange sky. Within minutes, it was the nastiest walk we'd known. We fell repeatedly over the treacherous stones, panicky with thirst in the thick darkness. At the beginning of real alarm, Mike spotted a point of light.

We homed in on André's hurricane lamp. In camp, I slumped by the fire, speechless. After five mugs of tea I managed to crawl into the tent.

'What a beautiful morning – just like spring in England.' Mike's voice invaded a dream about finding a phone in the tent and ringing home. A cassette of James Taylor singing 'Carolina' spilled over the campsite, flooding me with memories of hearing it on a Christmas morning amid kids and ruined parcels.

Mike and I walked out of camp for the very last of the filming – a distant shot of the hill behind the Bodi settlement. Marking our way with stones and branches we moved through the bush for about half an hour. The hill stood sharp against a flawless sky as Mike turned over for the final shot. Afterwards, we shook hands in a parody of Victorian exploration. We turned back for camp and in yards we were hopelessly lost.

There was no sign of our careful markers in the featureless bush.

'Well it seemed like a good idea at the time,' Mike said doubtfully.

'Who needed a shot of the hill anyway?' I groused. 'This is just silly.'

We tracked sideways into the walls of greenery, feeling for some familiar feature. In moments, we'd lost one another. I remembered we hadn't brought water bottles and it stopped being funny. Coming so soon after the shambles of last night's nightmare trek, it was obvious the accumulated weariness was making us careless and ragged.

I zeroed in on Mike's shouts and we groped on side by side, hoping to get lucky. A big monkey tumbled in the trees above us. And then, in a moment, it was over. We were on the track to Hana, still showing faintly the traces of our jeep's passage a month before. Navigating gratefully by the elegant palms along the Gura river, we stumbled into camp feeling hot and foolish. We arrived to find another mammoth packing session in progress.

David yanked a tent pole apart. 'The Bodi want us to move up to their village under the hill. They reckon it'll save time tomorrow.' I groaned inside at the prospect of yet more camp-building, but it was obviously a good idea. For Turton, there were other problems. 'The Bodi also want me to stay behind here to act as some kind of mediator with the Mursi. I've told them I'll be back in a few months, but they're not very pleased.'

A dozen Bodi girls wandered round the site, giggling at the panting white men. Strikingly pretty without the cut lips of the Mursi, they surveyed the possibilities. Soon, they had a bonus. Looking effortlessly stylish and flirty, they tripped round the site in a riot of bows, flounces, headscarves, miniskirts and sashes fashioned from our pastel yellow and green toilet rolls. They ran off shrieking with laughter, leaving the site littered like a fairground after a bank holiday.

It was time to lighten our loads for the final push. I dumped a pile of paperbacks on a film box and crawled back into the tent to hunt for other disposables. When I emerged with an expired insect spray, I found a couple of Bodi men peering intently at one of the books. I looked over their shoulders. *The Film Director as Superstar*, the title was. Not here, he isn't, I thought. Who the hell brought that anyway? But what was hypnotising the Bodi was the picture on the cover. It was a montage, with a cartoon figure standing against a photographic background of Hollywood. As the Bodi prodded the cover with inquisitive fingers, I realised they were trying to reach into the picture and touch the background. Clearly it was their first encounter with a two-dimensional image. The men looked at me and laughed. Then they threw the book on the ground.

A herd of zebra lifted their heads as we shambled past. It was a simply glorious evening, sunlight flooding the plain. Ahead of me, a girl with one of our huge boxes on her head had come to a stop. With her foot, she fumbled in the dust. I picked up the spent cartridge and gave it to her. She gazed at me steadily, with what felt like calm dislike.

As we approached the Bodi settlement, the returning flood of cattle merged with our file, and we arrived amid bells and gathering darkness.

The gunshot bounced off the hillside and echoed into the blackness behind us. After a moment, I could hear people running towards us from the settlement and angry shouting. 'Imagine coming through all this to be bumped off for the sake of a guinea fowl,' I murmured to André.

Turton arrived with the first of the Bodi. Their rifles glinted in the light of our fire. David was almost as edgy as the rest of them, and it took a little while to persuade him that it wasn't a Mursi raiding party, but Chris and Ulikoro out hunting for dinner. Then he was more furious than I'd seen him before. 'God, don't they know how dangerous that could have been, blasting away close to here. They could have started a full-scale battle.' He spoke to the Bodi and they went off, muttering tetchily.

'Well at least we didn't miss.' Chris was unrepentant, plucking with casual expertise. He worked on steadily as the earth began to tremble and a big herd of zebra thundered round us, unseen beyond the firelight.

Under a grand display of stars, we gnawed the fried guinea fowl. After the weeks of freeze-dried sludge, it felt very good to have something to chew on. As we ate, Mike stabbed the darkness with a torch beam, stirring the grazing zebra. From the Bodi settlement, the rhythmic slapping and ululating of a dance drifted down to us. The awareness of the space around our little camp was a liberation that affected us all, freed at last from the dense bush which had enclosed us for so long.

'D'you think there's a chance we might make it all the way to Hana tomorrow . . .'

'Maybe – depends how many porters show up . . .'

'It's going to be a hell of a push whatever happens . . .'

The voices blurred as the fire died. Hazy with Mandrax, Mike lay back with his hands behind his head. 'I love Africa,' he murmured, and I heard him laughing quietly at the exhausted sentimentality which had released a rush of forgiveness.

And in the morning, it did seem almost as though we'd achieved some kind of truce in our long tussle with the place. I jotted down the gathering excitements of the day.

'5.50 a.m. By lamplight. Our earliest rising for the big walk.

7.10 a.m. High marbled cloud, glowing with hidden early sun. The first porters seem to be straggling in.

8.20 a.m. Day heating up. First party away with Mike and Chris.

9.20 a.m. All away at last after endless squabbles over portering.

10.40 a.m. Halted at a river – women and men washing apart. Many stops, but we do move slowly forward.

11.30 a.m. Arrived at another little river. Everyone sprawled around as David begins his endless check and payment routine. Big question now – how many are willing to go on to Hana?

12.35 p.m. News via André. We all go on. Vast relief.

1.25 p.m. A stop after sloshing across the Hana river. Boots and socks now a quagmire. I don't care. The end's almost in sight.

2.45 p.m. HANA, HANA, HANA, at last at last at last. First news – the Captain says our plane's *tomorrow*.'

Of course within minutes it became clear that the plane was a false alarm. But nothing could dent our joy at having made it to scruffy, awful Hana. The diary told me it was Sunday afternoon, and suddenly it meant something again. In this desperate place we were back in our world.

The evidence was all around us. The Captain babbled of politics and rumours of revolution in Addis while women in cast-off dresses and men in ragged uniforms wandered round our campsite. A weary troop slouched to some sort of attention as an Ethiopian flag was lowered.

And already, the Bodi porters were uneasy outsiders. As soon as they'd been paid, they drifted away taking with them the way of life we'd known for the past weeks. Ulikoro, the powerfully built Mursi teenager we'd first met suckling milk directly from his cow's udder inside the defensive compound, stood close to us.

It was obvious that he shared Ulichagi's worries about finding himself in enemy territory. He also faced the prospect of following Ulichagi to an encounter with a far more alien place. Ulikoro had agreed to go with Turton to Addis Ababa for a few weeks to help with our translations.

I wandered off down to the river on my own. Floating in the rust-coloured water for ages, I registered the fact that we'd come through. It was a good time.

And then there was nothing to do but wait – and hope. The radio spluttered with news about army activity in Addis and we fretted about threats to our rescue plane. Now, it was supposed to come on Thursday. Meanwhile, Hana offered some distractions.

The Fukuis appeared even more improbable visitors here than

84

us. In his immaculate nylon anorak, Dr Fukui stepped tentatively on to our campsite with his elfin wife, Masuko, impeccable in pale blue sweater and slacks. It was clear that Japanese anthropologists found the Lower Omo no more welcoming than we had. The Fukuis' account of their chaotic attempts to begin fieldwork among the Bodi made me feel like a gnarled, bushwise veteran. Twice they'd overturned landrovers in flooded rivers; now they were desperately short of money. Standing in our sleazy campsite, they also gave us the startling news that they were planning to build a house. With a view to establishing this marvel in the bush about half an hour from Hana, they'd somehow portered in galvanised iron sheets, window frames, china crockery and tomato ketchup. Anecdotes about the Fukuis' domestic plans and problems were to illuminate our last days in Hana.

The prospect of more anthropologists on his patch didn't seem to please Captain Cherkole. But we were at least able to offer some compensations. There were twenty-six transistor radios in Hana, treasured possessions for bored policemen. Sadly, they all seemed to be very broken. A queue of hopeful owners waited patiently at Chris's tentside surgery, but the diagnosis wasn't encouraging. The innards seemed to have melted, while colonies of insects had made homes behind the dials. Chris did finally manage to coax a couple of the things into crackling life, becoming an instant hero. His success earned him a more serious commission.

The radio telephone was Hana's only connection with the outside world. It had stopped working weeks ago. In its warping wooden shed with a floor of earth, the shiny telephone looked oddly efficient; but it stubbornly resisted Chris's attentions. Policemen and children peered through the ruined walls and the machine buzzed with incoming static. It continued to refuse all attempts to transmit.

The broken radio telephone was a perfect image for the increasingly desperate frustrations of Hana's people, calling dumbly for help from an unheeding world. Pat and David talked for a long time with the sad medical orderly from the police post and he told a frightening story.

'I am here two months already and I have not even an aspirin for all these people. I try to tell men to dig latrines but nobody hears me.'

'Yes, we saw a man today with bad hepatitis,' Pat said.

The orderly pulled unhappily at the belt of his smart uniform.

'Look,' Pat continued. 'You really must try and get the men to dig those latrines.'

'The Captain asked them to do it six months ago, but no one volunteered.' The orderly's message was chillingly clear. The place teetered on the edge of mutiny and the Captain had to work for the consent of people who had nothing more to lose.

Late on our second evening in Hana, the Captain arrived in camp with a bottle of Tej. The locally-distilled honey tasted, like most local things, of mud, and the Captain was in no mood for revelry. Refusing to sample the Fukuis' leftover goat stew, he sat quiet and morose and soon made off into the dark.

'I reckon he's worrying about whether to try and fly out on our plane to get some supplies,' David said.

The world service had more accounts of confusions in Addis. I wondered again about our almost exhausted food stocks and about getting out.

Mike looked up from his book. 'Sounds like a plane,' he said. I snapped off the cassette of Carole King and we went very quiet. It was a plane.

Two minutes later, the Dakota slammed over us. André had already pulled on his boots and was running for the landing-strip. It was hard to take in, but it seemed to be for real. The plane was here, a day ahead of our best hopes. Pat and David came running from the river, their washing still dripping. In a confusion of joy, I began to attack the tents.

We'd reduced the camp to ruins by the time André came panting back. 'It's ours,' he gasped, 'but there's a huge bloody row with the Captain. He wants to fly to Arba Minch for supplies and they won't take him without insurance.'

The big police lorry lurched on to the site and we flung our boxes and bundles into the back. Ulikoro calmly laced up my borrowed orange and black trainers and climbed up into the lorry. Excited policemen were already scrambling for our discarded cooking gear. I walked towards the strip alongside the lorry feeling light with happiness.

The Captain was wearing his best uniform, and he was

fuming. The flight engineer smiled as he shook my hand and gave me the news. 'I'm afraid he's placed the plane under arrest.'

'How can he?'

'Well he has the gun, not me.'

André bowled the jeep's spare wheel across the strip. It bore no relation to the jeep and we hoped to submit it in evidence to the hirers of their useless spares. 'Where's the jeep?' asked the bewildered engineer. When I told him about our 150 miles of walking, he looked at me with something of the evasive pity often reserved for the mentally disturbed. Then he brightened with the realisation that he was to be spared the horrors of another jeep-loading marathon.

The handful of wondering Bodi retreated to the edge of the strip as the Dakota's engines screamed to power up the plane's radio. The pilot stuck a hand out of the cockpit window, thumb up. It seemed Captain Cherkole had clearance to fly.

'Let's go,' the pilot shouted. I caught sight of the Fukuis running towards the plane. They conferred desperately with a crewman. Then Mrs Fukui scrambled on board and we were away.

As we banked, the bush opened up under us. It looked hot and empty. There was no trace of the lives we'd been following over the past weeks, no evidence of war or debate or human passage. Sitting behind Ulikoro, I saw his face as he gazed through a window. He was impassive, his feelings as elusive as the land below us. I slept.

I came awake as we hit the bumping strip at Jinka. It was fifteen minutes later, it seemed. A policeman stuck his head through the door and talked urgently to Captain Cherkole. The Captain grinned hugely and crushed my hand. 'I am transferred here to Jinka and I have promotion.' He jumped down on to the strip where men rushed up and kissed him. Before I could focus properly, the Captain was back on the plane shouting joyous farewells to his friends and we were away.

In less than an hour, we were down again and with less cause for celebration. 'Didn't you smell something? Maybe we have some electrical fault,' the flight engineer said. We sat in the shadow of a weary-looking wooden hut alongside the grass strip at Arba Minch and waited. In the background, the pilot seemed to have found a telephone. He was talking to the Governor of the province, accusing Captain Cherkole of hijacking his plane. The Captain grabbed the phone and shouted his justifications.

With shocking abruptness, it was all rushing back – the world of phones and barbed wire and ragged kids who asked for things in English. It was too quick. I stared at a bright blue bicycle leaning against an oil drum and, for a moment, I felt as lost as Ulikoro.

After a while, the flight engineer came over to break the news. We were stranded for the night until a spare part could be flown in from Addis. It felt oddly inevitable after the unreal tempo of our apparent escape.

General Mebratu had a good grey suit, a smart white Peugeot and an exquisite English accent. For the first time, it occurred to me that we must look like the tattered survivors of some harrowing natural disaster. The General was too polite to comment. As the Governor of Gemu Gofa province, he was reponsible, in theory, for the Mursi and the Bodi. He seemed a nice man and remarkably hospitable in the circumstances. He looked at Ulikoro. 'Does he speak English?' the Governor enquired.

We jolted up a long dirt hill in a landrover, trailing through the Governor's dust plume. The corrugated iron roofs of Arba Minch glinted in the windy afternoon sun. It looked like a fair-sized place with the risky, temporary feel of a frontier town. On a dusty corner, there was Captain Cherkole shouting something as his hat blew away.

Then, in a dream, we came to a hotel. There were flowers round the door, and a terrace with tables and tablecloths. When the cold beer arrived, none of us spoke for a time. It came to me that we had to be less than a hundred miles from Mara. It felt like centuries.

Ulikoro handled his first knife and fork with instant aplomb. As the coffee followed the steak, I felt as though long-drained reservoirs were refilling at a rush. Tastes blossomed in my mouth again. But already, by the second beer, the thrill was blunted as the familar swamped in, dulling the marvellous shock of being back.

At the end of the day, in my hotel bedroom, I had a green tin reading lamp to write by: 'In bed, real bed, alongside a Donald Duck alarm clock. Fascinating to watch the shade-in to our world through Ulikoro's eyes. He astounds us all with his poise as his universe is overturned by the moment. In one day, clad in my trainers, T-shirt and dirty blue jeans he has flown in a plane, seen a bicycle, travelled in a land-rover, met a Governor in a suit, eaten in a hotel, encountered an ice-cube, watched table tennis, puzzled at a glass window and two cats and gone to bed in a bedroom, alone.'

Watching the Governor playing enthusiastic table tennis in the games room, Ulikoro had laughed and then I'd gone with him to find his bedroom. He turned on the shower and watched the flow of water with grave astonishment. When I said goodnight, he was standing next to the wall, switching the light on and off, on and off.

It was two days before we got out. Between frustrating expeditions down to the airstrip, we taught table tennis to Ulikoro who instantly beat me, ate strange things in a little shed like a voodoo temple and got to know the aircrew. I watched sinister black birds spiralling in the dizzying spaces over a lake like an inland sea far below the hotel. The Governor beat his staff ceaselessly at table tennis and I found a lizard in my room. Down at the strip for yet another futile enquiry, Mike and I took pictures of one another climbing long-abandoned aircraft-boarding steps towards a non-existent plane.

We were out of money and weary for home. I had a dream about getting demobbed after my military service.

'Our flying time to Addis Ababa will be one hour and twenty-five minutes.' At last there was a plane and it had real seats, even if most of them were jammed with our boxes. The jokey flight engineer in the red hat finished his announcement: 'Good luck.'

I woke from thick sleep and found Ulikoro, his face pushed against the window watching the vast sprawl of Addis Ababa slide below us. I could see light through the looping cut where he sometimes had an earring. I thought of our arrival at Hana and how much more strange and lonely this must be for him.

At the big modern hotel, Turton signed the register for Ulikoro. Under 'Profession', he wrote 'Farmer'. That evening, he told David he didn't feel like eating. I lay on my bed and I felt full and empty and more tired than I could ever remember.

★

The postscript was slow in coming, but memorable. In December, five months after we returned to England, both Mike Dodds and Chris Wangler became very ill. Chris ended up in a terminal ward over Christmas before the problem was finally diagnosed – malaria.

Both the crew were well and working again long before my memento arrived. On a frosty November night I collapsed in a London street. By then, of course, I knew what it meant.

The tropical medicine specialist was intrigued. 'It's a very rare strain, you know,' he said. 'If by any chance you ever pass that way again, would you mind popping a mosquito in a bottle?'

It seemed unlikely.

THE SECOND EXPEDITION

December 1981–January 1982

I

His arrival caused a bit of a stir in the bar of the Addis Hilton. Oblivious in lounge suit and green wellington boots, Ron from Oldham strode across to our table. 'Mine's a pint,' he said by way of introduction.

We talked for a while about his work prospecting for steam-power in the country south of Addis and his surprising sex-life in the city. Then it was time for business.

'All right, you can take the dinghy, but look after the bloody thing. The lads like to do a bit of water-skiing after work and they wouldn't be very chuffed if you got it gobbled up by some of them Omo crocs.' He gulped the dregs of his beer, and ploughed off through the assorted aid officials and world bank people just as another power cut dimmed the bar lights.

It was five days after Christmas 1981 and I was back in Ethiopia. It was still hard to take in, but tomorrow I'd be in the Lower Omo valley once again and with the Mursi.

As Ron's offer suggested, this was to be a very different kind of film, based on the River Omo; and it was about a very different theme. For some time, David Turton and I had been talking about a possible return to Mursi country with a quite new focus. This time, the logistical worries concerned hippos and crocodiles and the subject would be the strange relationship between the Mursi and a small group of people called the Kwegu who lived along the Omo. The Kwegu were those hunter-gatherers who had first drawn Turton to Ethiopia in the late 60s as a recently graduated anthropologist in search of a people.

A new series of 'Disappearing World' films, with André Singer now translated from jeep-watching to Series Editor, provided enthusiastic support for a return expedition. I never did quite decide whether André's enthusiasm for our date with discomfort might not have been in part some long-matured repayment for his weeks alone with the jeep.

Addis Ababa was transformed from the place I remembered seven years before. The city centre now was 'Revolution Square', where huge portraits of Marx, Lenin and Engels stared down on the herds of goats mingling with the rush-hour traffic. The imagery was eerily familiar to me. Only a couple of weeks ago, I'd finished a fascinating but exhausting year's project, a large-scale dramatised documentary about the birth of 'Solidarity' in Poland. Clandestine research in Warsaw and in Gdansk shipyards had made me a student of the heroic graffiti of socialism; it was curiously dislocating to find the bearded faces of those sombre European philosophers displaced from the frosty hoardings of the Baltic coast to the sparkling sunshine of East Africa. Emperor Haile Selassie was gone and Colonel Mengistu's picture hung in the lobby of the Hilton Hotel. For a visiting British film crew, the important place now was the Ministry of Information and National Guidance, and our Ministry man was Mohammed Idris.

I'd liked Mohammed on sight at the airport. Compact, able and friendly, his energy and intelligence had already seen us over a dozen hurdles but, as he sat with us now in the Hilton bar juggling with his orange juice, I was concerned about him.

A practising Muslim, married to Ethiopia's most famous popular singer, he seemed unprepared for the rigours of the lower Omo. Mohammed was due to come with us tomorrow but, sitting alongside him fastidiously dressed in slacks, sports jacket and suede shoes while he told me he hadn't arranged special footwear or malaria tablets, I was worried. It seemed strange that, coming from 3,500 miles away, I felt more aware of what we were in for on the southern edge of his country, but perhaps it was inevitable. Mursi country was still a uniquely difficult place to get at. And Mohammed had been crucial in solving the problem this time.

He was one of those people with a talent for friendship. Walking down a street in Addis with Mohammed was like strolling through a familiar village. At every turn there were greetings and handshakes. In the bank, a dramatic circular tower like a trendy cathedral, he moved quickly between embraces and hellos to track down our bundles of low denomination notes, vital for porterage and gifts. At the Red Cross offices, more handshakes and we'd come away with two huge tents. Permits and paraffin, Mohammed had fixed it all. But his major achievement was the helicopter.

David Turton had come across the possibility when a big Soviet-built M.I.8 rescued him from the fringes of Mursi country eight months earlier. One of the last Dakotas had got stuck on a muddy strip and the army helicopter had flown down from Addis to take him out after days of watching the Dakota sinking in the mire. Now with no Hana in the vicinity and no more Dakotas, we'd had to find a new way of getting to the Omo. It obviously wouldn't be easy to charter one of the precious army helicopters, especially with a major campaign being fought against guerrillas in Eritrea, but Mohammed had made it happen.

He spotted a friend as soon as we arrived at the Army aviation base. We followed the Colonel in his stylish flying suit past the giant portrait of Colonel Mengistu and into the cheerfully dilapidated officers' mess. Beneath posters showing Uncle Sam bombing the planet, we sat in ruined armchairs poring over Turton's sketchy maps of the Lower Omo. No helicopter had ever been there before, but the Colonel seemed intrigued to give it a try. I decided to worry about the bill later.

On the last night before the wilderness, I phoned home. I'd left behind a house and a family marooned in the depths of the wildest English winter in years. Digging my way out through snowdrifts towards the main road the morning after Boxing Day, I struggled to believe that within seventy-two hours I'd be sweltering beside an African river. My wife said it was still snowing hard in Macclesfield and we wished one another luck.

I lay awake in the dawn for an hour, listening to a Muslim priest wailing on a nearby tower, and worrying about the helicopter. But at the army base, there was no replay of the loading farce of 1974 and it all went with cool military precision. Not long after half past eight, we were clattering over parched yellow scrub.

There were six of us perched in the belly of the helicopter on our piles of equipment. Across from me, researcher Andy

Harries, boyish in lime green shorts, looked relieved. Before I arrived with the crew, his weeks of grappling with revolutionary bureaucracy in Addis alongside Mohammed had clearly been testing.

I'd worked with Andy a couple of years earlier in America, persuading suspicious television people to give us access to their programmes for a five-hour compilation of US television to be transmitted by Granada in Britain throughout the night that Reagan was elected for the first time. I got the impression that not even the most paranoid Californian media-hustler had tested Andy's persuasive powers as severely as those careful, quiet officials in their Addis offices. Most of all, I know he'd been concerned about whether the helicopter would really happen. Andy had earned his flight.

So had Phil Smith, though he looked more doubtful. Phil was our sound recordist, a big neat cockney and a self-confessed townie. He'd recently completed two years work recording Granada's lavish and much acclaimed adaptation of *Brideshead Revisited* for which he won a major award. It was hard to imagine a location further removed from Brideshead's hyper-civilised stately homes and European capitals than the Lower Omo Valley, and difficult to conceive of a technical challenge more unlike the business of recording Laurence Olivier's performance as Lord Brideshead. Now Phil fiddled with a very new-looking baseball cap and scanned a technical manual about his lightweight tape recorder.

'Hey, look over here!' Mike Blakeley was as restless as ever, scrambling over the piled equipment and balancing against a bulkhead to take silly snaps of the rest of us. The chopper bucked on a thermal as it skimmed a mountain top and Mike sprawled in the deflated dinghy, yelling with laughter. A stubble-bearded Mancunian, Blakeley has the build common to a surprising number of cameramen – stocky with the powerful shoulders you need to support a 14-pound camera for days on end. He's the veteran of a thousand documentary scrapes in odd places, unstoppably energetic and shamelessly optimistic. Mike's family had been in films since the early days of the century, producing hugely successful comedies as subtle as rude seaside postcards with Northern variety artists like Frank Randle, all false teeth and braces. He seemed to have inherited something of that re-silient good humour and I was glad to have him around. On top of everything else, Mike seemed to be the only one who claimed to know anything about outboard motors and inflatable dinghys.

David Turton studied a batch of aerial photographs, trying to work out where we would join the Omo and turn south into Mursi country. I could see he was anxious. Since the gathering Ethiopian Revolution in the late 70s, he'd only been able to return for a brief visit in April 1981, when he'd found that the war with the Bodi was over. Now we were relying on his best guess about where we would be most likely to find Mursi and Kwegu together, an island, uncovered at this dry season, on a bend in the Omo about forty miles south of Mara. The place was called Alaka.

A crewman came back from the flightdeck and startled us by yanking a window open. The domesticity of the gesture shifted the flight for a moment into the realms of a quaint Jules Verne fantasy; looking out at the vast sea of unvarying bush was an immediate dose of reality.

Mohammed Idris had sat quiet and brooding until now. Suddenly he got up, stretched, grinned and popped his head through the crew door. After a moment he turned back and announced: 'Arba Minch.'

It was a terrific ride down, like the best of Disneyland skidding low over silver rooftops, a market packed with bright crowds, a river and then a cloud of red dust, the strip at Arba Minch.

Finding myself here again had the quality of a circling dream, one of those where you're conscious of being inside the dream and will soon allow yourself to wake. I reached into a sweat-stained shirt-pocket for my new diary:

'10.25 a.m. Sitting on a seat at Arba Minch airstrip – the same seat where I played endless scrabble with Chris Wangler seven years ago. I never thought I'd end up here again, where we had the infuriating two-day wait on our way out of the bush last time.

It's soakingly hot as a battered truck with "Inflammable" on the side refuels our chopper. This place is sadly run down since I was here, no longer in use for regular flights – no planes left it seems. In a shed I found the same Ethiopian Airline steps on which Mike Dodds and I took photos of one another heading for nowhere.'

My superstitious alarms proved groundless, and Arba Minch made no attempt to hold us this time. In less than half an hour we were away, hammering up over wild empty mountains, munching our Hilton hotel packed lunches.

The pilot gestured Turton to join him on the flightdeck as the gash in the dark bushbelt ahead signalled the River Omo. I stood in the open doorway for a grandstand view as the horizon tilted and we swung out over the river.

A flock of white birds scattered below us, reflecting in the shallows. I felt excited and elated. Last time the Omo had been no more than a mirage on the horizon. Now we were there, skimming effortlessly above the remotest reaches of one of Africa's great rivers.

Even at the height of the dry season it was a majestic spectacle, coiling through the colossal empty spaces and slicing reflections of the sky into the tawny pelt of the bushlands. We banked and swerved to follow the river as it meandered between the fringes of bushbelt, undercutting pink cliffs of flaking rock and opening up shoals of white sand. There was no sign of human presence.

'There's Alaka!' David pointed through the glass bubble at a long splinter of land lodged in a sweeping bend of the river. We circled and Mike Blakeley jammed himself in the open doorway filming the sudden evidence of settlement – patches of bright green cultivation, a cluster of circular huts, running people.

The pilot heeled round for another circuit, scanning a wide shingle beach and trying to estimate if it would support a landing. I was making a real effort to resist the inevitable cliché, but it was proving impossible to shut out the echoes of that first moon landing.

Then we were slamming in, on to the shingle, committed. As we settled, a sandstorm boiled up and blotted out everything. My watch said it was five past twelve and in just three and a half hours from Addis we were in the heart of Mursi country, shrinking that interminable two week approach march of 1974 to a disconcerting morning's outing.

Out on the shingle the heat snatched at my breath. Andy Harries jumped down beside me. 'God, it's like standing close up against an electric fire,' he croaked. Phil Smith jammed on the new baseball cap and surveyed the prospects without enthusiasm. 'It's not always this hot, surely?' he said. It seemed best to let him down gently. 'Actually,' I said, 'it's a bit nippy this morning.'

Turton walked away over the stones, his shape shifting and wobbling in the heat, towards a line of head-high grass that masked the beginning of the island. There was still no sign of a reception committee. I turned back to the helicopter and began to help with piling boxes on to the shingle. When I looked round again, people were walking out of the grass towards David. I dumped my box and tramped off to renew my acquaintance with the Mursi.

As I approached, Turton was already surrounded and more people were coming down on to the beach. Soon I was in a throng of remembered faces, feeling my hands grabbed, my shirt and hair fumbled. Somehow it wasn't surprising when I heard someone saying 'Lesalee'. I turned round and found myself shaking hands with Ulikoro whom I'd last seen as a bewildered teenager newly arrived in an Addis hotel. Now I was facing a giant of a man, his biceps bulging as he pumped my hand and smiled hugely.

I'd been aware of a slender figure standing slightly apart from the press of people, self-possessed but in some way cordoned inside a reserve which separated him from the others who'd come to meet us. He greeted Turton with a warmth that suggested some special acquaintance and David motioned me over.

'Leslie, this is Darchu,' he said. It was a huge relief. Darchu was a Kwegu, the man Turton had most hoped to find at Alaka, someone he'd known since he was a youth a dozen years before and who we'd discussed as a central figure for our film. We shook hands awkwardly.

I still have this big blow-up of a picture of Darchu I took somewhere. It hangs over a staircase at home and visitors tramping up the stairs are often stopped by the thing. The head is turned aside emphasising the exquisite profile – aristocratic cheekbones, an aquiline nose, a jaw-line like a model girl's. The face is almost disconcertingly feminine, but there's a whippy conviction about the torso. The expression has a kind of poised melancholy, so that it's hard to look at this photo of an East African hunter-gatherer without thinking 'style'. These days, my daughter has another of my photos of Darchu, louche in my bush hat, on the wall of her room at university.

On the shingle at Alaka, Darchu looked an instant star.

★

It wasn't even vaguely like any other New Year's Eve. With the helicopter long gone and a handsome base camp blossoming in a big shaded clearing at the centre of the island, three of us followed a Mursi youth out across the shingle to a place he said would be safe from the crocodiles. It seemed a good idea to lean on local wisdom in choosing a bathing beach. Blakeley filled his hat with river Omo and rammed it on his head while I lay in the shallows and watched a man piloting a log canoe from the far bank. He stood in the stern with a long pole and after a moment I tracked down the odd feeling of familiarity.

It was a snapshot from student days thirty years ago of summer afternoons lounging on a river bank watching people in punts with straw hats and voices honed by privilege. Then a lanky figure glistening like a seal splashed across my field of vision and I had a giggling tussle with a Mursi claimant for my soap.

It was a sublime late afternoon, bronze sunlight flooding everything, and the river holding the colours of a greening sky. Hammocked in warm water, I thought about Yvonne at home in the snowdrifts.

'This is just perfect,' Andy sighed.

'It's certainly a marked improvement on last time,' I murmured. Maybe, I thought, just maybe it'll go on being like this. The possibility of a permanent base camp on this pretty island without those punishing forced marches of 1974, lulled me for a moment into a naive optimism. I was old enough to know better and I had been here before.

I became aware that the Mursi bathers around us weren't just shouting for our soap. They dashed out of the shallows, yelling and pointing. I could just see the tell-tale bumps moving across the surface that revealed the interested crocodile. We got dressed quickly and tramped back to camp.

A warrior with a beltful of cartridges was examining our tea-towels, his face alight with excitement. Another man gobbed hugely and snorted tobacco from a bullet case. I counted twenty-two Mursi visitors round the campsite.

Mike had almost completed his second table, manufactured somehow from branches and string; Phil was experimenting with freeze-dried beef stew, Andy found news of a coup in Ghana on the World Service radio, Mohammed loped in with yet more firewood, and David talked quietly with Darchu who'd arrived with his pretty wife and tiny baby. It was another evening in Mursi country and I was happy to be back.

'It looks promising for the film,' Turton reported after his talk with Darchu. 'Apart from his, there are two other Kwegu families close to here. And Darchu says there's a Kwegu making a new canoe a few miles down the river if we're interested.' I was interested.

Mohammed was talking to me about television and he said, 'Did you ever see a programme called "Invasion"?' This was something of a surprise since I'd made the programme a couple of years earlier, a dramatised documentary about the Soviet invasion of Czechoslovakia. I hadn't expected it to surface in the Lower Omo, but it seemed Mohammed had seen it on a borrowed cassette and he was a fan.

It had been a very long day. We toasted the new year in lukewarm Scotch and fell into the spacious new tents long before midnight.

1982 started early, and with a bang. 'Friday, 1 Jan 1982, 2.45 a.m.' I wrote by torchlight. 'Thunder, lightning, rattling rain. Up to dig out the fly-sheet. Happy New Year!'

2

For much of the flight out from London, David Turton and I had talked about the film. It was obviously going to be difficult. Last time, for all the nightmarish logistics, the theme had been plain enough. If we could reach the Mursi and shoot some debates, we should have a film. This time, instead of those startling, photogenic debates about a war, we had only an idea. And how do you make a film about a symbiotic relationship?

David had given me a notion about what seemed to be going on. It appeared the Kwegu had lived along the banks of the Omo for centuries, surviving through river skills and hunting. Much more recently, perhaps during the early nineteenth century, the migrating Mursi had arrived at the Omo on their wanderings from over in southern Sudan. Far more numerous and warlike, the Mursi had established their dominance over the few hundred Kwegu. But now, it seemed, things had become much more complicated.

As we flew over the edge of Africa in the dark, David talked about the strange relationship which apparently turns up again and again along the length of the continent.

'It's a curious kind of dominance,' he said. 'Since the Mursi are constantly on the move between their cultivation sites on both sides of the Omo and their cattle-grazing lands thirty miles to the east, they need the Kwegu who stay put at the river with their own cultivation. They call the Kwegu "people with no cattle" and look down on them as second-class folk. But they also depend on the Kwegu to watch over the canoes and to ferry them past those crocodiles to their cultivation sites.'

For the Kwegu, the value of the deal with the Mursi seemed more elusive — something between protection and patronage. 'The odd thing is though,' David said, 'far from feeling oppressed, the Kwegu seemed to reckon they're getting the best of the bargain.' It was plainly a fascinating business and we sat into the night chatting about parallels in Marxist descriptions of class exploitation and feminist analyses of male domination. It sounded good after a couple of bottles of Ethiopian Airlines red wine; but I wasn't any clearer about how we were going to make it all into a film.

Sitting hunched with fright in a Kwegu canoe as we edged across the Omo on the first morning after our arrival, I felt a long way from those comfortable theorisings at 35,000ft. I was sure we were going to capsize into the river, and it didn't help a bit that Phil and Andy were shouting from the bank that they'd spotted a crocodile. They'd both declined a maiden canoe trip, and I wished I'd had more respect for my own cowardly instincts.

I crouched in the rough hewn-out centre of the log behind David and Mike and tried to fix my eyes on a puddle in front of my feet and on a little tuft of grass which had bravely sprouted inside this thing. I was terribly conscious of being trapped at the shoulders by curving walls. Each intake of breath seemed to make us wobble alarmingly, but Darchu appeared not to have noticed, standing unconcernedly in the stern and poling us easily towards the far bank.

As soon as we hit mud, I was out, squelching gratefully through the shallows. We gathered the gear and hauled up to a ridge where a few huts overlooked the river. I slumped alongside Mike under a little shade tree. After a few minutes a man came out of one of the huts carrying a woman in his arms. She looked desperately ill, impossibly thin and frail with terrible exposed sores on her legs.

'She looks as though she's dying,' David said quietly. He handed the husband a course of Tetracyclin tablets and I donated a film can as a container. The woman spoke in a sad little whine. 'She's asking for more treatment, but there's just nothing we can do.'

As her husband carried her back to the hut, I remarked on his striking gentleness. 'Yes,' David agreed 'but there's no space for sentiment. The family will just accept what happens.' It was a bleak introduction into the hard realities of this beautiful place.

In the afternoon, it was time to tackle the dinghy. I didn't fancy any more canoe trips. For a long time, we wrestled with the perplexing instructions and then explored the heavy folds of bright red rubber. Scores of Mursi spectators watched in fascination as the thing began to swell into life at last, fat and incongruous in the middle of the campsite like some fantastic slug that had crawled in out of the undergrowth. Tomorrow, we'd haul it down to the river for launching. I tried to imagine what Oldham Ron and his chums would have made of it all.

To complete our offer of entertainment for the afternoon, Blakeley dug out the Polaroid camera. His energies undimmed by hours of tussling with the dinghy, he dashed around the audience firing off pictures and handing them out to the bemused subjects.

As each image seeped through, it was greeted by whoops and shouts of astonishment. Five minutes later, I found several pictures thrown away in the bushes. Turton told me a Mursi had said to him: 'Why give me this? I can't eat it or sell it.'

At the end of the day, I luxuriated in the river splashed by white sunlight and watched by a pair of pelicans. On the walk back to camp a fragment of film and a scrap of paper on the shingle felt like an upturned dustbin in an exquisite Japanese rock garden.

After dark, I came upon Mohammed and Ulikoro, the young Mursi who'd travelled with us to Addis. It seemed he must have picked up enough Amharic then for the remarkable business they were engaged in. By the light of one of our hurricane lamps, Ulikoro was clutching a biro and painstakingly copying out Amharic characters while Mohammed repeated the sounds for him. Within fifteen minutes, he was constructing basic sentences. I walked away quietly so as not to break the spell.

Just before tent-time, the camp was flooded with music. Somebody had dug out a cassette of the theme from 'Brideshead Revisited' and fired it into the African night. It was a sledge-hammer dissonance, as the stately strings which had accompanied the spires of Oxford and aristocratic anguish fought with the living uproar of the Omo valley after dark, and it had a terrific climax. As the Brideshead music soared to its end, I heard the clapping rhythms and driving chant of a night-time dance somewhere across the island. I had a flash of Lord Sebastian Flyte reclining on a lawn with Ulikoro and a Fortnum's hamper but it was probably the nightly Mogadon beginning to do its stuff.

We carried the dinghy down to the river next morning. I broke away into the bush for a moment for a photograph. It looked like some kind of awkward ritual procession, a party of celebrants shuffling across the shingle bearing this big red thing on their heads. Then they chucked it in the river and it was just an inflatable boat on the Omo.

I was very glad Blakeley was with us. He waded out with the baffling outboard engine and lugged it into place with obvious confidence, doing expert looking things while the rest of us stood on the beach feeling useless. Then there was no avoiding my boat trip.

I've never got on with boats. One of my earliest childhood memories finds me blubbing with terror in the back of a rowing boat on a municipal boating pond in Leeds. 'It's too near the water,' I'm repeating like a stuck record. As far as I recall, my most recent boating experience was going round in circles on a lake in south-east China that was sixty miles long and 5ft deep, expiring with tedium as our hosts pointed out yet another pagoda while politely evading all attempts to discuss a documentary. And that about covers it for me and boats – fear and boredom. A cross-channel ferry still looms like a prison sentence. Even my best boat trip, a week's filming on an American sixth Fleet aircraft-carrier hoping to be harassed by Soviet spy ships didn't really win me over. The breakfasts for 2,000 were fun, and the jets pounding into the deck were fun, but the Soviets didn't show up and the boat was still a boat.

I splashed out and clambered into the dinghy alongside Mike and a Mursi called Ba baiu who'd somehow become an instant stowaway. Captain Blakeley yanked on a string a couple of times and the engine ripped into life.

And then we were away, cruising down the Omo and it was terrific. Maybe it was just the awareness that we were first and there'd never been anything more powerful than a log on these reaches of the Omo; maybe it was the sheer rush of speed as we surged along under the pink cliffs behind Alaka while Ba baiu placidly surveyed the horizon as though he'd been doing this all his life.

Too soon, my first enjoyable boat trip was over and Mike was throttling back to skim into the shingle. Phil and Andy scrambled aboard for their treat and I watched enviously from the beach. The dinghy drifted in midstream, a lot less efficient than a Kwegu log as Mike panted on the string for minutes on end. 'It must be flooded,' he yelled, and I shouted that we'd meet them round the bend of the river where the current would carry them on to a beach.

It was a bit of an anti-climax, but at least we knew it could work. We dragged the boat on to the sand and headed for camp sprouting oars and fuel pipes on a really hot slog across the island, tramping through little settlements and stopping constantly to hand out penicillin ointment and bandages. Tiny kids scattered before us, screaming. 'It's hardly surprising,' David observed. 'I just heard a mother telling them to watch out or the white men would eat them.'

Our campsite was a bliss of shade and refreshment. Gulping down mugs of Mohammed's marvellous brew of Omo and lemonade powder, I revived enough to notice a strapping Mursi scrutinising something near the tents. I walked over and found he was looking at a picture postcard that had somehow found its way here with us, a street scene in the Eritrean capital Asmara, flat-roofed brown buildings, palm trees and a garish blue sky. I glanced over the man's shoulder and saw that he was holding the card with the horizon running from top to bottom. He laughed and passed the card to three friends. One after another, they all turned Asmara on its side and looked with interest at the horizontal palms and the vertical sky. It was for some reason genuinely unsettling and for a moment nothing seemed quite secure. Was it possible these people simply didn't see the world the same way at all? It was an echo of the way I felt during an earthquake in the Andes in the early 70s when the solid floor of the little hotel suddenly became undulating rubber and I couldn't be sure of anything any more.

Then David came over and turned the postcard back to match the world of buildings and streets, explaining as best he could notions of towns and pavements and photographs. I gave the card to the man who'd first found it. He looked pleased.

By the end of the day, a circle of men were sitting round Phil's tape recorder listening to recordings of our first solid filming. They seemed hypnotised and it had been an encouraging start. We'd begun at Darchu's compound, shooting a relaxed conversation between him and a bunch of Mursi while scrawny chickens grumbled around them. Even at close quarters, the Kwegu were physically indistinguishable from the Mursi, apart from the welcome evidence offered by Darchu's pretty wife, grinding sorghum in front of the hut, that Kwegu women did not cut their lips. Darchu was clearly bilingual in the Mursi language, shifting easily out of Kwegu and chattering with the other men. Again I was taken with him, poised, articulate and full of descriptive gestures. David murmured that the talk was about canoe-building and the differences between Kwegu and Mursi which sounded like a producer's dream, and before we packed up there was a bonus. Darchu sang songs about Elephant and Buffalo and Giraffe, and the sweeping melody broken by flurries of notes sounded like the rhythms of the hunt.

Under a shade tree on a ridge overlooking a dry tributary of the Omo we filmed Darchu playing a game with half a dozen Mursi. Below us, women toiled in the sun hurling stones at birds with designs on the lush sorghum crop. For a long time I watched the hands flickering over an ancient-looking carved wooden board, scooping up stones and distributing them along a row of hollows. It seemed to involve complex calculations done at lightning speed, but I could never catch up with the basic rules. A man crooned his cattle song as he made a successful play and I was as baffled as ever. Again Darchu had his place in the circle of Mursi men, and it was impossible to detect any sign of his second-class Kwegu status.

Only a few months back some chap with an eye for an obscure business opportunity wrote to me saying he'd seen the sequence in our film and he'd like to market the game in England if I could tell him how it was played. As I'd never got further than registering that the Mursi called it 'Huroi', I leaned on Turton and he sent the man a treatise by a learned colleague about the ninety-seven variants of Huroi played up and down Africa.

I'm still looking out for the jolly English version with Ian

Botham's recommendation on the box-lid and pretty pink plastic cups in the hope that I might at last get a grip on what they were doing under that shade tree.

It seemed to be our day for cultural collisions. After dark, when Turton had retreated to his tent to escape the tide of Mursi demands for clothes, razor blades, food, towels, money, a smiling man came over to join me in listening to a cassette of The Who's 'Won't Get Fooled Again'. The thunderous anthem for the lost illusions of the 60s really seemed to get through to him as he stood over me, head shaking, feet stamping.

In the silence after The Who, I could hear another dance crackling into life across the island. 'Let's go to the dance,' Andy said.

Outside the womb of our camp, the moon made hard shadows but the brightness felt like menace as we edged along tracks that were suddenly unfamiliar. I populated the bush with scorpions, snakes and leopard tracks and began to wonder if this was a good idea.

'Is this a good idea?' I said and then there was someone coming towards us. A smile jogged up to the track, resolving into Ulikoro with our battery lamp shining in his face. Mike pointed at the noise of the dance and Ulikoro led us towards the dark mass of the great shade tree.

As we got near, the hypnotic drone and slap of the dance reached out and drew us in.

I tried to put it in the diary: 'A powerful sense of dangerous excitement. Ulikoro snaps on the lamp and there are leaping figures in a chanting, shifting ring. No one seems surprised to see us, a dozen figures loom up to shake our hands. Why on earth do I remember those shining children issuing from the space ship at the end of *Close Encounters*? I switch out the light and there are just the dark shapes, moving against the moon. It feels like Africa, unchanged and unreachable. For all the welcome, we're outsiders, gauche gatecrashers. Ulikoro wants us to leave.'

Ulikoro was right. Back in camp, I felt I was waking from a dream. There was a humorous Mursi, with a smile like a sad car salesman, trying to flog a deer horn tobacco pouch to David. 'This man, Bekithi, once saved my life in a river,' David said mildly, but the chap had already turned his attentions to me. 'He says he saw you seven years ago at Moizoi, so where's his present?'

Dazzled by the cheek, I fetched him a razor blade. 'It's blunt,'

David interpreted, as Bekithi cut himself. This was clearly a vintage cadger. I hunted in the tent and brought him a disposable plastic razor with a bright yellow handle. He beamed and announced, 'That's a real present.'

Under the great shade tree, a Mursi with a deformed ear told us an old story about his people and the Kwegu.

'Ages ago, when our ancestors were on the way to the Omo, there were two brothers. When they got to the hill called Dirka, the older brother's wife was about to give birth. So the younger brother took the cattle ahead to drink at the spring. The other stayed with his wife who gave birth in the bush. And then he saw vultures and he said: "I will get meat so my wife can drink soup." So he followed the vultures and found some Kwegu eating meat. He took some of the meat and made soup for his wife and finished the rest of it himself. It was giraffe, something we have never eaten.

So, when his brother came back with the cattle, the older one said: "Don't come near. I have eaten giraffe." The younger one was shocked and said: "Why did you eat it?" His brother replied: "My wife was ill. You had better take the cattle on by yourself. I will become a Kwegu."

Later, the younger one came to see his brother here at Alaka. "Are you my brother?"

"I am he."

"Is this your place now?"

"Yes, it has become my place."

"Then let it become our land, and let us both eat from it."

So now I herd my cattle and the descendants of the older brother are my Kwegu. We are brothers.'

It's a story full of messages about how the Mursi view the Kwegu, as falling short of herding moralities, as inferiors, as people without cattle. It denies them even their integrity as hunters, depicting the Kwegu as cattleless herders who have taken to hunting until they can scramble back to herding.

Even after a few days acquaintance, it didn't seem to fit with Darchu.

From where I stood, it looked uncomfortably like a riot. I could still just see David, apparently struggling to stay upright in the midst of a couple of hundred screaming, jostling people. A few Mursi men lashed at the crowd with long whippy branches in an effort to impose some kind of order, stirring a cloud of choking red dust. It certainly wasn't the orderly payout we'd intended.

When we were first planning the film back in Manchester, I'd discussed with Turton how we could best offer some practical assistance to the hard-pressed Mursi and Kwegu. During his brief visit in April 1981 he'd found that though the food situation wasn't as desperate as we'd experienced seven years earlier, people were still hungry. But after years of failed rains up to 1980, there had at last been a wet spring and the prospect of a decent harvest.

Turton had been particularly impressed with the way that emergency grain from the military government, dumped of necessity at the fringes of Mursi country, had allowed the people to use the mechanisms and values of their own society to allocate the supply. Instead of becoming refugees waiting outside the barbed wire at official soup kitchens, the Mursi had worked out for themselves ways to distribute and share the grain.

Turton suggested our most effective contribution now would be money with which people could buy grain at highland market villages to help tide them over until harvest time. With Mohammed's help and know-how, we'd purchased in Addis £1000 worth of single Ethiopian dollar notes, a bulging parcel smelling strongly of the rancid butter which is used as a cosmetic by Highland women. The plan had been to hand out the money at a series of orderly gatherings during our stay. The chaotic scene I was looking at now revealed that it was going to be more difficult than that.

At last the crowd began to scatter and David walked wearily towards me. 'We're going to have to think of a better way,' he said.

We were crouching under a shade tree with a Kwegu called Kumuli when we heard the dance. The cracking precision of the clapping cut through the sultry afternoon like a volley of rifle shots. The sound was coming from the great tree where we'd had our encounter with the night-time dance. I stood up and I could just see the group of girls, collapsing in giggles now as the dance petered out and then instantly started up again. Without a word, we set up and began to shoot.

Over the next ten minutes, we gradually moved closer, anxious not to break the mood. But we needn't have bothered. By the time we were under the tree, the thing had exploded and we were irrelevant.

It was good being a wallflower at this dance, looking in on all that strutting vitality and sexy arrogance. A group of young braves arrived, wilder than any gang of painted punks. Fantastically stencilled with zig-zags and stripes and whorls on faces and bodies, some of them carried slender poles tipped with the white fluffy tufts of colobus monkeys, silly and sexy. A couple of the gang had racy white spectacles painted round their eyes, others flaunted long curling feathers. Cool as a troupe from *West Side Story*, the men stalked inside the circle of girls and went into their stamping, swaggering display. One brave jutted his colobus pole with the insolent provocation of a rock guitarist. Mike moved with them inside the circle, wildly incongruous with the camera on his shoulder but seemingly invisible. Around them the girls were a driving vortex of sound, miraculously synchronised clapping layered with cross-rhythms, over an insistent humming drone that had the quality of an incantation and a powerful animal bellowing in triumph.

Then I saw some tiny children had joined in, dust spurting under their feet and it was just kids having a good time – a livelier Sunday afternoon than most kids could hope for.

But it wasn't for everyone. Standing quietly outside the circle, excluded, I spotted Darchu. It was approaching harvest time and one of the few moments in the year when young men and women could get together, but not for a Kwegu like Darchu.

David had talked about the strict separation between Mursi and Kwegu when it came to sex. 'It's accepted that lots of Mursi men will sleep with Kwegu girls though they keep it quiet and it's said that the men's cattle may die as a result. But if a Kwegu man gets found with a Mursi girl, he's liable for a real beating.' It was the first time I'd seen real evidence of Darchu's Kwegu status.

'Terrific stuff,' Mike croaked, pulling his camera from his shoulder as another dance subsided. 'I reckon we've got it.'

'The last one was best for sound,' Phil added. They were both drenched with sweat after the exertions of the past hour but they looked happy.

We followed Darchu towards the river and the dinghy. After the cosy days on our island base, there was no avoiding the necessity of venturing out. Tomorrow would be our first voyage down river and Mike wanted to check out the transport.

The outboard fired, stalled, fired again, stalled again and then cleared, the uproar bouncing off the cliffs across the river and scattering a flutter of pelicans. It didn't exactly inspire confidence for our trip tomorrow. Mike throttled back and shouted to us. 'I'll take it round the corner to the bathing beach. It'll give it a chance of a run and we'll be a bit nearer where we're going tomorrow.'

He ripped out of sight and we flogged round the shingle which was by this time in the afternoon glowing like a fire-walker's ordeal.

Mike was wearing only his hat as we approached, but I could tell he was less cheerful than usual. He let me have it all in one burst. 'I got chased by a croc so I piled on the revs. I must have hit a submerged stone. It smashed off one of the propeller blades.'

'I don't bloody believe it!' I flopped on the wounded dinghy. 'We haven't even started yet and we have a rerun of the sodding jeep.' Mike looked chastened, but it was hardly his fault. It seemed that once again Mursi country was going to do battle with our machinery. I only hoped it wasn't going to win this time. I didn't fancy swimming.

Back in camp, we found a visiting well-wisher had left us three long white crocodile eggs. One more than the remaining propeller blades I thought.

But Ulikoro did help to restore some perspective. 'Would you ask if he saw television when he was in Addis with you in '74,' I said to David. At first, I wondered if he could have translated the reply properly. 'Yes,' Ulikoro said, 'and I saw the fish as well.'

'What can he mean, David?'

'Well I'm not sure you TV folk are going to like this, but it seems Ulikoro preferred looking at the hotel aquarium.'

3

I counted six of them as we swung into the narrows, and I couldn't really believe this was happening. We swept closer and they looked improbably huge, like out-of-scale models in a low-budget monster movie. As we came level with their shingle bank, the crocodiles slithered into the water and disappeared under the dinghy – I grabbed a rock from the bottom of the boat and allowed myself to admit that there was good reason to be very frightened.

When Turton had first mentioned the crocodiles in my Manchester office I'd struggled to take it seriously. I suppose I thought we might just catch a glimpse of a receding tail at the limits of our zoom lens.

Now they were somewhere just below us with only a floppy skin of rubber between their jaws and a five-course banquet. I had this inappropriate cartoon strip vision of the croc-punctured inflatable skittering off over the treetops like a burst balloon farting its way to the horizon.

Darchu's attempt at reassurance hadn't helped. 'The crocodiles won't bite the boat,' he said, 'only eat you if you fall in.' Turton's revelations about crocodile habits hadn't been any more comforting: 'Their teeth are too blunt to devour human flesh. Their tactic is to drown you and store you in a muddy hole below the water-line until you go soggy.' For all his academic detachment, he'd been the one who suggested we might load up with a few rocks.

I preferred to put my trust in Blakeley. He revved the ailing outboard, just enough to propel us past croc corner without fragmenting what was left of the propeller. We skidded away into calmer water and I began to unwind enough to let go of my rock.

It had been a morning of beauty and terror, miles down the Omo in the hope of filming the Kwegu canoe builders of Makaro. From the start, I'd thought it sounded like the title of an Edgar Rice Burroughs fantasy, and it had been that kind of journey. There were five of us in the advance party, Mike at the tiller, thank god, David and myself, while Darchu and Ba baiu did the navigating. We spluttered with the current past high flaking cliffs where baboons scuttled for cover, and banks of shingle interspersed with Mursi cultivation sites, lanky spires of sorghum flourishing in the floodlands beside the Omo. Two or three times we spotted people standing along the shore and Darchu shouted for advice about the shallows. A heavy brown bird flapped over us and we kept pace for a time with a magical red and white butterfly. After a while the dinghy was visibly deflating, but I began to feel less sure that this was where I was going to die.

Darchu pointed at the shore and we nudged into a beach of stones. 'I'm afraid this is as far as the dinghy can make it.' David was already helping to reflate the thing for the return trip to collect Phil and Andy. 'Ba baiu will lead the way to the canoe. He says it's just downstream here.'

I watched the dinghy claw its way back up river and out of sight and then turned to follow Ba baiu. I was carrying the camera in a black plastic bin liner and I quickly wished I wasn't. We fought our way along the bank in a ragged little procession, slipping down crumbling walls into the shallows, scrambling up an obstacle course of sandy dust. It was a muck-sweat of an effort, the first real flavour of 1974.

At last, as the legs were beginning to wobble, I crawled up into a clearing overlooking the river.

A 30 ft tree trunk lay on the floor of the glade, smoke drifting from a blackened trench cut into the bark. It was obviously the canoe, but there was no evidence of canoe-builders or canoe-building. I collapsed gratefully on a tree-stump, entirely alone with eight Mursi and their rifles. It occurred to me that I'd never been so isolated or exposed in my life, but it didn't really feel like that.

It had to be at least two hours before there was any chance of the others fighting their way back down the river and joining me. Meanwhile, I had the circle of staring Mursi for company and the diary:

'11.00 a.m. Activity on the canoe. A naked Kwegu wanders up, grabs a pot, drinks hugely and sprays water from his mouth on to the innards of the smouldering log. It looks very precise and presumably promotes the hollowing in some way.

11.20 a.m. A camera lesson for my hosts. One by one, they peer through the viewfinder, all for some reason with the left eye while I zoom in and out on their mates. Whoops of laughter.

11.35 a.m. A moment to count the bites on my hands: fourteen on the left, twenty-two on the right. A gorgeous dusty orange butterfly flaps past.

12 noon Awake from drowsing against a tree. Through my torpor, the Mursi chatter sounds utterly domestic and familiar.

12.25 p.m. Still waiting, stupefied. Ash drifts over me from the canoe.

12.40 p.m. Andy's cap visible through the trees.'

It was good to see them and to know the dinghy had survived another test. The arrival of the crew seemed to provoke a flurry of activity on the canoe. The man who'd sprayed water into the innards chopped away with a spear at the burnt wood to enlarge the hollow. Then he levered out jagged splinters with a creaking like the door of Dracula's castle. Finally, he poured water into a hole and began to make a muddy custard. It was time for Choya to step in.

David introduced me to the stately old Kwegu, a celebrated canoe-builder it seemed and Darchu's father in law. He stood alongside the log and explained his ancient skills to these strange white men who pointed things at him. Choya spoke in a whisper as hoarse as though he'd been dried out by the years of smoke and ash.

'I control the fire with mud, all along the canoe. Here I am now putting in fire, smearing, smearing it with mud.'

'The fire eats it,' Darchu explained, 'and then he puts in mud.'

With surprising delicacy, Choya scooped up a handful of mud and moulded it into the hot charcoal wall of the canoe. Mike straddled the log, risking a highly personal barbecue to get a better shot of the process and Choya looked up in alarm. He said something sharp and David interpreted quickly. 'Mike, it's considered very bad luck to step over the canoe before it's finished – could you stay on one side or the other?' Blakeley jumped aside as though a spark had stung him.

It seemed that the younger Kwegu was the eventual owner of the canoe. Called Nyomanikaulo, he was visibly proud of it. 'It's my canoe,' he said, slapping his chest, 'and later on when the moon wanes I'll pole it across the river so people can cultivate on the other bank. It's my canoe.'

Nyomanikaulo gulped from the gourd again and fired a spray of water into the roasting core of the log. Steam hissed around him as he spoke some blessings. 'Cut the water like a crocodile! Float like foam.' He sprayed again. 'Stay upright in fast water.' He seemed stuck for further suitable suggestions. A bystander offered another, rather less elegant variation – 'Cut the water like a hippo.'

The clearing was striped with long shadows by now, and it was time to face the river again. As we were stuffing gear into rucksacks, an extraordinary figure shuffled out of the trees. Bent and spindle-legged, the man had a face like one of those turtles that seem to have been alive for centuries. On his head, like a gnarled extension of himself, was a conical straw hat of un-imaginable senility. Doki, Turton said was the oldest Kwegu of them all. He looked like the father of humankind. David paid his respects and dashed away to distribute money to the Makaro people while we set out on the nasty little jaunt back to the dinghy.

Two hours later, Andy and I were still beached and waiting. It was a golden evening and Mursi youths splashed around us in the river, seemingly unconcerned about crocodiles. I sat on the shingle with Andy feeling like the Sheriff in *Jaws* in that scene where he was anxiously scanning the bathers for a menacing fin.

We had anxieties of our own. Where was the dinghy? Had the first boatload made it back to Alaka? Could Mike be back here before dark?

Just before 6 p.m., one of the Mursi made a whirring noise and pointed up river. I was more relieved than I dared admit.

The journey back up the river was like something out of fantasy fiction and I sometimes feel I must have dreamed it. It would have been a nightmare I suppose.

Backed by an exquisite sunset shading to violet in the glassy river we ploughed off upstream, this time against the powerful current. Soon, the penalty of the wounded propeller was alarmingly clear. At points where the river narrowed and the current was strongest, the dinghy hung almost stationary for minutes on end, Mike pushing the engine as hard as he dared to try and make some headway.

With the light draining away, it was a simply rapturous evening. We hung between a green sky and a gilded river patterned with the reflections of trees like oriental calligraphy. Darchu pointed and we spotted monkeys looping away through the high branches.

Then it was dark with a brilliant half moon standing over us. By now, Darchu and Ba baiu were reduced to navigating by sweeping the distant river bank with our handlamps. Although I was waiting for it, it was still a shock when Darchu's beam hit those shining points of light. We were navigating by croc's eyes. Sweeping further the beam caught a long grey shape sliding into the water.

I'd been dreading croc corner, the narrowest and most turbulent point in our journey. Fighting the scream of the engine as it struggled to make progress against the fierce current I yelled, 'Go for it, Mike!' The injured prop seemed a secondary problem, wallowing in the dark water and convinced we were slipping backwards. In the midst of it all we had an unwelcome distraction. Andy spotted that the dinghy was alarmingly crumpled and we scrambled amid the half-seen rubble in the bottom of the boat for the pump.

And then it was just absurd. We giggled uncontrollably, pumping to reflate the collapsing dinghy while Mike bawled at the protesting outboard, 'Come on you bugger!' 'I don't think I remember this in my contract,' Andy panted, taking his turn on the pump. With painful slowness, we began to move ahead and into easier water.

Under the dark mass of the familiar cliffs behind Alaka, we spluttered in. It was completely black as the dinghy bumped against the beach. The sand was still warm and I'd never have believed this could feel like coming home.

Mohammed seemed very relieved to see us. He'd stayed behind to watch over the camp, and he didn't appear sorry to have missed the adventures of the day recycled via our wide-eyed tales. There was a lot of loud laughter and a rush of competing bad jokes.

Amid all the noisy relief, it wasn't immediately easy to place the new voice: 'I've come to complain about this Parrot!' Then the classic Monty Python Parrot sketch filled the site from Andy's cassette player. It seemed an entirely appropriate way to celebrate the end of a silly day.

I fell into the tent and tried to write up some lessons. 'We mustn't get stuck like that again, on the river after dark. It's beautiful but bloody dangerous. So the boat made it after all. It's an edgy business, but we have to make at least one more trip to see the canoe-launching. Mike has done a terrific job with six trips up and down the river today, and although he's obviously enjoyed it, it must have been a real strain. I'm whacked now. Andy's already asleep.'

As I tumbled towards oblivion, I could still hear somebody replaying the Parrot sketch: '. . . an ex-parrot, he has joined the choir celestial, bereft of life, he breathes no more, he's snuffed it.'

4

'Mikey!' Blakeley's favourite Mursi tormentor, a roguish bald man called Ulilibai was already hard at it, bawling through the flap of their tent at the drowsing crew. It wasn't much after seven and we'd promised ourselves a quiet day after the trials of the river, but it seemed Ulilibai and the three dozen other Mursi visitors had different ideas. Through the mosquito net, I could already see David at work handing out money to a crowd of new arrivals. Andy stirred and groaned at the slum of our tent. 'Good morning camper,' I greeted him. 'Nobody gets a day off when the Mursi are around.'

We went through the motions of competing with the flies for breakfast and listened to a World Service news about snow, floods and rail strikes in Britain. A couple of Mursi dogs scuffled in the dust, and Terry Wogan's international request programme filtered through the fusillades of our gobbing visitors. It was just another morning.

The routines of water-purifying, equipment-servicing and Mursi-parrying were interrupted in mid-morning by a filming bonus right on our doorstep. Darchu had found a bees' nest in a tree yards from the camp. It could be a useful sequence for us, giving vivid expression to another Kwegu service much valued by the Mursi. Honey is a prized commodity in the Lower Omo, as it is in the rest of Ethiopia since it's the basis of Tej, the national drink. The Kwegu's skill in harvesting honey is something the Mursi are keen to profit from, trading it in highland villages for axes, knives, cloth or goats.

When we arrived at the tree with Darchu and our film gear, I already felt distinctly foolish. Cutting a protective veil from a spare mosquito net to wedge under my hat had seemed like a good idea, but already it was suffocating, scratchy and full of gaps. Worse still, it made the crew convulse with laughter every time they looked in my direction. Darchu, as usual, was more poised.

He began by performing a small miracle. In seconds, Darchu made fire. Into a notch in a twig, he inserted a stick, twisting it rapidly by rubbing between his palms. The notch began to smoke, Darchu piled on the dry grass, and then lifted the bundle to blow on it. Flame burst through the grass and I would have applauded if it wouldn't have wrecked Phil's soundtrack.

Darchu blew smoke from the burning grass into a crack to shift the bees away from the honey and then reached for a rather hopeless-looking axe – just a narrow blade of metal in a wooden handle. Every blow hit the mark, quickly opening up a hole in the side of the tree. Seeing the accuracy of Darchu's work Mike risked hair-raising angles with the axe falling right beside the lens. The chopping ceased and I could hear the angry buzzing of the colony inside the tree. To my alarm Darchu simply stuck his arm down into the hole and pulled out a honeycomb. The whole operation had taken about five minutes. It was a dazzling display of casual expertise and I doubted it could have been done quicker if Darchu had borrowed our matches and stainless steel axe. I threw away my improvised mask before we walked back into camp.

In the afternoon, there was more evidence of Darchu's talents. It was almost as though he was lining up the demonstrations in front of us. Phil was tinkering with a scheme to conceal a microphone in a bamboo stick to help with unobtrusive filming – 'My bush Nana Mouskouri mike,' he called it – when I spotted what Darchu was doing. Sitting in front of one of the tents, he was quietly dismantling and servicing a rifle. We began filming while, watched by the anxious Mursi owner, Darchu unscrambled the interlocking maze of springs and sliding chambers. David asked what the problem was and Darchu told him it just wouldn't fire for some reason. A shower of rust and earth accompanied the unstripping of every component.

Borrowing our oil and a scrap of sandpaper, Darchu worked away for half an hour. I was fetching a new roll of film from the storage tent when I heard a whoop of joy. The rifle's owner was hopping with excitement, watching Darchu firing the empty weapon at the sky with a series of triumphal clicks.

At the end of the afternoon, I joined David on our regular medical parade. It was hopeless really, but impossible not to make the gesture. Dusting the successsion of savage cuts and dabbing penicillin ointment on the terrible tropical ulcers was plainly a feeble response to an appalling health problem. I supposed the tiny baby with the worrying-looking foot would have a few hours of relief, but the inadequacy of an elastoplast was painful, and I reckon that the session did more for my Dr Schweitzer fantasies than for the long line of Mursi patients. Then David went off to see a woman who had sent word she was in great pain. It sounded like appendicitis, an unimaginable horror in this place.

He drifted into the camp like smoke and suddenly he was just there. Komorakora, the Mursi priest had come fifty miles to see us. I spotted the heavy ivory bangle and that face built for spirituality, unchanged it seemed by the years since I'd seen him last on the hillside at Ma'do after the great debate to strengthen the Mursi for war. He recognised me and it felt like an obscure sanctification.

Komorakora's other-worldliness survived even his raffish outfit – a dark-green velvety shirt and a multicoloured stetson. He sat with David and they talked for a long time. I could guess something of what must be passing between them since Turton had already told me what he knew of the Mursi migration. When he'd come here briefly eight months earlier, he'd heard about the migration and about the remarkable events which had been going on since the beginning of 1980. People told him: 'Since the rain has deserted our country, many have decided they must do the same.' It seemed that, driven by the drought years of the 1970s and the resulting hunger, something like a quarter of the Mursi people had set out on an exodus to higher, better-watered ground some fifty miles to the east in the valley of the Mago river. It brought them close to the fringes of highland Ethiopia and the outside world. The migrants had been led in what they called their 'search for cool ground' by Komorakora.

Now the Priest had made the long walk from his new home back to Alaka. He and David had a lot to talk about. When he finally moved away to sit quietly at the edge of our site, Turton came across. 'It sounds extraordinary,' he said. 'The Priest's talking about a major settlement of around 200 huts which is quite unlike anything they've built before. But they're obviously having a tense time with some of the highland people. It would be terrific if the helicopter could try and fly over the new place on our way out.' I caught some of David's excitement, but the prospect seemed utterly remote.

It wasn't only us the Priest had come for. He was also back in Alaka to see Darchu. It had occurred to me in 1974 that the whole of Mursi society numbers only about as many people as the small Cheshire village I live in, and I suppose I shouldn't have been surprised to find that two of our central characters were closely connected. It certainly helped the tidiness of our film that the Priest was Darchu's Mursi patron.

The patron–client relationship between individual Mursi and Kwegu is where the strange association comes into focus. A Kwegu like Darchu has a special connection with one Mursi and it's to this patron that he'll contribute most of his skills and services on the river or in hunting. That much I knew, but it simply raised a hundred other questions.

On a calm grey morning at Darchu's settlement, we filmed with him and the Priest. While Darchu's two wives roasted unripe sorghum over a fire and a tiny baby crawled around, we got a straight answer to one basic question – what's in it for the Kwegu?

'These are our people,' the Priest murmured, 'we marry wives for them. If he wants to marry, I give him a cow. I gave cattle for both his wives here. They were my cattle.'

Darchu told it as a tiny drama. 'If I want to marry, I go to see this man and say: "I've seen a girl." "She wants you?" "Yes!" "Get up and let's go." He gives me a cow.'

As we walked back to camp, David filled in the picture. 'Once a Mursi has handed over an animal to a Kwegu for him to get married with, that Mursi will have a special relationship not just with that Kwegu, but with his children and their children and so on.'

Quite how the Mursi had persuaded a people who had no cattle that they needed cattle in order to marry was just one of the questions we were going to have to spend time and film on. But it obviously gave the Mursi the most basic kind of control over the Kwegu.

Back in camp, I counted 137 visitors to the site. My ongoing bush seminar on symbiosis was going to have to wait.

'It looks like something out of *The African Queen*, doesn't it?' Andy said. He was right. We were pushing along a forest bank overlooking the Omo and through a gap in the trees we could see Darchu and Ba baiu up to their waists in the river dragging the dinghy through the shallows. They looked a lot less haggard than Humphrey Bogart.

Mohammed had said it was Christmas day according to the Ethiopian calendar and our present was to be another adventurous day trip. A Mursi had lost a rifle in the Omo a few miles north of Alaka and Darchu had been asked to try and find it. It sounded like a long slog, but there might be good film at the end of it.

Andy and I watched some small boys hauling in big fish with nothing but unbaited hooks and lines and then walked on to our rendezvous with the dinghy. After a short struggle upstream, we hit impassable shallows again and it was time for more walking.

Our little file straggled up through a ruined forest and out on to a vast shelf of shingle. It was difficult to imagine how this landscape must look in the wet season with the Omo swollen to several hundred yards wide and roaring over the stones we were crossing now.

'Jesus, how much further?' I could hear Phil panting behind me as we clattered across glaring white stones under a sky bleached by the sun.

I could see distant figures scattered by a bend in the river. We traipsed towards them and Darchu went on ahead to make contact. By the time we arrived at the river, he was nuzzling a rifle into his shoulder and taking aim. The crew were filming just in time to record the shot and the plume of water that leaped up from the river where Darchu had seen the crocodile. It seemed a casual enough precaution for what followed.

Even now at the height of the dry season, the river was roaring through the narrows where the Mursi said he'd lost his rifle. I tried to stand with the crew in the warm shallows, but just a few feet from the shingle it was hard for any of us to stay upright.

Wading easily against the rush of water, Darchu and a local Kwegu helper pulled a canoe towards the head of the creek. Then they climbed in and began to drift quickly downstream while Darchu probed the river bed with a long pole. For all his simple resources, he worked with the care and precision of a bomb disposal expert. Alongside me, the Mursi who'd lost the rifle chattered excitedly with a group of spectators. I noted they stayed well out of the river, and I didn't blame them. When I got David's translation of what they were saying, their caution seemed more calculating.

'I've brought this man,' the owner told the others. 'He's a Kwegu who can dive. If a crocodile gets anyone, I'll be responsible.' The value of this guarantee became even less clear when Darchu moved into the next stage of his search. Abandoning the canoe, he dived into the swirling water. As he swept downstream, he was clearly feeling for the rifle with his feet. We swapped tasteless jokes about the crocodile, but we all felt close enough to Darchu by now to be genuinely uneasy.

The Mursi rifle owner seemed unimpressed by Darchu's efforts. 'If only more Kwegu were here from upstream,' he lamented, 'they'd go in and look. They wouldn't be afraid of crocodiles. They're good in deep water.'

But even Darchu's energies were looking ineffective against the force of the river. He was constantly being swept away past the search area, fighting to the shore downstream for another attempt.

'Look what he's doing now,' David said. From the river-bed, Darchu heaved an enormous stone and held it above his head. It was a moment before any of us realised what was going on. Looking through the camera, Mike spotted it first: 'That's amazing – he's using the stone to weight himself down against the current.'

It was like watching one of those barmy gladiatorial TV shows where grotesque strongmen pull trucks up hills with their teeth – only this was for real and there no prizes, just terrible risks.

It was obviously hopeless. Despite the rock, Darchu was still being carried away by the current, and only his persistence made the hunt seem credible.

'Looks like he's calling it a day,' Mike reported. Darchu

dumped his rock and allowed the river to carry him to the bank a hundred yards downstream. Mursi kids began to play in the shallows.

I suppose it should have felt like witnessing some ghoulish ordeal dreamed up from the Labours of Sisyphus and the Roman Games with the Mursi rifle owner as Zeus-cum-Nero. But somehow Darchu's stylish performance had bypassed all that. It should make a terrific sequence, and heading back over the shingle it already felt like a possible opening to the film.

By the end of the day, the journey back to base camp, arriving scorched, dripping and filthy had mellowed to a diary entry; and there was even a moment for some stock-taking.

'A week into the Lower Omo tonight, good film I think and routines established. Hard days, but treasure stored. A most beautiful night now, lit by an almost full moon. A walk to the beach with Andy produces a *frisson* of pleasure at the soft blue light over the bush. A man lopes by playing a kind of bush xylophone, the unearthly metallic twanging a perfect soundtrack for the scene. Down by the river, fragmented silver, there's a quiet greeting and Ulikoro comes out of the darkness. He sits with us on the stones and he looks quite superhuman by moonlight. We flash the torch across the river and stab into eyes, five pairs along the far bank – crocodiles we presume. On the way back, tiny children run softly behind us and one holds Andy's hand. In camp, a man tries to sell us a lion's claw from an animal he shot about three miles south of here. Outside the tent now, I can still hear the chatter of a group of women.'

I heard Turton packing up his translation stuff and I called to him, 'David, how long are those women going to go on nattering out there?'

'You should worry!' he chuckled. 'They've just told me they all intend to spend the night in my tent.'

5

For the next two days, we were becalmed in domestic detail with nothing to film. The hours were full of water-purifying, inept and unproductive fishing, medical parades and cadgers. Mike felt unwell and then, thankfully, felt better. I grappled with a lethargy that lay on me like a dead animal and I finally got free when Ulikoro cut himself and I had to scuttle around with first aid. I found Phil reading his passport and the World Service had yet more news of English blizzards. But at least it all gave me time to talk to Turton about the film and about the Kwegu way of marriage.

He snapped off his cassette recorder and took a break from translating our talk with Darchu and the priest. 'What it comes down to, I suppose, is that the Mursi have managed to control the means of Kwegu reproduction, their continued existence in fact. A Kwegu can't marry without the help of a Mursi, as the priest told us, because a Kwegu has to hand over livestock to the father of his Kwegu bride. Since the Mursi have all the cattle . . .'

I smacked an insect on my arm, but it was too late. 'How on earth do the Kwegu feel about all this?'

'Well they feel dependent of course, but they don't seem to resent it. If you ask a Kwegu, "What do you get from your Mursi," he'll always say, "Cattle to marry with." Actually they do have a tradition of marrying in the past without handing over animals and if you ask them why they need livestock nowadays they'll admit it's because the Mursi insist on it.'

A man was hovering, trying to sell us another rubbery hen for dinner but I tried not to catch his eye. 'Surely the Kwegu father-in-law can't even keep the animals with all the tsetse fly there are at the Omo?'

'No, that's right and that's the basis of the whole thing. The Kwegu marriage arrangement is really a deal between two Mursi, the groom's patron and the patron of the bride's father who takes the livestock and herds them away in the plains on the other side of the river.'

Some answers, a lot more questions, but another man was hovering now and he was someone we did want to hear from. For several days we'd been waiting for news of negotiations about a Kwegu wedding which was due to happen miles to the south downriver. This was the man who might be bringing some word.

'I'm afraid we're going to have to dash – it's going to be this afternoon or tomorrow morning.' David was already chucking things into a rucksack.

Memories of those frantic evacuations of 1974 thumped over me and I didn't want to know about bridewealth discussions miles away down the river Omo. It was already almost two in the afternoon and we were faced with a journey that would take us way beyond the canoe-building site. At the very least, it promised a night-out of special vileness. And then there was croc corner . . . I tried to displace my worries with the logistics of travelling light.

Five shattering hours later we seemed to have arrived some-where and I took it all out on the diary:

'On a riverbank overlooking the Omo. A sublime evening light and an absolute ecstasy of physical discomfort – soaking wet boots, itching limbs, nothing to sit on and the prospect of a night out of doors in the dust. We sprawl here waiting for our gear being carried down from Alaka; nothing to eat, nothing to be done.'

The river had been like some dream. Baboons stared out at us, we slid over silky water in unearthly light and even the crocodiles seemed like mythical beasts on the borders of our fantasy. Then we moved beyond the limits of that last expedition to Makaro and the canoe builders and it all became uncomfortably real. In endless muddy shallows spiked with rotting branches we heaved and grunted to pole the dinghy along. At last Darchu had pointed at the shingle and we drifted in, tramping miserably through green mud to be told that this was the wrong place. A local Kwegu crammed himself into the dinghy practically sinking us and we pushed on south, boots immersed in the filthy water swilling round the bottom of the boat.

We chugged round another bend, and there was another outcrop of sorghum, another shingle beach and Doki, the oldest man on earth, waiting to welcome us.

The immediate good news was that the bridewealth negotiation wasn't until the morning – maybe. Doki led us up to our dust-heap and we waited for the porters bringing our life-supports as a delicious light brown moon drifted up over the river.

Sometimes I almost catch hold of the texture and flavour of that night, taking it by surprise like seeing a star more clearly by looking askance at it. Piling layer upon layer, it became one of the most extraordinary clusters of images and emotions I can ever remember. In the middle of it, I scribbled by moonlight: 'An indescribable evening. Words run out of traction in such a place on such a night.'

The ingredients were banal enough, God knows. The five of us lay shrouded in net on improvised frameworks of twigs, rooting for half-thawed fragments of space food in silver bags. Andy twitched a transistor hunting for rumours of World Cup soccer. And then there was the dance.

All around us was a circle of leaping bodies dressed in moonlight. Without any prospects, I took a photograph. Somehow, it trapped the thing. The giant moon is a lozenge of light, the figures hang on the sky like vapours, the stars skitter into triangles and squares.

Then something odd started happening to the moon. For a while I looked at it and wondered if it was just me; after all it had been a long day. Eventually I took the plunge.

'Andy, can you see anything wrong with the moon?'

'I've been bothering about that. There seems to be a bit missing.'

Now the Mursi had certainly noticed it. The dance came to an abrupt stop and people ran away. I thought I could hear some screaming in the distance.

'Yes, it's an eclipse alright,' David said. 'That's a bad omen – it's really upset people.'

I hope they don't decide it's our fault I thought, and then I fell asleep and dreamed I was studying English at Liverpool Polytechnic.

When I woke, the sky and the river were salmon pink, and all the birds and monkeys in creation were shouting their heads off. Sticky and bleary, we groped for the gear and shambled off to look for a wedding.

We came upon them as a man was being smeared with streaks of white mud. The bride's father was an amazing sight, like a man who's just had a disastrous time trying to decorate the ceiling; but he carried a powerful sense of occasion. He sat looking out over the river, still veiled in early mist, as the first negotiators began to arrive. They took up their positions inside a flimsy cage of sticks close to the river and we set up as un-obtrusively as we could with the camera looking through the bars. Before eight o'clock around two dozen people, negotiators and interested relatives including Darchu were assembled and ready to begin the bargaining.

There was no sign of bride or groom; this was strictly a busi-ness occasion. David had alerted us to the main players. Sitting opposite the bride's father, sombre in his white daubing, there was a big man dressed only in a surprising tangerine-coloured linen jacket of some elegance. He was the groom's patron, a Bodi who'd travelled down the banks of the Omo from beyond the northern border of Mursi country to be here. The Kwegu have the same patron–client relationship with the Bodi as they have with the Mursi and the groom's patron was here to give away as little as possible. Almost inaudibly, he began to speak.

For more than an hour, as the sun burned through the early mists, they talked and we filmed. After their night on the ground, Mike and Phil had a morning to remember. Shuffling round the bars of the cage, sliding down the crumbling river bank, juggling with film and tape, sweating to follow the un-predictable flow of events and speakers, it was about as awkward and demanding a sequence as the Lower Omo could provide. And of course, like them, I had no real idea of what was going on. Relying on whispered consultations with Dr Turton, the crew's instincts and whatever luck was around, we roared through six magazines of film without a pause.

It wasn't until weeks later in the haven of a Manchester cutting room, armed with David's painstaking translations, that I really began to understand what had been happening. Trapped on the little screen of the editing machine, I was looking again at those people sprawling on skins and bargaining with bullets on the dusty edge of a remote African river. But now I was looking at a story that could have come from the boardrooms of 'Dallas', full of intrigue and double-dealing and stitch-ups. More than anything, it was a revelation about the sophisticated human complexities that underpin the seeming simplicity of life in a place where the markers are often too blurred to help us see past the surface of preconception and easy prejudice. David dropped into the cutting room at the end of an afternoon when we were working on the sequence and he passed on a favourite quote. It was from the philosopher Gabriel Marcel and it spoke about 'the familiar at the heart of the remote, an elsewhere that is also a here.'

The Bodi patron began formally, using the convention that he was about to marry the bride himself. His opening statement wouldn't exactly win the hearts of Western women in the 1980s.

'Give me your daughter, so she can get me water and fetch firewood for me and become mine. I am asking you, the father; you and the grandfather are here.'

The bride's father wasted no time in getting down to business. 'It's time for serious talk. There's a big problem here.' The problem was that his daughter had already had a child by the groom before any bridewealth had been handed over. Seizing the advantage of the wronged party, he asked to see what the patron had to offer.

'Wow, look at that!' Mike had murmured as the heavy copper bullets spilled out of the patron's bag. The Bodi was going to buy the bride with the rifle bullets, a valuable commodity in these parts as I knew from a multiplication table David had taught us: 5 bullets = 1 goat; 24 goats = 1 cow; 4 cows = 1 rifle.

The groom's patron laid out bullets on a skin in four batches of 5, and they were immediately joined by a further 20, poured from a tin by a man sitting next to the bride's father. He was an uncle of the bride who had apparently already got the bullets from the Bodi on condition that he display them now as part of the bridewealth. The uncle's intervention made it clear why there were so many people jammed into the compound. He'd got in early for his share, but there were many relatives who'd be expecting their portion of the bridewealth. Well aware that he might see little enough of it in the end, the father looked unimpressed by the 40 bullets on offer.

'40 would have been good if the girl had no child and things were normal. I would take 40 and we'd be brothers. But she's been speared. We're enemies.'

The big Bodi laughed till his jacket shook: 'It was only a blunt spear – no one died. The child has been born, mother and child are well. It has ended well.' He went on to list other items of bridewealth that had already been handed over including several goats and a rifle. But the bride's father complained the rifle was broken; and then the father's Mursi patron stepped in with a breathtaking escalation.

'I want those 200 bullets I know the groom's got. This morning, you've insulted us.'

The Bodi made no attempt to deny the fact of the 200 bullets. We'd seen something of the goldfish-bowl quality of life here on our own campsite and it was obvious there could be few secrets in a society as public as this. The groom's patron tried to bluster his way through.

'Marriage talk is like this. The father bargains hard. But soon you'll sleep with my women in secret. It's just a short war. We bargain hard, but it's nothing too serious. This is bridewealth talk. We talk about women this way – we fight, tomorrow we're friends.'

But the bride's family stuck at it. The father asked for 38 more goats, the Bodi offered 28, notional bullets were bargained. It was becoming increasingly clear that people were getting impatient as the day stoked up and Phil captured a fine outburst from Blakeley's favourite tormenter, Ulilibai.

'Hurry up! We're suffering in the sun. Throw in more goats, get on with it!'

It seemed almost as though it was the mounting temperature that melted the decisive concession. The groom's uncle, a man in a striped T-shirt sitting alongside the Bodi spoke quietly. '60 bullets are upstream. Send a boy with us and he'll bring them back.'

The total of 100 bullets had done the trick. There was a stir of acceptance in the bride's family. But her grandfather, the venerable Doki still had something to say.

'If we've been hard on you, it's because we gave you many girls in the past. They've all been my girls. So I expected much more for this one; before, you've had my girls for just two goats. Now this is my last girl, so you should give us a lot.'

A gourd full of what looked like weak tea began to circulate to seal the agreement. I popped a purifying tablet into my water bottle and we passed it around, celebrating with mouthfuls of swimming pool.

Afterwards, David found out from Darchu what had really been happening. It seemed that the whole thing was a public performance to complete a deal which had been worked out in private the night before. The 100 bullet settlement had already been agreed by both sides, but it was important for the bride's father that the morning's negotiations should give the appearance of tough bargaining to squeeze those extra 60 out of the groom's Bodi patron. The reason for the charade was to help the father head off the demands of relatives who had a claim to a share in the bridewealth.

He'd be able to say that by the time the extra bullets reached him from upstream, they'd already been claimed. He'd be able to say 'no' without making enemies. It was a solution worthy of J.R. at his wiliest.

We were still bundling up gear when David gave us the news that Andy and I would have to walk back as far as Makaro to help lighten the dinghy for the shallows.

At least it allowed me to bore Andy with how it had all been as awful as this back in 1974 and what an easy time he'd had. That walk to Makaro was a vintage hike, right up to the grisly standards of seven years before. We snarled on thorns, and panted up dust piles, following the river northwards with a file of porters who displayed a dismaying tendency to break into a loping run from time to time. After a couple of hours, we came out on to a high ridge with stunning views south to the ends of Mursi country and a mountain called Dara. I recalled David told me he'd once climbed Dara with a Mursi guide. After several gruelling hours, they were within fifty feet of the summit when the man sat down. 'Why go any further?' he said. 'You can see the top now.' Pondering his curious British obsession with goals and conquests, David had pushed on alone the few yards to the top.

Approaching Makaro, we came into the clearing where the canoe was still taking shape, now visibly leaner and more convincing. 'Hey, look at that! I reckon we came the tourist route after all.' Andy was pointing through a break in the trees which framed the dinghy party, clearly having a hellish time manhandling the boat against the current. A few minutes later, our path came down to the river and a reunion.

We watched them slosh towards us, still dragging the thing, and I was very glad I'd been walking on dust rather than struggling through water. Andy and I tried to wade out and help, but the current simply tossed us aside. Dripping on a rock while my sodden diary dried in the sun, we marvelled as Darchu strode on easily upriver hauling the loaded dinghy on his own.

Mohammed, who'd once again gamely stayed behind to guard the camp looked particularly relieved to see us after that scrambled departure twenty-four hours before. Standing behind him was someone I recognised.

'Ulichagi, good to see you! A chali?'

'A chali hang, Lesalee,' he said with the familiar shy smile. He looked older and more tired but there was no mistaking the man who'd shared so many of our trials last time. He'd made the long journey to see us from his new home with the other migrants in the Mago valley. We had a lot to talk about.

I walked to the river to swill off the day and Ulichagi strolled alongside me carrying our orange plastic bucket. It seemed he'd staked his first claim.

6

Ulichagi peeled the skin from the plant and in moments it was a cord of tough string. He began to tie knots along its length and it came to me that it was his diary – eighteen knots, one to be untied every day until the helicopter took us away. I made a note in my diary while Ulichagi told David we white people seemed to be obsessed with paper.

He was right. Our restless concern with recording the passing of time and of things seemed particularly out of place on this quite glorious afternoon, standing on a hill that seemed to command the prospect of half of Africa. It must have looked this way for thousands of years, soaringly handsome vistas north to Mount Smith, westward to the 8,000 ft peaks behind Maji, south to Dara. Under our feet, David said, were countless Mursi dead, unmarked.

Ulichagi pointed to the east and David followed the line of his arm with a compass bearing. Somewhere in those green hills was Ulichagi's new home in the Mago Valley and the rest of the Mursi migrants who had gone in search of that cool ground and a better life.

We seemed to have reached the still, dead centre of the filming, half way through and drifting between the tumbling events of the past days and the uncertainties to come. At the very least, there was another river safari to be faced for the canoe launching and still much to do to fill out our account of the elusive business of Mursi and Kwegu.

My diary was littered with the trivia of those quiet days:

'Darchu offers 4 cows for my daughter, then ups it to 5. He says he'll live six months in Manchester, six at the Omo . . .'

'Phil burns ants off the tree that threaten to march on our water-purifier; Mohammed's writing an article about Soviet social realist cinema and studying Italian . . .'

'A riotous half hour with a group of locals teaching us Mursi. As they work through the parts of the body, we inevitably end up miming "bum" and "balls" and "dick" to gales of laughter . . .'

'World Service has more mad weather in England. Wales sounds impossible, minus 27 in Scotland . . .'

'Emerged from the river bath tonight to find my watch on a Mursi wrist, my boots on Mursi feet, my towel round a Mursi waist . . .'

'A rare dream about this place – David talking to Mursi from a minibus on a suburban street . . .'

The outboard was sulky again and we just about made it across the river to Darchu's wet-weather cultivation site. Immediately, it was a dense tangle like an English orchard run wild. The autumn-coloured trees were from some suburban weekend walk but they made an effective obstacle course for a film crew with all their encumbrances. We groped our way along cursing routinely and I anticipated a routine morning's filming of Darchu chopping down undergrowth, an excursion largely to break the tedium of another day in camp. As usual Darchu had a surprise for us.

I suppose the design of Darchu's dik-dik trap can't have changed in ten thousand years, but I couldn't imagine it being executed with more casual elegance. First he tied a sisal cord to a whippy branch, anchoring it under tension to a twig hammered into the earth with a stone. Then he scratched a shallow hole with his hands and balanced sticks against one another to form a trigger. The hole was covered with strips of bark and an open noose at the end of the cord laid on the bark. Finally Darchu scattered earth to conceal the trap. The whole thing had taken less than five minutes of our film.

Darchu stuck branches to the ground to funnel the dik-dik towards his trap. He talked as he worked: 'Little antelope! Now that I've set this trap come tonight. Tread on it! Tomorrow

I'll eat you and get indigestion.'

And there was more. Under a shade tree, Darchu bit the end off a tree stem and began to roast it in the fire. It seemed we were in for another demonstration from the man's inexhaustible store of skills and it was like witnessing a dazzling improviser spilling out chorus after chorus. When the branch was blackened, he gripped the tip in his teeth and twisted the bark fiercely, releasing it from the wooden core. Then, like a conjurer he was drawing out the tube of bark and he had a flute. When I held the warm shell in my hand, it felt too insubstantial for survival. Then I thought: Same neurotic Westerner's obsession with permanence and hanging on to things. Darchu will just make another when this one breaks. David was telling me about the flute: 'He'll cut finger holes when it's cooled . . .,' but Darchu was already away at something else.

There was this singing bush. Somewhere in the middle of it was Darchu, hacking and slashing and singing. We were trying to get through to film him, but it was just ludicrous – microphone cables and shirt sleeves snagging in branches, hats snatched from blundering heads like a routine from a 'Three Stooges' movie. At last the three of us fought our way through to find Darchu, totally naked amid the thorns and thickets demolishing the forest with a blunt bush knife and punctuating his blows with bursts of triumphal singing. Finally, with a couple of well-aimed slashes, an entire tree toppled into the scrub. Even Darchu had managed to work up a light sweat and the sudden flurry of slogging work was a useful reminder that what was another handy sequence for us was survival for him. As a result of his efforts in clearing the forest, he'd be able to plant crops in the next rainy season and feed his family. Dik-dik traps might be aesthetically pleasing and juicy to film, but they were about getting enough to eat in a very tough place.

Darchu buried his bush knife in the clean wood where the tree had split and looked up full into my face. For a moment we made and held contact; then he laughed and moved away. It was an odd jolt, a spark of real recognition across the gap, my first I suppose in all those encounters with Mursi. I know he'd registered my fascination with him and it was apparent he knew something about his own charisma for us; but I had no way of guessing what he made of me, so strangely met here.

★

At the end of the day there was a message from Choya, the canoe-builder. The string he'd sent said the canoe would be ready for launching when we'd untied ten knots. That would be perfect for us, four days before we were due to be picked up, and it was marvellous to have such solid information to plan round instead of the usual swamp of uncertainties.

'Leslie, you remember Ulijekholi?' David had arrived with a powerful-looking man in a startling orange Hawaiian shirt and natty slacks. It was the ear I recognised, an extraordinary mis-shapen jumble of flesh like a strange fungus clinging to the trunk of a tree. I'd last seen Ulijekholi as a young man driving his cattle on the ridge at Ma'do and I could still recall the swaggering assurance with which he'd flung his sheet over a shoulder. It was obvious he hadn't lost any of the assurance, but it was harder than ever now to recognise him as the Priest's brother.

We'd talked about Ulijekholi and he had an interesting story. The sharp clothes weren't just a lucky accident but a bonus of his new job. With the Revolutionary Government in Addis making real efforts for the first time to reach out to the remotest limits of their huge country, the struggling administration in Hana had recently appointed Ulijekholi as a tax collector for the northern area of Mursi country. Looking round the campsite at the dozens of lounging warriors it seemed a preposterous notion, but it clearly represented the stirrings of something entirely new in their lives. Ulijekholi was going to need all his assurance to persuade the proud and independent Mursi, with no experience of subjection or even of a chief, to hand over anything to some unknown authority beyond the horizon. I didn't envy him his new job.

We had a particular interest in Ulijekholi as the Mursi patron of a Kwegu living at Alaka called Kumuli. When the morning's squadron of flies zoomed into camp, I left David to explore the possibilities of a filming session with Ulijekholi and his Kwegu client. From the way he was eyeing up some of the items around camp, I thought we might be able to come to an arrangement.

David handed out the paper and the coloured felt-tips and I thought that no schoolmaster could ever have had less pre-

137

dictable pupils. The dusty bunch of Mursi kids giggled and looked uncertain.

I knew Turton had been involved in a long-term study with Mursi children in an effort to try and understand how they saw the world and how they might represent it. It was something that fascinated me. Having watched my own kids blossom from scribbling wavy onion-headed martians with tendril limbs to drawing recognisable versions of humanity, I wondered what these children of people who looked at postcards a different way would come up with.

The kids began to investigate the strange materials they'd been given and David talked about a similar exercise he'd tried years before. 'The chap produced a mass of squiggles and stripes on the paper and when I asked him what it was, he said, "A man". "It doesn't look much like a man to me," I said. And then he made me understand that the paper itself was the man's body and the patterns were his body decorations.'

Half an hour later, the kids' papers were a mass of colourful squiggles. 'They're cow patterns,' they said, or 'body paintings'. Then I found a boy who'd drawn an entirely convincing red crocodile, complete with a jawful of teeth. Alongside him, another boy was quietly producing green mules – upside down. A tiny girl was finishing a purple elephant with a baby elephant in its stomach.

I walked over to the tent to shift my newly washed bedsack into the sun. I wasn't there any more. When Darchu found the thing in the bush outside camp a few minutes later it was torn into three pieces. He reckoned it must have been grabbed by some kids while their chums were busy with the felt-tips. It looked like a mammoth sewing session if I was going to keep out the mosquitoes tonight.

By the end of the day, I'd managed to lose my hat as well, left behind somewhere on the bathing beach. I felt jaded when I got back from a fruitless search to find an extraordinary scene being played out in the middle of the campsite.

Dozens of little boys were sitting in lines, facing a grilling from Ulijekholi. One lad tried to make a break for it and received a rather half-hearted thrash with a branch. I found it hard to keep my face straight during the awkward little drilling and saluting session that followed, but it was intriguing to see how quickly those police drills Ulijekholi must have seen at

Hana were becoming absorbed.

I guessed the strange little charade must be something to do with my bedsack, and Turton's presence amongst the stern-looking elders confirmed it. When the boys were dismissed to scuttle away into the bush, he came over. 'Yes, of course it was partly for our consumption, but it's also in line with the way the Mursi kids are kept in order by the Rora – the young men's age grade.'

The faint echoes of cadet-corps pettiness had depressed me and I was ready for the tent soon after nine. The diary caught my mood:

'Early to bed, weary and a bit low with camp routines and discomforts, rubber chickens, heat and squalor. We need a second wind to gust us through to the end. Again, I feel submerged in the experience, miles below the surface of the real world. Still, tomorrow we're on the upward swing.'

I could see the ants swarming up Mike's legs, but I didn't like to interrupt him at his work. And after all, we'd been waiting for days to get our talk with Ulijekholi and Kumuli.

We were set up in a little compound a few minutes from our base, a couple of conical straw huts, a few hens and, we'd now discovered, a large ants' nest exactly under the spot where we'd placed our tripod. By now Mike had registered the ants, but he liked the shot and after a cursory swipe with his hat, he carried on filming.

It was a telling shot. Sitting side by side, Ulijekholi and Kumuli made the single most striking image we'd recorded of Mursi dominance over the Kwegu. Massive and coolly self-possessed, Ulijekholi cradled his rifle and patronised the camera effortlessly. Hunched beside him in a ravaged red shirt, Kumuli was a bit drunk.

The Mursi patron spelled out some realities: 'This man is my man – he has no cattle. I married each of his three wives for him, all with my cattle. So he's really my Kwegu. That's how it is.'

He looked across at Kumuli as the Kwegu told us how it seemed to him. 'The Mursi are good. But if we did something bad, they'd toss us in the Omo. When I carry this rifle, I say it's Ulijekholi's.' He prodded his patron's massive shoulder. 'If I go on a journey and they think the rifle's mine, they'd take it from me. But If I say it's Ulijekholi's, they're afraid to take it. It's like that – a Kwegu's things can just be taken and nobody cares.'

We fled the ants for the haven of base camp. Turton had passed on the drift of the talk we'd just filmed and it seemed we'd at least reached some kind of bedrock. 'Yes it's true,' David said. 'In the end it's the threat of force which keeps the Kwegu in their place, and it's the threat of force which ultimately sanctions the relationship. And it's that threat that lies behind the Kwegu's acceptance of what looks to us like second-class status.'

'But they still don't seem to talk about that, even in private.'

'No, that's true. They don't say it and they don't even seem to feel exploited.'

We were interrupted by a domestic crisis. Ulikoro had arrived in camp with a worrying story. His wife had given birth to their first child the night before, but the placenta had failed to come away. David looked very concerned.

'Even if we knew what to do, it wouldn't help. The Mursi have a taboo against intervening to remove the placenta. They won't even do it with their cattle.'

Ulikoro slumped on one of our boxes looking desperate.

'You're going to like that!' Mike looked up from the eyepiece and snapped off the camera with a satisfied flick.

He was right; it was an impossibly pretty picture – flawless skies reflected in an unruffled river, a man moving across the frame with rustic conviction. Kumuli drifted past us again, poling the canoe, and Darchu splashed himself on a foreground rock, folding up with laughter. It wasn't until I got David's translations that I realised they were sending us up.

'You look crazy,' Darchu was saying, 'cruising up and down to nowhere while these white men point their things at you.'

We'd been rumbled in the heart of the idyll, reconstructing reality in the way documentary always must on its way to try and tell true stories.

We sat around after dark, uselessly debating what we might do to help Ulikoro's wife. It now seemed likely she might die before morning and it felt impossible not to make some effort to do something. The white men who'd arrived from the sky with all their clever toys were proving as powerless as anyone else when it really mattered.

Distant thunder rumbled over the mountains and the place seemed tensioned tight with heat. We'd just about decided to head off for Ulikoro's compound when the man himself walked out of the darkness. He was smiling hugely and we didn't need David's translation.

I rummaged in the storage tent and broke out the precious bottle of brandy. There could never be a better excuse to raid it. We let out our relief in chatter and a cassette, while Ulikoro sipped his tot quietly, his eyes shining by the light of the fire.

7

On the sand in front of me, I could see sinuous trace of a tail marking its slither towards the river. It occurred to me it was an odd way to spend Sunday afternoon, hunting for crocodiles with a film camera. Odder still perhaps was how quickly croc corner, only a couple of weeks ago a location of nightmarish fantasy and real alarm, had now become a spot for an afternoon trip.

Out on the shingle with no possibility of shelter, the sun gorged on us. The light was like a bombardment, ricocheting from a billion brilliant corners. Picking his way ahead of me with the tripod on his shoulder, Mike's figure buckled and shimmered, blurring his outline until I could almost confuse him with the lanky pelicans idling along the edge of the river.

For an hour we tiptoed across the stones, whispering our guesses about the best places to look. Finally, there was no avoiding the suspicion that the killer monsters of the Omo were rather shy. We settled for our catch of two snouts and a tail and collected our headaches for the trip upriver to Alaka.

We rounded the last bend and with the home beach in sight, Mike made an unwelcome suggestion. 'Why don't we try and get up that cliff across the river? I reckon it'd be a terrific shot from up there.'

I took in the hundred-foot-high wall of flaking sandstone and tried to think of an excuse. The afternoon's mauling by the sun and a total intake for the day of a single glacier mint left me disinclined for the effort, but it was obviously a good idea. I cursed Blakeley's fearsome energies as we spluttered in to the base of the cliff.

To my dismay, Darchu led off straight up the crumbling wall. It was almost vertical, but somehow he seemed to be running. I clawed my way after him, choking in a shower of red dust and dragging the tripod behind me. With arms and legs quaking, I heaved myself to the top.

'It's like the sodding lost world up here.' The jungle of overgrown vegetation made it impossible to see over the edge and down on Alaka which was why we'd flogged up here. 'Well there's got to be some way through,' said the unstoppable Blakeley.

One step at a time, Darchu began to clear a track into the maze. We crawled after him, tumbling over roots, ripping on bushes. Even Mike began to lose his enthusiasm for the venture. 'I hope this is bloody worth it,' he grumbled between pantings.

It was, oh it was. Suddenly we were through to a thrilling prospect back over Alaka, held in a bend of the Omo with the mountains behind, all washed in a perfect evening light. Far below us in the river, microscopic boys flicked a fish out of the water, invisible until it flashed silver. On the beach lads were practising a donga fight and the crack of the sticks reached us with a weird clarity. Somewhere, a flute was being played.

And there was the whole map of our lives for the past weeks, laid out before us; without warning I caught myself choked with affection.

Filming was less enjoyable. We began to shoot with my innards already queasy at the void in front of me and immediately a big section of the cliff edge only fifty yards along from us fell away and tumbled into the river with a muffled roar. Darchu leaped backwards even more quickly than us so I knew it wasn't a freak. We completed filming with Mike flat on his belly, hacking away with a branch at an intrusive stalk on the tip of the precipice.

The air was foggy with mosquitoes as we headed into a blinding sunset to look for a way down. We slithered shamelessly on our bums as far as we could, and then Darchu had to cut footholds in the sheer wall to the river.

It was almost dark by the time we were tramping across the

island towards camp, too whacked for words. A slow shooting star arched across the sky like a rescue signal.

I'd been discussing for days with Turton how we should approach our vital talk with Darchu in front of the camera. The man was hardly a reluctant performer, but we wanted the most relaxed situation we could find, well away from inquisitive Mursi. The best bet seemed to be Darchu's wet-weather cultivation site over the river where we'd filmed him at work a few days earlier. We decided to take some food and the remaining Scotch and settle down for the day with our star.

Inevitably, he seized the opportunity for some work. Until the day came to the boil, he slashed away at the bush, singing somewhere in the greenery as we set up our stuff. By noon, we were all stretched out under a shade tree for vegetable soup and warm Scotch. It had faint overtones of a schoolboy picnic, playing truant from the world on a safe little adventure.

We moved into the filming without fuss. Darchu sat easily in dappled light at the edge of the shade. David asked him one question about the origins of the Kwegu and he was away, a torrent of talking only stemmed $10\frac{1}{2}$ minutes later by Mike's announcement, 'Out of film.'

We shot four magazines, almost three quarters of an hour of film with Darchu and it looked to be everything I'd hoped. For Mike, I could see it was less of a treat. He muttered on about 'bloody impossible contrast' and his problem was painfully clear in the enormous differential between Darchu's dark skin and the glaring brightness of the bush behind him. Each time we reloaded, we had to ask him to edge back further, following the movement of the sun as it began to slide down the afternoon sky. To my relief, he seemed quite unthrown by our antics and ready to go on forever. When I finally called 'cut', David looked happy with it all. He'd been giving me summaries of what Darchu was saying every time we stopped to change film, but it wasn't until I saw the full translations that I knew how rich it was.

'We Kwegu have always been here,' he began, 'always . . . and nowhere else. We've stayed here at the river, always. People died, but we stayed through the generations. Our ancestors lived on honey and hunted animals, chasing them in the mud when the rains came.' He made the sounds of splashing feet and paddled with his hands to mimic the hunt. 'They ran in the thick mud and speared the animals. That was the Kwegu way.'

It was all like that, intensely vivid and immediate, packed with those little dramas which seemed to be Darchu's instinctive way of talking about his life. I was struck most of all by a passage where he imagined a dialogue which felt to go to the heart of the Kwegu's relationship with the Mursi.

'If I have no Mursi patron, and I'm clearing, clearing – when I've cleared a place, other Mursi come here. They say: "We planned to clear this area."

"It's my place isn't it?"

"It's not yours – get off into the bush, you Kwegu!"

"What's all this about?"

"I don't want to argue – just go! My stomach wants no words. Stand aside! I want to clear and cultivate."

I say to myself: "If I argue, he'll beat me up." So what can I do? He takes the place over and I go back home. If we're caught without our Mursi patron in a place with no people, other Mursi would tie our feet really tight,' Darchu grunted with effort as he acted out the binding of the rope, 'and throw us in the river. Or they'd take us right out in the bush and hang us up out there. Back at home, they'd say: "He's gone into the bush. He must have been gored by a buffalo or a rhino. He's gone!"'

Darchu slapped his hands dismissively, his face set in an act of contempt. Then he brightened and turned to talk about life with a good Mursi patron.

'I carry on clearing with his protection. I clear and clear. If our Mursi is strong, our land is safe. People will fear our Mursi.'

'I still don't really get it.' I was sitting with Turton round the fire, munching our after-dinner glucose tablets and talking, inevitably, about Mursi and Kwegu. What Darchu had said only seemed to throw up new questions.

'Even if they can't do anything about it, why don't the Kwegu at least recognise how the Mursi exploit them?'

'Well they simply don't see it that way,' David answered. 'They don't see themselves getting less out of the relationship than the Mursi. In fact the Kwegu reckon that the things they provide are pretty trivial.'

'But what are they getting out of it?'

'You saw the answer the other day at that bridewealth negotiation. The Mursi give them livestock and without that they wouldn't be able to marry and have children.'

'Sounds like a mafia protection racket.'

'I'm beginning to think it might be a good deal more interesting than that.' There was a pause while David hunted, as usual, for the precise words. 'It's a pattern that may help to explain how many dominated groups came to accept their unequal position. The key thing could be for the dominators to persuade the underdogs that they're actually getting the best of the bargain.'

'It's an interesting thought. And my feminist friends would find it particularly interesting.'

As we finished our talk and David moved off towards his nightly translation stint, two men I didn't recognise walked into the camp. They'd come from Makaro with news of the canoe. Launch date had been advanced to three days from now, but there was a problem. Someone had carved too much off the front and there was a hole that needed patching.

'D'you reckon we might be in at the maiden voyage of the Titanic of the Omo?' was Andy's tasteless comment.

A lime-green snake as fat as my arm slithered across the path just in front of us and Ulilibai froze, blocking our way with his hand thrust behind him in warning. We were on our way to another impromptu bush studio for a talk with Ulilibai who, Turton said, had a revealing and mournful story about his Kwegu.

Under sober grey skies, Ulilibai squatted against a backdrop of skeletal trees and told us of his troubles: 'I have no Kwegu – none at all.' He spread his palms and spat with resignation. 'There is one but he's upstream – a Kwegu called Bawen. He has brass earrings. He and his people have always been ours.'

Ulilibai polished his teeth with a stick and continued his story. 'He's gone to the Bodi, given me up – he's really given me up.' Then he rallied and looked more hopeful. 'I'm going to get a Kwegu called Ofinay. I want him. Later, I'll take a cow and marry him a wife. All the Mursi want a Kwegu.'

At last I was beginning to feel that I might be able to see some pattern in the ambivalent dance of these people.

★

'9.15 p.m.' I wrote. 'Early to bed tonight with the prospect of a dawn rising to shoot the day's beginning at the nearby settlement. Then the trip south for the canoe-launching. I feel an odd apprehension about the big expedition, the last real target of our shoot. We're at full stretch down there, physically and logistically and I only hope our fortune holds. If it does, it should offer a smashing climax to the movie. Meanwhile, it seems the canoe-builders are claiming that the hole in the prow resulted from the evil luck of Mike's jumping over the canoe when we were filming down there. More money in compensation, naturally. A week tonight, the end of filming for the final wrap-up. Much luxurious talk of cold beer and home.'

It was still dark as we filed out of camp, soon after half past five in the morning. I paddled along in the puddle of my torch beam, less than half-awake and hazily relieved that we didn't have far to go. Well before the sun, we were at the settlement.

In a lovely silvery half-light, we whispered as we set up the gear. A paring of moon lay on its back against a sky browning with the implication of sun and we watched the scatter of huts begin to gather shape. We were shooting with the first stirrings, women crawling out of the black doorways like something being born with the day. As colour began to seep in, the noise of the bush fired into life. In moments, the din of birds and insects swamped over us, almost painful after the stillness ahead of the sun.

By the time Darchu emerged from his hut, to sit like an Indian chief wrapped in a sheet against the dawn chill, the geography of separation was clear. The six Kwegu huts like Darchu's were grouped in a circle at the end of the settlement, set slightly apart from the string of Mursi houses. The Kwegu circle looked in on itself to confirm a vivid metaphor of people connected but held at a distance.

With the sun now flooding the settlement, Mike began a last long pan across the huts. He was reaching the end when a Mursi youth stepped across and thrust his face right into the lens, ruining the shot. I saw Mike reach round the camera and slap the boy and instantly we had a nasty situation. Phil, who was recording a few yards away thought Mike had been attacked,

147

the Mursi lad was shaping up for a scrap and Turton was understandably furious.

'You just can't go hitting people like that, Mike. It's un-forgiveable!'

Abashed and repentant, Mike immediately apologised to everybody and I suggested it was time for breakfast.

'I know it was just spur-of-the-moment frustration,' David said as we walked back through a blizzard of morning flies, 'but thank God he didn't hit an adult.'

That last voyage down river for the canoe-launching was like an act of forgiveness on both sides. We loved the river, and the Omo put on its most perfect show. I recalled that only a few weeks ago I'd entertained the possibility that this was where I was going to end my life.

Now, the river was a sequence of exotic reunions: baboon cliffs, croc corner populated this time only by three sleepy vultures, and all those fearsome twists and narrows tamed by routine to almost theme-park cosiness. I took the tiller while Mike filmed and for some reason I steered into a sudden current of simple happiness, fed I suppose by endings and home thoughts and a sublime afternoon of sky and water.

By four o'clock, we were sitting alongside the completed canoe, white and almost elegant, set in the centre of the glade like some sacred object with offerings of sunlight slanting down through the cathedral of trees. Dozens of kids milled round us, including a gang of pretty teenage girls with freshly-cut lips bandaged in green leaves.

'Mikey!' Ulilibai's yell announced the arrival of the porters, an hour ahead of any expectation with our basic camping gear. David wandered across from a conference with the venerable Doki to give us a bulletin.

'It seems they're planning to launch tomorrow morning, probably around 8.00 a.m.'

'Sounds good,' I said. 'Let's get the tents up.'

Andy and I were still going through the routines of snapping tentpoles together when the horn blasts ripped across the clearing. Turton ran past us, shouting, 'I think they're going to launch the thing now!' and triggered one of the more extraordin-ary hours of my life.

For a ghastly half-minute, I was certain we were going to miss the climax of the film. With people and racket erupting all around us, we tore open boxes and groped with the clumsiness of nightmare to assemble the gear. I snatched up every spare magazine and lens I could find and ran, cursing the contrariness of reality in the Lower Omo.

Even the tidily edited final film retains something of the panic. The shot is a tumble down the bank at the foot of the clearing, captured as Mike grabbed the camera and switched on at the run. The picture swipes over a crouching Andy and falls through space to follow the headlong rush of the canoe bearers.

When we picked ourselves up, I saw with relief that we were ahead of them now. The canoe was obviously far too heavy to be carried to the river in a single surge and I could see it lumbering over the lip of the clearing while men streamed down the bank beside it and plumes of dust backlit to gold billowed into the trees.

We were on a wide shelf overlooking the river and I couldn't conceive how sheer muscle-power could possibly shift the massive log across this hundred yards of cracked mud and down to the water. Immediately the huge thing toppled out of the clearing and thumped into the earth below driven by scores of whooping, singing men. In moments they had become a team of devotees, hauling the juggernaut towards the river with long sisal ropes while the soundtrack went crazy. Now Phil had to capture a wild symphony of noise: triumphal singing, a shrill counterpoint of ululating women, whistles, the non-stop rasp of the horn, shouting, laughing and the yelp of the occasional trodden dog.

The canoe moved forward as each surge of energy, powered by a hypnotic rocking of the log from side to side by dozens of hands, climaxed in another brief rush towards the river. Soon, the whole procession had flowed down to the dusty cliffs over the Omo and the prow of the canoe jutted high over a bank like a sinking liner in its death throes.

For us, scrambling to find positions there was a new crisis. Since we'd been so totally unprepared, we were now shooting with three half-consumed magazines and struggling to calculate how much footage we dared to spend before we risked losing the moment of the launch. Mike and I swapped magazines time and again, shouting our estimates at one another through the uproar.

A memory hit me from nowhere, and I knew at last where the faint echoes had been coming from. No wonder I hadn't made the connection sooner; the situations could hardly have seemed more remote from each other. It was a sweltering night in Miami Beach almost ten years earlier, the climax of the National Democratic Convention which nominated decent but doomed George McGovern. I was filming on the Convention floor amid the chaos of waving banners, tribal skirmishing and political hussles, trying to record the infighting in the Pennsylvania delegation. We had one of those rare moments when people were a lot more interested in what they were doing than in the presence of the film camera and I knew we were getting terrific material – only we were running out of film and we were on the floor illegally so there was no way to get out for more. The frantic calculations of film stock flowed and merged with the intriguings of the delegation to make a night which had resurfaced now on the banks of an African river.

Focussing again the din and confusion of the canoe-launching, it felt as though the parallels might go beyond our problems with film stock. With the canoe still grounded in a gulley while the hordes of followers juiced themselves up for the final push, there was a moment to take in some details. On a little ridge just above the canoe, I saw Doki flicking water over the prow with a wand of leaves in some kind of blessing. The droplets showered down like scattered silver coins against the declining sun and the dust kicked up by hundreds of feet was like blue smoke. Despite Doki's blessing, it was overwhelmingly a Mursi event. A Kwegu might have made the canoe, a Kwegu might be its owner, but the Mursi were running the party.

A forest of arms pushed up from behind the gulley to tilt the canoe over the pivot of its last obstacle. With a final irresistible rush, the massive log was launched into the river. The proud owner stood alongside us and smiled shyly at the camera. Then he waded out and climbed into his brand new canoe, poling it easily towards the far bank. Mike filmed him, standing up to his knees in the warm water while dozens of boys and men piled past him to fall in the river and swim after the canoe, yelping in celebration.

We slammed on the final identifying slate and hurled joyous obscenities in the air and I luxuriated in the certainty that we had a film. Mercifully, it hadn't been quite the same cliffhanger, but the last hour had enriched and shaped the story in a way that reminded me overwhelmingly of that final day of ritual and debate on the ridge at Ma'do seven years earlier. We'd got lucky again, just in time.

The diary reminds me of just how forgiving I must have felt that night. 'In the tent, still high from the launch, sellotaping dirty torn banknotes, happy. Even the unspeakable dinner of half-thawed space food and blackcurrant-flavoured Omo couldn't dampen our spirits tonight.'

8

On our way back upriver for the last time, we stopped to film the Mursi cattle. We waited on a shaded hillside overlooking a handsome swerve in the river, listening for the sound of bells. After the bonanza of yesterday evening, we had time now for anything and the mood was languorous and replete. Phil had some mellowness of his own to contribute. He'd just returned from helping David with a local pay and sick parade while the rest of us flopped in the dinghy, alleging guard duty while we glutted ourselves with sun in prospect of a return to an English February.

'You know,' Phil said, 'after the first few days, I thought I'd made the worst mistake of my life coming here. I wasn't going to go on about it, and I knew I had to get through it somehow. But helping David with that medical session this morning has finally shifted something for me. If you ever come back here, count me in.'

I could hear the bells now, and then the leaders of the herd came out of the trees behind us and ambled towards the river. Soon, there were hundreds of them, clanking across the shingle patrolled by a few spidery-thin herd boys. It was a spectacle with something of the momentous swagger of an epic western and I knew it was a rare enough sight. It's only at the height of the dry season for a few brief weeks when the tsetse fly are less of a danger at the river that the Mursi can bring their herds in from the plains twenty miles away to drink at the Omo. There were also daily rumours of skirmishes with their southern

June–July 1974

Debating the war, June 1974

Farewell to the dead jeep

Chris Wangler and Mike Dodds greet the day at Moizoi

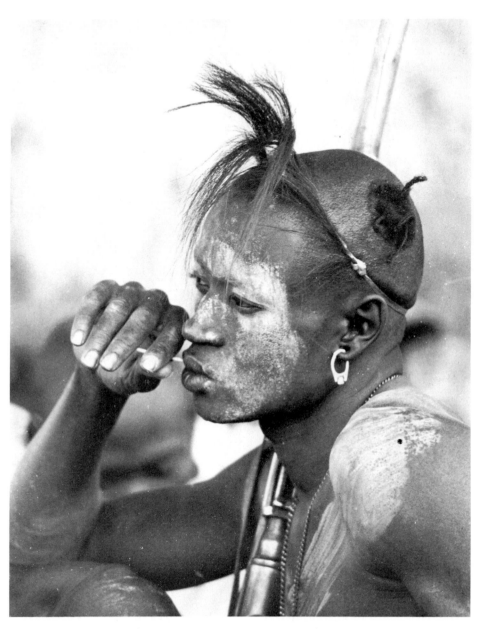

Mursi warrior returned from a skirmish

The ceremony of 'Spearing the Priest' begins on the ridge at Ma'do

Mursi woman wearing her lip plate
(photo. Chris Wangler)

Ulikoro's first encounter with table
tennis in Arba Minch

December 1981–January 1982

Darchu at Alaka, January 1981

Arrival at Alaka

Base camp. Turton toils, Blakeley and Smith purify yet more water, Mohammed Idris ponders, Andy Harries pursues his researches

A Mursi pastoral: cattle drink at the Omo, sorghum prospers in the foreground

Phil Smith, Mike Blakeley and the wounded dinghy

Working on the Kwegu canoe

Waiting for the dinghy, sharing worries with the diary

The bridewealth negotiation, bullets for a bride

A messenger of change: Ulichagi points eastwards towards the Mago Valley
where he has moved with the Mursi migrants, in search of 'cool ground'

April–May 1985

Komorakora, the Mursi Priest. Mago Valley, April 1985

A sticky interview with Kelithee

Local film crew ready to roll

The Priest's settlement at Banco. Filming amid ruined sorghum, devastated by the plague of army worms (photo. David Wason)

Mursi women in Berka market – dealing with the outside world

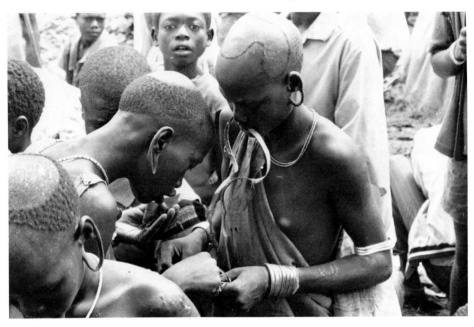

Television's newest audience. The Mursi at their forest preview

Though life is changing for the migrants, most girls still cut their lips...

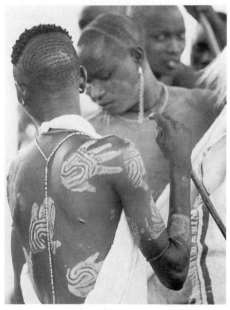

...and young men decorate themselves for a dance

Camp visitors study a German newspaper which somehow came with us
to the Mago Valley

Journey's end – for us, a drowned landscape after a 50-mile trek for nothing...

...and for them – 'cool ground', the Mursi migrants' new homeland in the Mago Valley

neighbours, the Hamar, and the riverside settlements offered security to the precious herds.

I was looking out on an almost unnaturally perfect image of traditional Mursi life, like one of those Victorian paintings packed with good works and affirmative incidents. Sorghum flourished in the foreground and healthy cattle drank contentedly in the river while herdboys moved amongst them in fulfilment of their traditional roles. I watched it all, I suppose, with the ironic concern of an intruder from the world of flux and future-shock, wondering mostly how long it could all stay like this after the stories we'd been hearing of migration and shifting values and contact with the outside world. Well, for what it was worth, the image would be held on our film, but maybe that in itself would be another agent of change.

Mike nursed the outboard round croc corner for the last time past a couple of bored residents and we began to think about base camp and our twenty-fourth successive lunch of packet soup. Instead, we found ourselves becalmed a few minutes later by a really loony little incident. We'd given a lift to a Mursi acquaintance of Turton's but when we arrived at his settlement, the conversation seemed to go on for ages. At last, David snorted in exasperation.

'What's the problem, David?'

'Oh, he wants me to give him money or he won't get out.'

For a maddening quarter of an hour we drifted and fumed while the man nattered on. Finally, David solved the dilemma with admirable decisiveness, simply chucking the man into the shallows. He came up laughing and sloshed his way home, still asking for money.

Mohammed was a terrific audience for our traveller's tales of the canoe launching. 'Now you will have a great film, I think,' he predicted. I felt more indebted to him than ever for his forbearance in staying behind yet again to watch over the camp. The long hours of studying Italian and watching out for rope rustlers can't have been much fun, but Mohammed's cheerful support had never wavered.

With less than a week to go before we could hope for the helicopter, the days dribbled towards demob and my diary was full of endings.

'Stirrings for home everywhere. David labels cans, torches, knives with local names. I sellotape yet more banknotes for our final payouts with a million flies for company . . .

Dreamed I was at a grand dinner and had to join a male chorus line to dance and sing 'There is nothing like a dame' . . .

Darchu's wife safely delivered of a baby girl after he made a late-night dash to find a tree which promotes contractions . . .

Ulichagi is back after a round trip of a hundred miles from the new settlement. It's going to get very crowded here over the next few days . . .

Another day in the goldfish bowl. Weary of heat, discomfort and remorseless interrogations every minute for everything we possess . . .

Finished my novel at last, feeling deprived.'

The novel was *Daniel Martin* by John Fowles and reading it in this place had provided at times an almost grotesque counterpoint to the days of dust and insects. The story of Fowles' people and their highly strung gavottings through Oxford and Claridge's and Hollywood had I suppose both anchored me here and provided its own disturbances. Those exquisite sensibilities, infinitely alert, passionatly introspective and redeemingly ironic seemed to throw into greater relief the areas of life here I still found it hardest to relate to. It had burst out sometimes in exasperated diary notes: 'So hard to deny myself value-judgements when even a Fairy Liquid bottle is an object of wonder and mystery and I find myself fighting to repress an unworthy and patronising conviction that they just haven't done enough with the opportunities of being human.'

I'd been here before, of course, muttering sourly into the diary in much the same way seven years before. They were, I suppose what a Mursi anthropologist might have called the tones of a Western middle-class man, mistrustful of instinct and what one of my friends wonderfully described as 'educated beyond my intelligence'. But I felt closer this time, especially through Darchu, to some awareness of complexities below the surface of lives that had seemed limited and diminished. I'd been fascinated to talk with Turton about the striking absence of emotional illness among Mursi and Kwegu and I had quite enough evidence now to mess up my tidy balance sheets.

Then I came upon this sentence almost at the end of *Daniel Martin* that helped to focus my blur of conflicting responses. The context could hardly have been more remote from the Lower Omo as the hero confronted Rembrandt's awesome late self-portrait. But it seemed to say something useful for me as I sat reading page 667, surrounded by staring naked men: 'It is not finally a matter of skill, of knowledge, of intellect; of good luck or bad, but choosing and learning to feel.'

We came upon Choya the canoe-builder sitting on a bank looking out over the river. He was back in Alaka now, and in his own place he seemed ageless, wrapped in a kind of stoical sadness. We were here for the last of our filming, a talk with Choya and his son-in-law Darchu about how they saw the future for the Kwegu. They sat side by side on their ancestral ground and contemplated the end of things.

Choya spoke in a whisper: 'Now we Kwegu are finished. We are with the Mursi, we're together here along the banks of the river. We're finished.'

'Yes, we'll become Mursi,' Darchu said. 'There'll be no Kwegu. The Kwegu are finished and we'll become Mursi.'

We walked back towards camp, relishing the end of shooting which was being celebrated by the most perfect sunset we'd seen, palest orange draining to subtlest violet behind trees as still as plastic replicas.

David reflected on what Choya and Darchu had said. 'I reckon we're watching the evolution of a sort of class system. The Kwegu are really becoming a Mursi underclass rather than a separate people. Everybody says that the barriers between them are collapsing and the taboos are fading.'

'What sort of things do you mean?'

'Well, I can remember a time when the Kwegu weren't allowed to visit the Mursi cattle. These days people even admit there's intermarriage. Remember how Ulilibai said that now Kwegu women were marrying Mursi, their customs were gone?'

I found I was carrying our clapperboard for the shot numbers. Mike had printed across it before we began 'Disappearing World' – THE KWEGU.

They were arriving from miles around now with only three days before we were due to go. I had a vision of people consulting knotted strings all over the place and heading off hopefully for 'London', the name they'd given to our base camp.

All day long we were surrounded by bargain hunters, eyeing up the possibilities as we began to sort out things to be left behind before embarking on our mammoth packing session.

It was increasingly difficult to find anywhere to sit down, and when Bekithi sat on a scorpion after dark it seemed painfully inevitable. I heard his roar through the tent wall, and we lurched out to find him hopping with the unimaginable discomfort of it, but Turton's composure as he handed out the painkillers told me it wasn't terminal.

Bekithi's manic laugh woke me next morning to announce his recovery and soon he was laying vigorous claim to my green towel.

The outboard roared into life for the last time and Captain Darchu had his chance. We'd agreed it would be nice if he could pilot the dinghy round to our boating beach so that we could begin to dismantle it, and he skimmed away with Mike as though he'd been doing it all his life. I walked round the shingle with Andy who was hailed ceaselessly by his well-established name 'Lusi London'.

Finding the dinghy beached amid a circle of kids, I saw just how lucky we'd been all these weeks. As well as the missing prop, the other two blades showed deep cracks and were obviously on their last legs. I preferred not to think about how it might have been or about what we were going to say to Ron in Addis.

It seemed a good time to call it quits in the battle between our machines and Mursi country with the score at one each now: a jeep for Mursiland – a dinghy, just about, for us. I'd got to know the astronaut David Scott in the late 70s, the man who commanded Apollo 16 and drove that extraordinary lunar rover across the surface of the moon; but I reckoned even he'd have acknowledged that the Lower Omo was tough territory for imported transport. Blakeley, of course, was undaunted and mused on about microlite aeroplanes as we attacked the stained rubber with washing-up liquid and pan scrubbers.

At the end of the last afternoon – always, we guarded ourselves with 'maybe' – we had reduced our lives to bundles and boxes.

The dinghy was by now a shrivelled carcass washed up on the shingle, watched over by Ba baiu and Ulikoro from a little blue tent we'd put up. A huge cardboard box was filled with goodies to be handed out as soon as we heard the helicopter, an inventory of our cast-off treasures: shirts and trousers, pans and knives, string, plastic bags, empty bottles, film tins and disposable razors.

On a perfect evening, I took a sentimental stroll to the bathing beach and as I lounged in the warm river our neighbourhood crocodile popped up a few feet out to signal a frustrated farewell. After dinner, we voted for a last dance.

Walking along those utterly familiar paths across the island under pink cloud towers, we moved past families huddled over evening fires. At the shade tree it was the way it must have been for centuries, the ring of slender silhouettes veiled in dust and bonded by the slap of hands; but tonight there was a marvellous dance we hadn't seen before. The dancers stalked the ring miming a buffalo hunt and in the midst of it was Darchu, a hunter now, dramatically scanning the horizon. Already, I thought, we're gone for him and our little interruption has been absorbed.

Back in camp, a flurry of warm rain drove us into the tents. I thought about climbing into the bag, but I should have known it wasn't going to be quite this easy. It was two hours later before I was back in the tent with the bedtime diary. 'A barmy final evening verging on low farce. With the rain, from nowhere a sudden blast of wind. Soon after, Ba baiu and Ulikoro, speaking fast and looking worried. David translates: the tent on the beach has gone. Off we traipse into the dark. No tent, but the boat bits are intact. We swirl the torches, and there's the tent blown fifty yards into the bush in a tangle of tubing. A mad scramble in the dark to rebuild the big tent, and at last it's done and lashed to the outboard. Just now, more animated chat between Ulijekholi and Darchu. It seems they're afraid the people from Kuduma and Makaro will turn up tomorrow, nick things, and blame the folk here at Alaka. An all-night guard is to be posted, and tomorrow should be interesting. Over the river now, a vast glow in the night sky from a bushfire.

And suddenly it's the last night and the last tent. Quite unbelievable. No one dares think what happens if the chopper doesn't come. Milk, sugar, tea, coffee and most food gone now.

Being marooned would not be amusing. I pray for the sound of that helicopter tomorrow.'

I was loading up for the fourth time to ferry stuff down to the beach, and as I fended off yet another enthusiast for my shirt, I could see Turton was having a tough time. It wasn't half past eight yet, but already there were hundreds of people milling around in expectation of the great give-away.

I'd walked over to commiserate when Bekithi cocked his head and said something to David.

'Not yet surely?' I didn't dare to believe it.

'Well, I can't hear anything, but he seems certain.'

It was minutes before I picked up the first faint throb of the rotors and by then I was running for the beach. I came out on to the shingle and there it was, skimming round a bend in the river, only feet above the water, the most beautiful helicopter in the world. A pulse of simple joy went through me and I shouted something obvious, very loud. Alongside me, Phil had this sensational smile.

Thrilling and impossibly intrusive, the big brown machine walloped round the cliffs and then thrashed towards us, settling with a flourish of dust smack on the target of bedsheets we'd stretched along the beach. In the gale before the engine subsided, scores of Mursi flattened themselves on the stones. What was that song David had passed on, the one they'd come up with after seeing the helicopter that rescued him last year?

'It rises from its back! It's too thin – give it an injection to fatten it up!'

Now I could see the captain striding towards us, and I woke up to how shabby and crazy we must look. In his stylish blue-green flying suit and sun glasses, he was like one of those soothing beings from pulp fiction who come to us from a wiser planet to sort things out. When I shook his hand and said, 'We're very glad to see you,' my sincerity was painful.

'How was it?' he asked, and I couldn't think of anything to say except 'fine'.

I led our rescuer back into camp, finding myself possessive of it all, conscious of showing it off to this intruder who could never know how it had been. We found Turton ambushed in the midst of his bumper hand-out. The captain looked disbelieving and worried, but it all seemed orderly enough. Then things began to get ragged. A pan was grabbed, the crowd pressed forward and in a moment it was moving towards pandemonium. Ulijekholi slashed uselessly at the mass of bodies with a branch, but now there was nothing to do but go.

We walked away from the shelter of camp for the last time and I felt like an official in a deposed regime, fleeing into exile. Out on the shingle it was impossible, running the gauntlet of crowds desperate to make the most of their last chance. We trotted towards the helicopter, trailing people tugging at our clothes.

I looked round at the press of faces but there was no sign of Ulikoro, or Ulichagi or Darchu. Then, alongside the helicopter they were all there. We mumbled hopeless, emotional goodbyes with the rotors already swishing over us. In gathering uproar, we scrambled on board – but where was David? Andy spotted him, still on the shingle handing out the last of our money. We yelled, he dived in, the engine screamed and we were away. In seconds, we spiralled up leaving flattened people, red cliffs, an island called Alaka, a shrinking river and it was all too quick, much too quick. I found myself choked with feeling and I knew I couldn't speak without tears.

We fell back on the grubby rucksacks and for a brief space there was nothing to say. Then we actually shook hands and wallowed in the exhilaration of going home.

I suppose I wasn't even particularly bothered about finding the new settlement now. We had a film, we had come through. But David was on the flight-deck talking to the captain so why not spend a few minutes scouting along the Mago valley in search of the Mursi migrants?

We battered along just above the treetops, scattering a herd of antelope with our shadow. Soon we were banking over the brown gash of the river Mago, set in a startling rush of greenery. For minutes we circled over empty bush. Enough, I thought. Then David banged on the bulkhead and there it was.

On a bare brown hillside some way back from the river, the new settlement was an astonishing spectacle. There must have been a couple of hundred huts, most of them huddling together in a big circular compound utterly unlike anything we'd seen in Mursi country. It looked like a beleaguered garrison, abandoned by a retreating army and the settlement seemed shaped for de-fence against hostile neighbours.

Mike wedged himself in the open doorway, filming the place as we circled twice on a steep angle. There was almost no one to be seen. We came level and now I was aware of the mountains along the horizon.

'See that column of smoke,' David shouted, 'that's Berka.' Berka, I knew, was a highland village, the first outpost of modern Ethiopia, the place where those Mursi migrants were beginning to make contact with the outside world.

We slammed the door shut and headed for home.

THE THIRD EXPEDITION
April–May 1985

I

I came awake in the darkness as my bed collapsed, and for a moment I had no idea where I was. Then I heard the crazed chatter of a colobus monkey somewhere overhead and I knew I was back.

Away in the world it was Good Friday 1985; in the Ethiopian highlands it was a time of catastrophe, and in the Mago Valley it was the first dawn after our arrival. I gave up the hopeless struggle to rebuild the bed under me and lay soaked with sweat in the half light, wondering why I'd done this to myself yet again.

It had been a crowded three years for me since we'd circled over this place on our way back from the second film. I'd been in China filming the beginnings of a consumer revolution; and for a series about other people's television, I'd interviewed Mrs Gandhi and filmed awful Filipino game shows. In Brazil I'd gaped at glossy soap operas where beautiful people bitched in wine bars offering visions of the good life to a TV audience who often lived in a squalid cardboard box. Then on one frantic day, I'd filmed Ronald Reagan making the same electioneering speech five times as I joined the White House Press circus, descending with the camera-laden hordes on little farming towns and ending up memorably at a place called Media. Meanwhile, between the films we'd moved out of the house in the snows, my daughter had started university, my son was wandering somewhere in Nepal, we had a new dog called Rosie.

But from time to time I remembered that settlement on a bare hillside in southern Ethiopia and I'd find myself in a Manchester traffic jam wondering how it was with the Mursi migrants. And somehow, the Mursi wouldn't quite go away. The Kwegu film won a grotesque chromium cup at a French Festival, and I carried it through the Paris rush hour concealed in scraps of newspaper; I talked sometimes to David Turton's students about our films; and every day I met that picture of Darchu on the wall at home.

Then in the autumn of 1983, Turton came back from a field trip to the Mago Valley with extraordinary photographs and a story I couldn't get enough of about how the Mursi migrants were beginning to make regular contact for the first time with the outside world. The pictures showed Mursi women in Berka market haggling with highland Ethiopian traders, money in their hands, a school and police station in the background. David also had stories about how the tsetse problem in the Mago Valley was challenging the Mursi attachment to cattle and shifting people away from the mobile herding life towards a new existence as sedentary farmers. I found myself more excited by the prospect of making another Mursi film than by any project I could recall. With the accumulated experience of the earlier films, I felt we were in a position to record a life-change for an entire people. For me, there was also, I realised, a special motivation. The notion of a trilogy of Mursi films seemed to offer a unique possibility of shape and coherence among the scatter of documentaries that had been the business of my life over the past twenty years.

It had taken a while, but I'd got here. The months of negotiating and persuading in Manchester; the worrying phone calls in the middle of the night from researcher David Wason, gone ahead of me to Addis and concerned about the cost and availability of the helicopter; the weirdly familiar rerun of the Addis Hilton and the bank-raid with Mohammed for those piles of rancid notes – somehow, through all of it we'd moved towards another film.

Addis itself I'd found bizarre, the Hilton still teeming with guests in gold jewellery considering crowded menus and well-tanned world bank people beside the swimming pool, while the world's TV screens were groaning with the terrible images of the famine holocaust just over the horizon. The revolution seemed to have gathered conviction and the latest gossip was that all officials would be compelled to wear imported Korean cadre suits in lurid royal blue. We looked forward to seeing Mohammed in his. Meanwhile, a local wag had told Wason that the huge triptych of posters in Revolution Square were now known as 'Marx, Lenin and their minder'.

But Mohammed's boss Comrade Teklu Tabor had smiled on the project. We talked in his office under a big colour picture of Colonel Mengistu and I quickly became aware that for Comrade Teklu and government people in Addis, our new film with the Mursi might be much more than an anthropological record of a remote people somewhere out there at the limits of the country. As we described our intention to explore how the Mursi were beginning to make contact with modern Ethiopia, Comrade Teklu visbily relaxed. It seemed our theme would be in line with government plans to take Revolution and Development to every Ethiopian, though it wasn't easy to relate enthusiastic talk about the Literacy Programme to my memories of the Mursi. Teklu looked even more pleased when we talked about how the Mursi migrants had moved spontaneously to the Mago Valley. With the regime now under increasing international criticism for allegedly enforcing the movement of people out of famine areas and away from Eritrean rebel influence, a film which would be an undeniably genuine record of spontaneous migration was happily timed. I left Comrade Teklu's office newly alerted that our third film would inevitably echo the Mursi's increasing contact with the political realities of Ethiopia in the 1980s.

Mohammed had done his stuff again, and the nice man at Army Aviation had been as efficient as ever. The helicopter had worked its miracle and seventy-two hours after leaving Manchester, I was sweating in a tent in the Mago Valley.

It seemed a pity to drip all over the new diary, but it would have to learn.

'6.30 a.m.: My hen has just arrived to shout us into the day. Not a bad first night till the bed collapsed, and a pretty morning through the net at last with pink bands of cloud breaking into fragments. Now the hen insists, and I suppose I must face the horrid get-up routine.'

Two of the crew at least had the benefit of ignorance, being new to these parts. David Wason, who'd shared my television wanderings the year before in India and the Philippines was coming fresh to the special pleasures of 'Disappearing World'. Even without a collapsing bed, he was already bemoaning the effects on his back of unloading giant boxes and then sleeping in the Mago Hilton. During the Indian shoot, Wason and I had discovered we were linked by a ludicrous sartorial telepathy which found us turning out day after day in identical clothes, like two members of some over-regimented 30s dance band. Scheme as we might, we'd find ourselves matched yet again every breakfast time. Here at last we were released since the khaki war-surplus cast offs we'd all bought, plus the matching mud, were already rendering us interchangeable.

'How was your first night?' My polite question was addressed to the other first-timer, sound recordist David Woods.

'Ugh!' he said, but I knew he was a witty man.

The filthy little Mursi dog howled as I sawed away with my battery razor and it occurred to me that not only were three of my colleagues called David which was going to get very confusing, but I was the only member of the team who didn't have a beard. Somehow, for me the burden of grimy stubble on top of everything else outweighed even the obvious convenience; and the macho image didn't seem likely to register here.

Blakeley turned his awakened energies to my broken bed while I crunched resignedly on a dreary health-food bar, my invariable breakfast in Mursi country as a man with a pathological aversion to porridge and all things gluppy. Tasting that familiar sawdust lolly was my Proustian memory-reviver: now I knew I was really back.

A quarter of an hour out of camp, we walked into a strange landscape. More than anything, it reminded me of one of those World War 1 battlefields – shattered trees, like the ruined skeletons of prehistoric monsters strewn over charred black earth. Then I spotted the tiny spurts of green, pushing everywhere through the scorched ground. The whole valley was a Mursi farm and we were walking through the first hints of a promising sorghum crop.

Looking at the awesome impact they'd had on the riverside forests, clearing and burning off huge tracts of land in not much over a year, Mike was moved to grand speculations.

'Just think what somebody like Darchu could do with this if we set him up with a couple of those bandsaws I've brought with me.'

'I reckon they're doing just fine as they are,' I assured him and it was apparent the migrants were really settling into their new homelands now. Turton had already discovered that they'd long ago abandoned the big defensive settlement we'd flown over three years ago and their gathering assurance was obvious all round in their clearance and occupation of these riverside territories.

It was a spectacularly beautiful morning, and with the jagged green mountains standing clear on the far side of the river, I could almost have believed I was walking in the Lake District if the temperature hadn't been in the 90s with humidity to match. After a soaking half hour we tramped up a rise and into Nyomaniali's compound.

If anyone stood at the centre of our third film in Mursi country it was Nyomaniali. As a Mursi with the title 'Chairman of the Mago Valley Farmers' Association', he was striking evidence of the migrants' new and increasing involvement with modern Ethiopia. Somehow or other, officialdom had reached out there and made this handsome man in surprising blue underpants and battered plastic sandals a 'Chairman'.

It was easy to see how Nyomaniali had got the job. His intelligence and restless energy were apparent as he sat in his neat compound talking to Turton. I was less clear what his title actually meant and what sort of official functions he could conceivably fulfil out here in the Mago Valley. It might be a lot closer to the frontiers of my world, but it was still a wild and remote place.

In the doorway of their hut, Nyomaniali's wife cradled a tiny baby. I noted that she hadn't cut her lip and mentioned it to Turton.

'Yes, that's interesting. He says it wouldn't be fitting for a "child of Mengistu" to cut her lip. It seems some official he's met has passed down the word that the government doesn't approve – not in line with modern Ethiopia, they reckon.'

Colliding so immediately with the themes that had brought us back here was almost unsettling, but we made a date to begin our filming tomorrow via a talk with the Chairman.

★

Exactly twenty-four hours after our arrival, we crowded under one of our new canvas awnings, sheltering from a torrential downpour. I gave thanks that we hadn't been trying to land our helicopter in all this and attempted to edge in enough to stop the rain running down my neck. It was proving difficult to take full advantage of the shelter since a dozen Mursi visitors were occupying much of the space and all the picnic chairs.

Otherwise, the crews' domestic arrangements were prospering. With a simple syphon, Mike had ended the water-purification drudgery of earlier expeditions. More ambitiously, Blakeley and Woods had lined the black tube that transported our camera tripod with a bin liner and were now embarked on a bold experiment. Mike assured me that the humid conditions should be ideal for brewing beer from the kit he'd brought with him. I had more confidence in Wason's bush oven, a metal box with a thermometer on the door which he planned to stick on the fire and make bread. Andy Harries had promised us bread rolls but delivered stones at Alaka, solid enough to do duty as anti-crocodile ammunition. This time, Wason looked smugly confident.

Turton was talking to a splendidly muscled young man, making notes about his family tree.

'Leslie, you'll remember this chap's father from that debate at Mara in '74. He's called Rabithella too.'

The young Rabithella crunched my hand, and again I had that sense of coming back to a village of old acquaintances.

As the rain subsided, we took the priest on one side and gave him a splendid sheath knife and belt which he accepted with the calm assurance of a man receiving his dues.

Another of our visitors was more critical. I saw Turton talking to the man, and suddenly he exploded in laughter.

'He says if he sees his dead brother when we show the '74 film, he'll spear us to death.'

We all laughed a lot.

It's hard to read the diary sometimes through all the damp smudges.

'3.00 p.m. Raining again. We're still feeling for ideas, events, sequences, people to tell our story about the Mursi's meeting with the twentieth century. Inevitably, it's more complex and ambiguous than it seemed in Manchester. There's no big defensive settlement any more, the cattle are still around – the priest's based with his about four hours away – and there's no current dispute with the highlanders. But the theme does hold and change is in the air if we can only get it down on film with clarity and feeling. It'll be tough, with a lot of bloody walking, but it must be possible.'

I watched a tiny kid meticulously gathering our spilled soap-flakes one at a time from the pebbles. Then I teetered into the river with Mike's newly manufactured soap-on-a-rope hanging round my neck like a talisman against the torrent. Bathtime on the Mago was much more of an adventure than it had been at the Omo. It might be too narrow for crocodiles, but the rush of water following the afternoon's rain was daunting. I clung desperately on to a half-submerged branch and let the current drag me horizontal. Suddenly, Mike's branch snapped and he was whisked away with a receding yell like a cartoon cat falling over a cliff, disappearing rapidly downstream. For a moment, I was alarmed, and then he stood up about 100 yards away, laughing uproariously. Alongside me and my pudgy colleagues, Mursi youths sported in the shallows like seals.

Back in camp, we had a new visitor, an alert-looking young man called Bedameri. I watched him talking to Turton, and even at a distance I could feel his springy intelligence. David had told me about this man, the only literate Mursi; he'd learned to read and write while imprisoned in a highland jail for alleged cattle-rustling. I'd seen photographs of him in 1983 when he'd been the essential figure in an extraordinary scheme, involving written passes, which the Mursi had worked out with their angry highland neighbours to resolve a dispute about the theft of honey. Bedameri's Amharic was clearly excellent and he was soon chatting away with Mohammed.

Wason's bread was a triumph, but my suspicions about Blakeley's beer were proving well-founded. As we sat around after dinner spitting out insects, I noticed the puddle seeping from the tripod box distillery. The ants had spotted it too and it was already seething. The crew scurried around clucking with concern and soon had the precious stuff rebottled in our plastic water carriers, leaving the site stinking like a brewery and the spectators very confused.

I fell asleep with rain pattering on the tent.

'6.30 a.m.: A little surprised that the camp has survived an apocalyptic night. Wakened around 2.30 a.m. by a colossal storm, lightning like a disco strobe, a bombardment of thunder and torrential rain hammering on the tent. An hour later it was still going flat-out. If we can sustain that, it can hardly throw much more at us. Now it's bashfully calm, a dawn chorus of bells and coos from all the birds in the Mago and only a huge puddle on the site to show for it all.'

Turton had a breakfast horror story.

'A couple of days ago, an 8-year-old boy was walking down to the river close to here and he was grabbed by a python. It got a real grip on him, but a crowd of local women were passing by and they stabbed at it until it let go and slithered away.'

We gagged on our porridge etc., but it seemed we were stuck with snakes for breakfast. David suggested that the worst of the bunch we were likely to encounter round here was the green mamba.

'If you're bitten by one, the important thing is to relax. The Mursi bury bite victims up to their necks so they can't move and circulate the venom.'

As we considered the advice, the World Service announced the opening of the English cricket season.

Our first shot was of one of those luminous green shoots pushing its way through the ash-blackened soil, as relevant an image as any I supposed to begin a film about the Mursi's new life on what they called 'cool ground'. Mike zoomed out to include the devastated landscape of the Chairman's cultivation site, studded now with the evidence of a promising harvest. After the overnight deluge, the earth positively breathed fertility and I felt I could almost hear the sorghum sprouting. It was a morning rich with reasons to support the migrants' decision to come here.

We moved into the compound to film a talk with the Chairman. He squatted in front of his hut while his wife fed their baby in the doorway. Immediately, it was obvious Nyomaniali was a terrific talker, charismatic and voluble about the migrants' changing lives.

'Now we've become the governments' people,' he said. 'Now that the people have heard the word, the old ways have gone.'

After a while, he walked over to the hut and asked his wife for something. She emerged with a goatskin container and Nyomaniali pulled off the lid with a plop, drawing out a bundle of folded papers. The documents were ragged now and the edges looked mouse-eaten, but the circular blue official stamp was still clearly visible.

'They look like government communications,' Turton said. 'Something to do with cattle-raiding, asking him to look for the culprits.'

The Chairman couldn't read the papers, but he was in no doubt about what was expected of him.

'The government says, "Don't steal other people's things." If someone steals cattle, they should be arrested. That's the government's way.'

But it seemed the distant government weren't having it all their way.

'The government says women shouldn't cut their lips. One or two have heard their word. But our ancient custom is to cut the lip, like that!' The Chairman made a slicing motion at his mouth. 'We've always done it. It's a very good thing.'

As we filmed, a trio of teenage girls watched us through the doorway of a hut, their slashed lips jiggling as they chattered.

'Hello Mohammed, this is Leslie. Can you hear me?' I spoke into the walkie-talkie feeling rather foolish and to my considerable surprise, it crackled into life almost immediately. 'Yes Leslie, I can hear you!' So the thing worked, at least over the half-hour's walking distance back to camp. It was a comforting toy, and I thought how often on those earlier films – for André alone with the jeep or Mohammed left behind in camp while the rest of us were down river – the walkie-talkie would have been a lifeline. Now it had an immediate practical value.

'We're on our way back. Could you brew some lemonade?'

Back in camp, we had another technical novelty to unveil. Turton had brought with him some equipment borrowed from Manchester University's audio-visual department: a little monitor and video recorder which we hoped would allow us to introduce the Mursi to television through a viewing of the two earlier films we'd made with them, and also a small amateur video camera. His students had always asked what it was actually like when we made the films in Mursi country and now David planned to record a simple visual diary to give them an idea.

As he sat with the Chairman and Mohammed trying to understand more about those tattered government letters, I wobbled around them with the video and pressed the button to start David's home movie. Immediately, we had a fascinating and revealing story. It seemed there had been a debate here a few months earlier where it had been decided that the Chairman should go and ask the government for Aid. He'd walked up to Berka and got a scribe to write the letter we were looking at, clearly signed with the Chairman's thumbprint. Mohammed gave us a translation of the careful Amharic script.

'It starts by saying "Application" – that's the modern way of making this kind of request – and then it says: "I, the Chairman of the Mago Farmers Association, Nyomaniali Komode, explain the situation of my district as follows. As a result of famine, the people of this sub-district are exposed to disease and death, and so far three people have died. I would like to inform you that the situation is so serious that unless food is immediately given to the people, their condition will be very bad." '

Mohammed looked up, and behind him the Chairman whittled away at the handle of an axe with one of our knives.

'At the end, he says, "We shall build the People's Democratic Republic of Ethiopia!" '

And it had worked – 370 sacks of wheat had arrived in Hana. The picture it revealed of the Mursi suddenly doing business with modern Ethiopia on its own terms of letters and officialdom was startling. To confirm the point, Bedameri kneeled alongside Mohammed, studying the scraps of a letter and murmuring to himself as he read.

The episode also alerted me to some uncomfortable realities that seemed likely to be an inescapable part of our third film. All this talk of distant places, Berka, Hana and doubtless more to come, was bringing back unwelcome memories of those interminable marches in 1974. Mike videoed a brief state-of-play chat between Turton and me, and it's perhaps as well that I didn't realise how prophetic my comfortable campsite speculations would turn out to be. Lounging in a picnic chair, I suggested to David: 'It looks as though the biggest logistical problem we're going to have is that, compared with the Kwegu film, this one's going to involve an awful lot more moving around. We're going to have to take to our feet and cover a lot of ground.'

But I didn't reckon on 200 miles.

We huddled under the awning, trying to hide from the nightly invasion of flying monsters, listening to an old Tony Hancock tape and demolishing the last of the Scotch. Soon, we'd gathered an audience of a dozen teenage girls, most of them proudly displaying new pink elastoplasts provided by David Woods at his afternoon clinic.

'Shall I show them the family album?' Wason suggested.

They gazed at the photos of David's faraway home-life in a Derbyshire cottage, those unfathomable scenes of sledging in the snow, cricket on the lawn, prams and picnics and each turn of the page provoked whoops of disbelief.

I was waiting to see what would happen when the last page was turned. Wason had taken some polaroids of the girls themselves looking at the photos and slipped them into the end of the album.

The shrieks of amazement, jabbing fingers, hands over mouths were duly delivered. There was something else though, something I tried to set down in the diary.

'A quite overwhelming culture collision. We can't begin to know what we do. But under it all, there's a curious shared humanity, a coming together beyond our utter separateness. To put it another way, one nubile girl suggests that Wason might fondle her bottom. Time to go home.'

2

'Dog,' the Mursi said.
     'Rosso?' I enquired.

'Rosso – dog' several voices confirmed, and there were smiles of encouragement in the gloom.

The object of our studies, a diminutive mud-spattered pup called Tini nosed even closer to the fire.

It was my very first time inside a Mursi hut. There were twelve of us in here, plus Tini of course, sheltering in Ulikuri's house from a sudden downpour. I was surprised how spacious it was inside the curving straw walls while we hunched round the fire in a circle swapping vocabulary and dog stories.

'They keep the dogs to give warnings about hyena attacks in the cattle compounds.' Turton wiped his smoke-stung eyes.

'I reckon the postman at home would warmly recommend our spaniels for a job in that line.'

We'd sloshed across the river on a dramatic afternoon, with the hills to the north lit by white sun leaking out under threatening skies. On the far bank, we gasped our way up a steep track towards Ulikuri's settlement, watched over by a lad on a high platform of branches who Turton said was keeping a lookout over the sorghum for raiding baboons.

From the first moment I'd set eyes on him, I'd found Ulikuri a rather alarming figure, 6 foot 6 inches tall and straight as a duelling pole. Turton had hired him as one of our camp helpers and he had a revealing story.

Ulikuri had spent his boyhood on the fringes of Mursi society, hanging around the highland town of Jinka and his recruitment into the Ethiopian army was perhaps inevitable given his warrior's build. He was one of those very few Mursi who'd seen something of the world outside, fighting in Eritrea and Somalia with Colonel Mengistu's armies. Eventually he'd been wounded and had chosen to return and join the migrants in the Mago valley, marrying a strikingly pretty woman called Kelithee. I noticed she hadn't cut her lip.

Now the rain stippled the puddles outside the doorway while thunder grumbled in the mountains. Ulikuri was passing round a couple of neat red boxes and when they reached me I found his war medals, shiny gilt stars to recognise his time as a soldier for revolutionary Ethiopia. He was obviously very proud of them, and I was extremely glad I hadn't met up with Ulikuri as an enemy.

I stood in the drizzle on a ridge overlooking the river and helped a young Mursi with a cheeky face called Sigi to operate the walkie-talkie and speak to his chums back in our base camp. Like everyone else who's ever used the things, he couldn't quite think of anything to say.

We waded back across the swollen river Mago, me hanging on to Ulikuri's massive hand to save me from an ignominious plunge. Woods was less fortunate, sprawling full length in the water just as he reached the shallows. When we saw he wasn't carrying his recorder, we felt safe for a barrage of scathing comments. We slopped into camp to find Mursi visitors packing our canvas awning like a Wimbledon crowd on a wet Saturday afternoon. I spotted a very familiar face and it was Ulichagi.

After dark, Ulichagi sat with us and told a sad story. As we'd found in 1982 when he visited us at Alaka, he'd been one of the original migrants, but after a couple of hard years here in the Mago valley, he'd moved back again to traditional Mursi lands and to his cattle. Now it seemed, things were really tough for him.

'I've lost everything,' he said, and he looked in a state of shock. The recent torrential rains had washed away his crops, four of his eleven children and his three wives were all ill, he'd missed out on the Chairman's delivery of Aid grain. Even the knife I'd given him in 1974 had been destroyed in a fire.

Then he looked more cheerful and spoke to Turton for a while, looking at me repeatedly. 'I hope you're ready for this,'

David warned. 'Ulichagi says that now you're here everything will be fine. When he heard the day before yesterday that you were back, his family smiled.'

Feeling hopeless, we gave him brandy and glucose tablets, and I promised money and clothes and a new knife. Ulichagi smiled and spoke again.

'If you lived here, you'd have many cattle,' David translated.

'He should have a word with my bank manager.'

At bedtime, when even Mike had called it a day with his efforts to mend a Mursi rifle with a cannibalised fish-slice, I wandered over to find the flap of our tent putting on a spectacular display. It was too dark for a photograph, so I told the diary.

'There must be several hundred creatures seething on the tent, all different like a plate from an Encyclopedia − brown buttons with horns, a white moth with fine black chevrons, a delicate pink stick, a huge humbug with feelers, subtle grey striped things, nasty little functional beetles, an exquisite white lace job, a giant moth, 5 inches across with concentric pink circles on its wings like RAF insignia. Round the nearest storm lamp, squadrons zoom and bank like one of those hyperactive space fighter attacks at the end of *Star Wars*.'

A late colobus monkey in a hurry to be home rattled round the circuit of our treetops and I realised we'd been in this extraordinary place for almost a week. Once again, it felt like months.

It looked as though Turton had really sorted out his money distribution this time. For the second successive morning, he sat behind a neat table in the debating area beside the river, noting the name and family of each woman as she arrived in front of him. The Chairman and Ulikuri counted notes into bundles of around £4 each and David handed them over. Despite the uncomfortable reminder of colonial imagery, it was plainly working far better than the awful scrums of our earlier expeditions, and several people had told us that the money would make it possible for them to buy grain until their sorghum ripened and as a result they'd have more energy for vital weeding. The scale of need in the lines of patient women with their tiny undernourished children remained fearful and it was hardly surprising when things began to look less orderly. Soon there were groups of women standing round the table while men waved their arms and shouted. David wisely folded up his table and left them to sort things out with the Chairman's mediation.

An hour later, on a morning of great heat, we walked out of camp with Ulichagi to look for a suitable place to film a talk. Wason lugged Turton's little video camera and his record of our confusions over the next hour remains a chastening memento, painful to view even now.

We set up at the edge of the grassy space where the helicopter had landed, and fiddle for long hot minutes trying to frame a river background. The tripod collapses, the foreground's too messy, the sky's too bright, and all the time Ulichagi sits resignedly in the sun. At last we start rolling, and immediately a file of women troop by. Turton gets up, unhappy.

'He's troubled by those people, and he's very hot.'

'So we'll have to find a new place,' I say with audible exasperation.

We move off the track and the background's too contrasty. We move towards the river and the soundtrack's too noisy. Finally, we trail into the forest with the long-suffering Ulichagi, and the video captures a Tolkien fantasy of gossamer webs strung through the trees. After a few yards we can see that every strand is an umbilical for a tiny green caterpillar. For several more minutes, we shamble about with the gear, looking for a location.

'Just like the Cheshire countryside,' Mike says, dumping the tripod. 'A bit warmer though.'

At last, the video finds us installed in front of an acceptable tree-stump and we begin filming. Allowed to speak at last, Ulichagi laid out the dilemmas of the migrants' new home here with the lucidity of a man who'd had to grapple with them as a matter of survival.

'There are tsetse here, so if cattle come here, they're bitten and they die. If there were no tsetse here, we'd all come to this flowing river. There's grass and a river. It's very good. It's just the flies. If we had a powerful medicine to kill the flies, there'd be no one left at the Omo. They could cultivate here – there's lots of water here. It's very good.'

★

For the second time in twenty-four hours, we were sheltering from the afternoon downpour in Ulikuri's hut. I passed a moment photographing the beads of rain hanging from the straw fringe of the doorway. Across the compound under a dripping tree, Blakeley and Woods were teaching a couple of teenage girls to play pat-a-cake, slapping palms and laughing in the rain.

Before we were rained off, we'd been filming a talk with Ulikuri, sitting in his compound while a group of women worked and chattered with their children round the fire. One mother bathed her baby with a skilfully directed jet of water from her mouth as Ulikuri talked about his travels with the army.

'I saw everywhere,' he said. 'It's all Ethiopia. We're one people.'

I thought of the Mursi in 1974, so recently scarcely aware of a world beyond the horizon. We changed magazines, and Turton summarised what Ulikuri had been saying.

'He admits Mursi customs will disappear and some of the girls are already not cutting their lips.'

We began filming again, and then I saw the dark spots of rain on Mike's shirt. Without warning, one of our Mursi porters carried a metal box right across the picture and into the hut.

'I think we'd better cut,' I said.

When I emerged after the shower, Blakeley was already re-cording his protests for the video.

'I'd like to point out that I stayed outside while the producer sheltered in the hut!'

I added my message. 'That's because I'm the producer.'

Wason kept the video running as we tried to interview Ulikuri's wife, Kelithee. The filming was hopeless, but the video remains instructive. After only a couple of minutes, Turton turns to me, and I say, 'Cut,' with pointed weariness.

'She's not relaxed,' David begins. 'She's combative, she answers every question with another question. But we've been here a long time, we didn't prepare her, there are all these people standing around. We shouldn't be surprised if it doesn't turn out right.'

It was a familiar frustration. Over the years, we'd always failed to film successfully with women, and failing again on this damp afternoon with a screaming baby alongside me, I felt a rush of exasperation with David. While Kelithee got on with her cooking, we continued our tiff in front of the video.

'David, we really are going to have to pour some effort into making some real human contact with a Mursi woman.'

'Exactly, I agree. But what I'm saying is this woman's young, she's truculent, she's, I don't know . . .' He pushed back his hat in frustration, 'She's not someone we can get to know.'

'That's extraordinary, because on a person-to-person basis as we just saw over there, she's self-confident, cheerful, approachable . . .'

'Well, if we could film her like that . . .'

'I suppose you may be right,' I conceded.

'The set-up here isn't helpful, unfair even. But I'm not sure I agree with you that she's a person who's incapable of . . . Let's just give her more time, stick around more. Let's come back several times and see if we can make progress. OK. Let's thank her, and get our feet wet again across the river.'

While the crew were packing the gear into the rucksacks, the conversation simmered on. I supppose I was still blaming Turton for the maddening elusiveness of documentary film.

'Over the ten years, we've had real problems even getting pictures of women. But I'm beginning to feel we bear some guilt for this. We just haven't put the same kind of detailed effort into trying to make that contact as we have with men.'

'That's true,' David admitted, 'but we haven't tried to make contact with just any old man either. They've been very specific people. I think where we're guilty is that we haven't spent the same kind of effort choosing the right woman.'

Mike had been listening as he dismantled the camera. 'Don't we compromise them sometimes, filming people in their own environment?'

David had the last word.

'Imagine a film crew coming into your own front room with all your friends standing around and then saying: "Tell us about the important things in your life!"'

Uligidangi was a natural clown. Turton had hired him from the start as one of our camp helpers and we'd all quickly learned to enjoy having him around. Enormously tall, and spindly as a colt, with a comic's mobile face, he used his jester's skills shame-

179

lessly to cajole tobacco out of the crew. He also performed daily miracles in conjuring flames out of our rain-sodden firewood and carried water from the river in containers I could hardly lift off the ground.

Now Uligidangi was capering round the camp, as giddy and gangling as his name, showing off his new shorts donated by David Woods. The four inches of slack waistband were gathered up by a length of clothesline and somehow the man inhabited the ludicrous bloomers with huge style.

With Ulichagi dapper in Mike's red and black striped underpants and another brave in his blue Y-fronts, the camp had a festive feel after the rain. Two butterflies the size of small birds hovered over Wason's bread mix.

Then after dark, something awful happened.

'8.35 p.m. Ten minutes ago, a little boy of about 8 stumbled into camp. He's been bitten by a snake near here. His eyes are wide and he says his heart's beating fast. We're appallingly ignorant of what to do. We've given him morphine, found a campbed and two sleeping bags. He's lying still now with two tourniquets.'

Ten minutes later, the boy was vastly sick and Turton found in a medical book that morphine was the last thing we should have given him.

'9.00 p.m. The parents have arrived. Mother looks stunned, Father sits at his head. The boy's been sick again. Hopefully he's got rid of the morphine. We've given him Temgesic instead which must be dissolved under the tongue. He looks wildly as people tell him what to do. His father tells him he couldn't have been bitten at a better time as we're here. Lightning like artillery fire behind the trees.'

After another half hour, we began to relax a little. There was no sign of swelling in the boy's bitten foot, and he was calmer. We had a few minutes to say goodbye to Ulichagi, off with the dawn for the fifty mile walk back to his cattle. I handed him a Woolworth's bag containing three shirts, a pair of trousers, a sheath knife and £50. He'd also claimed one of our picnic chairs. After taking possession of it all, without a pause he asked for a plastic jerry can as well.

We talked until almost midnight with Turton about the harshness of life here while the worried parents kept vigil and silent lightning flashed round the eastern horizon.

After a night of stupendous rain, hammering on the tent like a firehose for hours on end, in the morning the campsite was a muddy lake. But the boy's parents were smiling and the crisis had passed.

3

Mohammed had a grim story. He was talking about the terrible scenes he'd witnessed in a highland refugee camp on a recent visit to make a documentary about the government's famine relief work. He spoke of shattered families and dying children, bringing a sharp personal focus to those numbing pictures we'd been seeing on our television screens in Britain. As he talked, I could see a couple of Mursi visitors chortling over the pin-ups in some German newspaper which had somehow found its way here with us. Life might be tough here, but at least the migrants seemed to have avoided the catstrophe that was devastating so many of their fellow Ethiopians. A few minutes later, we heard about the army worms.

Worried men arrived in camp and sat with Turton. He reported the wretched news. Swarms of army worm parasites had been found in the Mago Valley and the vital sorghum crop was threatened. Now, there was to be an emergency meeting of local men to discuss the crisis.

At first, it felt like an odd rerun of 1974 and those scrambles to film the debates. We dashed down to the debating area alongside the river to find a couple of dozen men talking quietly under the shade tree and we were shooting in seconds. Soon, it was apparent that this was a discussion rather than a debate. Men were exchanging views with low-key passion, but there was no formality of set speeches or oratorical pacing around.

I spotted the Chairman who seemed to be taking an important part, but, as so often, we were pouring film through the camera without any clear understanding of what was going on. All I could see for sure was that it was an occasion of real gravity.

As we changed magazines, Turton whispered that the purpose of the discussion was to decide who might be the right person to perform a ritual of purification. When we started filming again, I could see that the attention seemed to be focussing on a tall man with a hawklike profile called Miradowa. He looked reluctant and dismissive.

The Chairman spoke for a time, and I heard him use Miradowa's name. The man continued to look unimpressed, poking at the earth in front of him with a stick. Then Miradowa spoke, and I could see him indicating the height of the sun above the horizon with the slope of his arm. After another brief exchange, it was over.

'I suspect everybody knew it was going to be Miradowa,' David said as we gathered up the gear, 'but they had to reach a public agreement because he'll be doing the ritual on behalf of the whole community. He was the obvious candidate, because his grandfather was a Chachi from over towards Sudan and those people are supposed to be experts in dealing with the army worm.'

'He didn't look exactly thrilled with the suggestion.'

'No, that's right, but that's the way people with supernatural powers are supposed to respond when they're asked to use them for the community.'

The army worm sounded like a potential disaster for the migrants, but conscious of documentary's heartless appetite for strong incident, I knew it could prove important to the film.

I remained unconvinced that the ritual would ever happen. Having spent weeks at Alaka waiting for a crop-purification which never took place, I wasn't holding my breath for Miradowa to get to work.

In camp, we had another crisis. Bedameri, the literate Mursi who was now one of our helpers, was ill. He huddled wrapped in a sheet, shivering and looking wretched. Turton talked to him for a while and then reported the diagnosis.

'He's in a very troubled state at the moment because he feels that, probably as a result of all the people coming through the camp, someone's bewitched him – call it what you like, evil eye or whatever. Our helpers are always worried by that kind of thing, because lots of people come here every day and they're often people they don't know at all.'

'Can't we cure him?' Wason asked.

'No, we can't cure his concern,' David replied. 'We can give him our medicine and he's quite happy to take it, but it's no substitute for the traditional healing he wants now.'

Turton had talked about Nga Jareholi, the healing woman and I'd looked forward to seeing her. We found her in her compound, gnarled and self-contained, with half a dozen women working round her, grinding, cooking, playing with babies. A teenage girl was dangling on a string a furious baby baboon. It was a beautiful place on this mellow afternoon, commanding grand perspectives back over the valley and the compound held a sense of order and calm.

Under a dramatic ruin of a tree, Nga Jareholi began her healing of Bedameri. She sat behind him on the red earth, stroking his back rhythmically, slapping her hands and hissing. We crouched nearby, filming, trying not to fracture the mood. I couldn't conceive of any location more removed from a hotel bedroom in Manila, but for me the scene was an inevitable echo of those Filipino psychic surgeons ten years earlier.

That must have been the oddest film I was ever involved with. I'd flown to the Philippines along with a party of twenty-four seriously ill patients who had signed up with an outfit called 'Christian Travel' for a desperate and expensive last hope of a cure. On the far side of the world, amid the sweaty uproar of Manila, we'd filmed what happened.

In an impersonal hotel bedroom, the patients took their turn on the table in front of the psychic surgeon. At first the thing was impossible, but my scalp shifted with the reality of it. After mumbling some prayers, the man plunged his bare hands into the soft tissue of the patient's stomach and rummaged for a moment, his eyes squeezed shut in a grimace of ecstatic possession. Then, suddenly there was blood and the surgeon was holding up a grisly piece of something. Immediately, he wiped away the blood and the skin was unbroken. The surgeon declared he'd removed the diseased tissue and a cure would surely follow. The donation could be left in the envelope provided.

We filmed the process dozens of times, deeply sceptical but baffled. Then we got hold of a piece of the tissue and found it was chicken liver. The 'Christian Travel' people became suspicious and hostile and we had to hide our film. The British patients were astonishing, alight with the possibility of cure but passionately determined we should be allowed to find the truth. It wasn't until we got home and showed the film to a stage magician, the young and then unknown Paul Daniels, that he pointed out what was happening. He revealed a simple conjuring trick, palming the blood capsule and tissue for release at the right moment. 'I wish I could earn my money as easily,' Paul said.

By the time we screened the film, several patients were already dead. They were the ones who'd been sold the most reason to hope. The whole experience had angered and depressed me for months.

It was apparent that Nga Jareholi was some kind of psychic surgeon. After a few minutes of stroking and clapping and hissing, she called Turton over and showed him what she claimed she'd removed from Bedameri's back. On David's palm, we filmed a microscopic fly and then she urged him to throw it away before its evil influence could do more damage. The trickery was unresistingly obvious. Equally plain was the fact that Bedameri looked a lot better.

I'd changed, I realised. Those angry journalist's certainties of the early 70s felt less secure now. It wasn't of course that I thought Nga Jareholi was pulling insects out of her patient, but I knew more about holistic medicine and the powers of the body to heal itself. And I was a good deal more in sympathy with Malinowski's marvellous observation about science and magic: 'Science is founded on the conviction that experience, effort and reason are valid; magic on the belief that hope cannot fail nor desire deceive.'

Turton put it well as we packed up for the tramp back to camp.

'Bedameri's better not because she's cured his illness but because he's feeling better. He's in a much better state to fight his illness than he was before.'

Once again, Mursi country was giving my rationalist streak a hard time.

Uligidangi saw it first. He pulled Turton away from our breakfast chatter and I watched him gesturing anxiously at something on the ground with a crowd of worried-looking

Mursi. We wandered over to discover a scene from horror fiction.

Oozing out of cracks in the earth were long skeins of slime, coiling over the ground with a loathsome, glistening sense of purpose. As we watched more slime writhed into sight. A couple of Mursi talked urgently to Turton while others shouted their alarm. Mike came across with the video at the ready.

He panned up from the slime to find David telling me about the Mursi's worries.

'They say it's a bad omen. If you find these things in your compound or even worse in your house, unless you take some ritual means of protection by killing a cow or a goat and spreading the blood about, you're likely to die.'

'We'd better get hold of a goat!' I said.

Our insect spray was closer to hand and I gave the slime a good blast. The effect was devastating, the seamless cord breaking up instantly to reveal a mass of wriggling grubs.

'They certainly don't like that much,' Wason observed, and the Mursi guffawed with delight. Never one for understatement, Mike made a suggestion: 'How about some meths and then set fire to it!'

The flames flickered out to reveal a grey dust like iron filings. 'Barbecued slime,' I announced, but breakfast appetites seemed to have vanished.

The three Ari men walked into camp, bringing with them a sense of another place. The highlanders were short and copper-skinned, dressed in garish striped pullovers and baggy shorts made entirely of patches. They carried sticks of sugar cane taller than themselves and they brought oranges and papaya for us from their headman. I watched as they walked over to our Mursi visitors and helpers and unexpectedly shook them by the hand. There seemed to be no sign of the tensions that had almost led to war between the Mursi migrants and the Ari over the disputed honey not long ago.

I was fascinated to see the highlanders with the prospect of our first major journey tomorrow up into their country. Ever since Turton and I had begun to discuss a film with the migrants, I'd been vaguely dreading that toil up to the village of Berka, on the top of a mountain 4000 feet above the Mago Valley. But

I knew it was almost certainly the most important sequence in the third film, the place where the Mursi were making their first regular contact with the outside world at Berka market. Now it was almost on us.

The Ari left as quietly as they'd arrived, taking away medicines and a sheath knife. It was a grey afternoon, punctuated by splutters of rain as we prepared for the big journey. I'd had to ask Wason to stay behind to watch over the camp with Mohammed as we'd be gone for at least two nights, and he was busy compiling some useful Mursi vocabulary to cope with our absence. 'How do you say "Sod off!"' he enquired. Meanwhile Woods played a Wham cassette to some visitors through his headphones. 'It seems George Michael's still Number One around here,' he reported.

Word arrived that Miradowa's crop ritual was postponed yet again. A boy had been sent up into the mountains to fetch a vital plant. We left a couple of visitors sawing up Mike's discarded fish slice to make earrings and went for a final sluice in the river. It was almost chilly after the sunless day, but I had no idea when there'd be another chance of a real wash.

'9.15 p.m. An early tent with the trials of tomorrow to come. Extraordinary how this wild place has already come to seem like home and how the move out feels alarming in prospect. Heaven knows where at this time tomorrow. As we settle down, a firefly winks outside our tent lining. Just when we're enjoying it, I notice a simply colossal spider trotting down our net. I hose it with insect spray, but the bugger survives to crawl away. From the slime beneath the earth to the horrors of the night, the day has been bracketed with monstrosities.'

Miradowa's timing was impeccable. After a morning of trying to stuff our lives for the next few days into a couple of rucksacks, word arrived around three in the afternoon that the crop ritual was imminent. We were due to head off before the end of the day to try and get some miles behind us on the long haul up to Berka, but it seemed that at last, in the nick of time, we were going to get our crop purification.

It was an extraordinary occasion, one of those events like the ceremony of 'Spearing the Priest' in 1974 that we could film but never enter. And like that earlier ritual, it told about ways of being and feeling and understanding which confirmed the complexity and depth of lives I'd sometimes naively thought were lacking in dimension.

Miradowa stood in the middle of his sprouting sorghum with another man. On the ground at their feet was a cluster of things, simple but powerful – gourds of water, plants, coloured dyes, materials for fire. All around them, the sorghum was heavy with the awful black worms. As Miradowa began, it was with that same disconcerting blend of the magical and the mundane that seemed to be a constant feature of Mursi ritual.

First, he wet his hands in water and then anointed the faces of his reluctant young daughter and baby. His daughter grizzled, and he ticked her off:

'What a fuss! What's going to eat you? What bad children!'

'What a pest!' he said as he anointed the baby.

Then Miradowa kneeled on the earth and rubbed away with a stone to produce a glowing red pigment.

'Do we smear the clay on before we light the fire?' his assistant asked.

Wetting his fingers with the red dye, Miradowa decorated the face, upper arms and wrists of the other man. Next, the man plucked one of the wriggling army worms from a sorghum leaf and handed it to Miradowa who took a piece of fat and rubbed it on the worm to ritually seal its mouth.

Something weird happened then. As Miradowa bent back his arm to hurl the parasite away, a crack of thunder rolled across the valley. It was still rumbling when he commanded the worms to be off.

'Go away! Go with the river!'

We looked at one another in disbelief and it was hard not to burst out laughing at the impossibly well synchronised apocalyptic sound track.

'They'll just never believe we didn't dub it on,' I whispered to David Woods.

The two men made fire with the same casual ease as Darchu, and soon white smoke was drifting up to attract the attention of Tumwi the sky god. Miradowa moved the firesticks in an elaborate sequence, pressing them under his arms, and then standing to drive the sticks between his legs, bending low and shouting to dismiss the parasites: 'Listen worm! I'll give you milk from the black cow. Leave us and go to Yal! Go and eat grass in the bush! Go back to the sky!'

The crew followed him for a distance, walking across the sorghum, flicking water on the shoots from a gourd and still calling on the worms to go. Then it was over, and it was just another wet afternoon.

As the rain pattered on the sorghum, we spent a few minutes kneeling on the sticky soil and filming the ugly black caterpillars clinging to every leaf. I reckoned it would need all Miradowa's power to get rid of this lot.

We walked back to camp in a warm downpour to load up for the journey to Berka and another world.

4

'D'you know that poem by Gerard Manley Hopkins?' I murmured to Turton, 'the one called "A Starlight Night".' He made a negative noise.

'It starts "Look at the stars! Look, look up at the skies! O look at all the fire-folk sitting in the air! The bright boroughs, the circle-citadels there . . .!"' and then I trailed away, old memories giving out.

Dribbling on about a nineteenth-century Catholic poet on a ridge in Africa was perhaps an exhausted indulgence, but it was that kind of night. I'd just never seen such a vast sky, such a towering display of stars. Another fragment of Hopkins floated back, something about 'a May-mess, like on orchard boughs.'

We lay on our backs in the grass, starbathing and swopping contented nothings, drunk with the space around us. I hadn't known Mursi country so beautiful as it had been this evening, a shifting miracle of sky and landscape viewed from a grandstand on a green hill. As the sun went, we'd looked out down the vast sweep of land towards the distant Omo under skies marbled pink and yellow and green, surrounded by the exquisite silhouettes of our Mursi porters. Not even a century of clichéd photographs could drain the quality of how things looked that evening in the bronze glow before dark.

It had started wretchedly with a sweat-blackened march up out of the river valley and on to that huge bare hillside where we'd discovered the migrants' original settlement in 1982. There was almost no evidence now of that big defensive compound and the abandoned cultivation areas were wildly overgrown.

The last quarter of an hour, straight up the steep hillside had left us incapable of speech or movement for minutes while the porters slashed at the waist-high grass to clear a campsite.

There were just the four of us now, the crew, David and me, with the Mursi porters gone to stay the night in a settlement in the valley below us, signalled by a pinprick of fire in the blackness. Occasionally, a laugh or a word would drift up to us on the wind. After space-food goulash from a silver bag on the camera-box dinner table, I extended the walkie-talkie without much hope.

Wason came through clear and cheerful from back in base camp. 'Mohammed's just turned down the offer of a Mursi bride,' he reported. We talked about torch bulbs, and even the radio signals felt like a kind of friendly pollution in this special place.

As our fire died, we stayed out in the warm darkness for a long time, savouring the night.

I dreamed about taking my lightweight suit from a wardrobe to find it covered in flies and woke to find my hands filthy with no possibility of a wash.

On the walkie-talkie, Wason reported a pan, a knife and a cup had been stolen from base camp at dawn. It was a morning of torn cloud hanging on the mountain tops ahead of us. Somehow, by the end of this day, we hoped to be up there. It seemed inconceivable.

After a breakfast of tea sweetened with a lemon glucose tablet, we moved off down the hill. In minutes, I was gasping for breath, heaving up a track towards a wooded ridge. Behind me, I could hear Woods and Blakeley panting like a couple of St Bernards in a heatwave, and we didn't even have any brandy. I really began to wonder if this was possible. And then, on a bend in the track, we were saved.

Standing quietly with their ragged drivers were three mules. They were scraggy and verminous-looking, but to me they seemed like creatures from a fairytale. I knew Turton had sent a note ahead days before, but I'd never dared believe the mules would ever happen. We staggered over to our transport, radiant with relief. Woods' choice promptly tried to bite him, but nothing could spoil the blissful encounter – except perhaps the sudden realisation that there were three of them and four of us.

'I'd rather walk for a while anyway,' Turton said, and he actually seemed to mean it. We didn't argue.

Apart from childhood donkey rides and an unspeakable few minutes on a manky camel called Cadillac at the Great Pyramid, I can't recall ever setting bum on an animal's back before. I knew Blakeley had bounced around the steppes of Northern China on a pony a couple of years earlier for a film about the Kazakhs; but I was pretty certain Woods was as much a novice jockey as me. He scrambled aboard and his steed headed off immediately into thick bushes, pursued by a muleteer waving his rolled umbrella. At least he wasn't around to witness the shame of my attempt to mount my mule Mutati. I hoisted without conviction into a battered stirrup and the whole saddle slithered sideways, to Mutati's obvious contempt. Wearily, the muleteer refastened the frayed girths and we shambled off.

After a protracted spell of hanging on shamelessly as the mules scrambled straight up the precipice of a path, I risked a glance over my shoulder. There was David Woods sweating on a mule, and behind him it seemed we had half of Africa, an endless receding perspective of hills and plains and sky. Then it was snatched away and my hat with it by a thick branch and we were plunging through a head-high maze of soaking greenery.

'Steady on Dobbin,' I heard Woods protesting somewhere behind me, but I couldn't see much point in expressing an opinion. We were borne upwards, will-less, and I was conscious only of the joy of not walking. Ahead of us somewhere, Turton raced on with the Mursi porters, clearly revealed now to the three of us documentary mortals as some kind of superior being.

At last, somewhere near the middle of the day, the mule under me seemed more horizontal and we were bumping through a crazy overgrown garden full of bananas. We came out into a clearing and the mules were surrounded by stocky people in woolly jumpers, a parade of pink and green and orange stripes to signal that we'd crossed the front line of that other world.

We munched bananas, sitting in the gloom of Balamer school, and I felt overloaded by the glut of information round me. I reported to the diary.

'A sudden new universe – tidy, substantial compound, this confident building, twenty feet round with a stout centre pole and immaculate circles of thatch.

On the wall, bold kids' drawings of Jesus and the cross, and printed homilies full of smiling Ethiopians. The Mursi porters sit around looking out of place and ill at ease. I suppose this Ari village is the last whisper of twentieth century Ethiopia, but it feels like a trip to New York.'

We straggled round the Ari settlement in a drizzle, filming defeated by walls of wide-eyed spectators. Turton overheard one of the Mursi instructing an Ari in how to behave for the camera: 'Act naturally,' the Mursi said, 'and don't look at them.'

I made faint contact with Wason on the walkie-talkie, shouting pointless messages into the mist. Reluctant to load up for more punishment, we hung around the Ari compound and were rewarded with a charming fragment of film. Ari kids gathered round a simple zither and sang a pretty song while one of our Mursi porters stood and listened with his arm round an Ari's shoulder. Then it was time to go.

Two hours later, we sat on the ground, numbed at the edge of a forest. I looked at the others, spattered in red mud, sweat-soaked, knackered. 'The weekend starts here,' I said. Nearby, the astonishing mules cropped the grass, unconcerned after their heartbreaking hours of slithering and skittering up and down vertical mudslopes, and stumbling to their knees in cruel gulleys. But at least we were in it together. Woods had fallen twice in rivers and I knew it must be getting tough when even Turton accepted his turn on a mule. Then I heard a Mursi actually panting behind me and a moment later one of them slipped on his backside.

Now I leaned against a tree and closed my eyes. 'It gets steeper here,' I heard Turton say. 'We have to walk and leave the mules to meet us higher up.'

That last hour up through the forest towards Berka was, I think, the most exhausting thing I can ever remember. Not even those nightmare marathons of 1974 came close. The near-vertical hillside was glazed with red mud, oozing down the slope like chocolate sauce on a glutinous sundae. Soon, the only possible way to make progress was by hauling hand over hand on exposed tree roots. Somehow, the desperate jokes kept coming, fuelling us like gulps of oxygen.

'How many Mogadons d'you reckon I'd need to kill me quickly,' Woods wheezed and then fell over again.

Ahead of me, the slope went on forever and I couldn't see the sky. When even the jokes were giving out and mutiny simmered, there were the blessed mules waiting for us. We slumped on to their backs and were carried on up.

It was chilly now, 6,000 feet high with dizzying glimpses of the plains we'd left behind. We plodded along a deep green valley and the mules came to a halt. Nearby, a pipe gurgled mucky water into a ditch and a scatter of children in colourful frocks stood around collecting the stuff in battered tin cans. We seemed to have arrived somewhere.

But not quite yet. The Mursi sloshed themselves from the pipe, gleaming blue-black, watched with obvious suspicion and alarm by the light-skinned highland kids. We managed a bit of filming and then piled on to the poor mules for a final plunge up a mud slide and out into the main street of Berka.

I thought Chaucer's England must have looked like this, and then it seemed more like a desperate frontier town in the real wild West. Ragged people stared at us from corrugated shacks as we squelched along the wide gash of mud that served the place as its only thoroughfare. 'What a crazy place to put a village, right on top of a mountain,' Mike said, but I could only think about coming to a stop very soon.

Under a tree that stood at the highest point of the settlement, we met a man in a brown sweater and flared trousers who greeted us in English. 'Welcome,' he said. A man built like a bouncer in an olive anorak and a sten gun looked more doubtful, but then he recognised Turton and smiled his policeman's smile. A sombre chap in a dramatic white sheet introduced himself as the director of Berka School and led us along a track. We came to rest in a field with football goal-posts where a circle of neat schoolgirls were playing ring-a-roses. I was too weary to care if I was hallucinating.

For the next hour, I was distantly aware of some kind of hunt for the key to the schoolroom which it seemed was to be our haven for the night. I sat on a bench, drained of everything. Eventually, I unfurled the walkie-talkie and went through the motions of calling Wason at the pre-arranged time. Unbelievably, he answered through a haze of crackles, burbling on maliciously from 4,000 ft below us about beer and brandy.

At last, the classroom key was discovered and we moved in. Before it got too dark to see anything, we surveyed the prospects: A flimsy wooden shed, a mud floor, lines of rough-hewn desks and benches. There was only room for one tent. In the space near the blackboard, Blakeley and Woods set up their yellow igloo. It squatted like a lunar module on the mud, a surreal dream. Turton supervised the Mursi lodging, a desk each to lay on in another classroom. For him and me, it was the floor.

From somewhere, Mike found the reserves to teach a couple of Mursi to arm-wrestle on a desk. After a trip to the alarming latrine, balancing on a plank over an unthinkable pit, even he fell quiet. We sat almost wordless in the darkness, scooping shampoo-flavoured curry from our silver bags while fireflies fizzed past over the soccer pitch. By half past eight, we were finished. Discovering a stub of candle, I moaned at the diary:

'Desolatingly uncomfortable bedtime – dirty, smelly, huddled on the mud floor over a plastic sheet, torches broken, fumbling in gloom.

Now Turton lays out the bush knife and tells us to watch out for snakes. It has to be the most uncomfortable night of my life.'

It didn't improve.

'6.20 a.m. A night of ultimate discomfort, awake for hours on the granite floor, assailed by a chorus of dogs, snores, cockerels, insects, rain, lizards on the roof, and finally mad dreams about missing today's market by oversleeping until 11 a.m., then finding Berka's a modern town of trains and taxis and having to go back to Manchester for weekend talks. It's almost a relief to be here in the scruffy, hilarious dawn with that unimaginable journey to be done all over again.'

We ate hard-boiled eggs out of our hats and went off under grey skies to find Berka market. Immediately, there was a bonus. Dazzling in the mud, a trio of Coptic priests, robed in orange and black, moved from door to door chanting for alms under multicoloured umbrellas.

'Of course, it's almost Palm Sunday,' Turton remembered, and we filmed as each household was given a long green stem. It was another reminder of how this little outpost of Christianity and schooling and policemen was now closer to the Mago migrants than their traditional lands in the Omo valley.

We dug in on the muddy slope above the water pipe to wait for the Mursi. Before 9 a.m., the first file of women were approaching along the valley, dramatically different in their brown goatskin sarongs amid the bright rags of the local kids. Just below us, we filmed a Mursi girl lending a hand to haul an Ari up a slippery track. As she passed by up the path, Mike tried to pan round with her. Losing his foothold on the slope, he pirouetted on to his bum to the enjoyment of passing water carriers. We gathered our spattered gear and clawed up the hillside back into Berka.

From a position under the big tree, we watched as the market began to blossom.

I've always enjoyed those little markets that seem to flourish at the edges of things, the last breakers of the world's tide of recycled junk. I remember a dusty square in the Andes, packed with the hot colours of fruit and rugs and old batteries, crowds of Indians in bowler hats and a light that stung the eyes. Then there was Namchee Bazaar on the approaches to Everest, yak blankets scattered with Tibetan trinkets and cast-off tinned sardines from old expeditions. Most of all, I remember those interminable street markets in India, hub caps and broken dolls and dead TVs and surgical instruments and congealed sellotape and frayed toothbrushes spilling over the earth. But none of them was like Berka when the Mursi arrived.

At first, the women stood apart on a mound, waiting for others to come. Mike scanned the street with the zoom lens, picking up the Mursi amongst the arriving highlanders. Many of the women carried bundles of firewood on their heads; one had a whole branch. Turton had explained how the migrants would sell the dry wood they'd brought to the highlanders to help them buy food. Soon there were dozens of Mursi walking up the slope towards us.

Standing alongside me, Turton confirmed the significance of what we were watching. 'They're becoming dependent on the market here in much the same way that they used to be dependent on cattle – as a means of seeing them through times of hardship.' In the hungry weeks before the sorghum harvest in the Mago valley, the crucial importance of Berka market was obvious. 'We're looking at one of the main reasons why they moved to the Mago,' Turton said.

The first traders arrived, flinging their bundles from the backs of their wretched mules on to the ground. In minutes, the muddy space in front of us was transformed. On sheets of battered polythene, they laid out their stuff – grain, salt, spices, cloth and the usual eccentric scatter of batteries, pencils and soap. We moved down into the throng.

It was every bit as chaotic as I'd anticipated, trying to record the dozens of bargaining sessions going on in the crush of people. To add to our problems, we'd picked up a tiny starstruck boy at some point and every time we tried to shoot, his pale blue sweater with the orange stripe was hogging the middle of the picture. Ploughing through mud and cowdung, we sought help in technology.

Turton had met up with someone he knew, a witty and caustic Mursi woman called Nga Lugu, and we asked whether she'd let us rig a radio mike in her skirt. God knows how Turton explained it, but the thing worked beautifully. We filmed as Nga Lugu haggled for bananas, and the encounter was full of messages about how the Mursi were taking on this new place.

'I don't want the bad ones!' Nga Lugu insisted. 'Those are the ones I want.'

The highland woman did as she was told, but Nga Lugu hadn't finished with her yet.

'Give me some more! Just those few? You give your own people more!'

It was plain that though they might be new to all this, the Mursi could look after themselves. We moved across to the main group of traders, arriving just in time for a row. A Mursi girl was giving a salt trader a piece of her mind, waggling her finger and then chucking his salt back at him. In the end, she seemed to get what she wanted, but it wasn't until Turton examined the film weeks later that we understood how tough she'd been. The girl claimed she'd given the trader two 10 cent pieces, and he'd only given her one measure of salt.

'I'm not having this!' she yelled, her cut lip quivering in righteous indignation. 'Do you want me to call my people?'

The trader wearily gave in; but on our soundtrack, David heard the girl telling a friend that she'd already smuggled back one of the 10 cent pieces in the confusion.

But despite the Mursi's market cunning, there were signs that they weren't having it all their own way. Turton had observed that 'once a person has tasted salt in their porridge, they don't want to do without it', and it was apparent how quickly items like salt which used to be luxuries for the Mursi were becoming necessities for the migrants. We filmed a Mursi doing business with a streetwise money-changer in a pink shirt, and the highlander shared a knowing glance with the camera that seemed to say 'I'm from your world and we both know things this guy has no idea about.' I realised I'd been feeling a protective affection for the Mursi all morning and that they seemed much closer to us than these worldly highlanders. And all the time, the lowering figure of the policeman had moved through the crowds with his machine-gun on his shoulder.

Before midday, it was all over and Berka was an empty quagmire again. Back in the classroom, we loaded the rucksacks for the awful journey down the mountain. Then, for almost two frustrating hours, we were becalmed. Most of our porters, it seemed, had been seduced by the high-life of Berka and Turton had to go and round them up. At last, under gathering rainclouds, we skidded off down the mudchute while the mules cantered into the undergrowth pursued by their yelling drivers.

The first hour was a huge relief. Mercifully, we were led down a route that avoided the vertical forest, winding instead along a steep open track. Why we hadn't been allowed to come this way on the outward journey was unguessable, but maybe the Mursi had wanted us to sample the scenic route.

After fording a little river, we found the marvellous mules waiting for us, one each this time, and climbed gratefully aboard. On a soporific Saturday afternoon of veiled sunshine we plodded along through a landscape like a messy garden, passing dozens of laden Mursi on their way back to the Mago. After the settlement at Balamer, we moved down into the wide-screen extravaganza of the Omo valley. The crew's mules had tumbled ahead of Turton's and mine and we teetered downwards together, enjoying the huge generosity of sunlight and space. Far away to the north a purple stain of cloud told of a distant rain-squall, but it seemed too remote to concern us. We passed the point where we'd first met up with the mules and I felt I was on home ground.

'I'm saddle-sore,' David said. 'D'you fancy a walk?' Numbed after the hours of hanging on and happy with Berka behind us, I consented. We dismissed the mules and stepped out for camp. Feeling perky, I reached Wason on the radio and asked him to lay on the lemonade in about an hour.

The rain hit us from behind without warning. As we moved out on to the bare hillside with no possibility of cover, the storm drove into us. I pulled on my waterproofs and in a moment they were plastered to me, useless. We trudged on soaked to the skin and I began to fall behind. In an old cultivation area where the track held the water ankle-deep, my left foot began to protest. The rain hosed down, obliterating the landscape and at last my trusty boots gave up the unequal struggle. I could feel the mud squelching between my toes and I began to know I was in trouble.

My left foot burned with pain and I was reduced to hopping through the flood. I came upon Turton talking to a woman with a baby and she piloted us along the Venice of pathways towards the river. I hobbled on fire and water. We met another woman and for some reason she wanted to examine my sopping hands. The narrow tracks were greasy sewers now, impossible to navigate without slipping on the steep sides.

We came to the first sorghum plantation to be yelled at by a woman complaining about how the crews' mules had churned up her land. I kept on walking while Turton apologised because I didn't dare to stop.

I limped into camp to be greeted not with lemonade but by Wason pointing the camera to record my soggy return for the video.

'I have a statement for the camera,' I croaked. 'I'm very, very wet; I'm very, very dirty; I'm very, very tired, and my boots hurt. A 50 mile round trek, 4,000 feet up, 4,000 feet down – it's a long way to go for a minute and thirty seconds of film . . . and I'm knackered.'

I fell out of Wason's shot. But at least I was wrong. Berka made seven and a half minutes in the finished film.

5

'It says "heed not puff". What d'you reckon that might mean?'
Wason crouched under the awning of the tent trying to de-
cipher the instructions of our Chinese-made paraffin cooker while
the rain thrashed into the puddle that used to be our campsite.

I'd dreamed I caused a tidal wave in a seaside village by
rocking the landscape and then woken to the roaring downpour punishing the tent. Now we were still stranded hours
after the usual get-up time, wrestling with the Chinese cooker
in the hope of breakfast. There seemed no prospect that even
Uligidangi would be able to create fire from the quagmire
outside, but the oriental import was proving maddeningly
inscrutable.

A few minutes later, Woods had destroyed the cooker in a
pyre of flame and Uligidangi's soaking sticks had become a
cheery blaze under our kettle.

It was mid-afternoon before the sun was in business. With
every available surface heaped under steaming laundry, we
rebuilt our dank lives and gathered strength to face tomorrow
and a lot more walking. We were flirting with notions of a
marathon expedition to traditional Mursi lands fifty miles away
in the Elma valley to film a spectacular stick-duelling event, but
mercifully that was still no more than a distant threat. Meanwhile, my damaged foot was considering the possibility of a
four hour hike in the morning to the Priest's cattle compound at
a place called Madadari. As the nearest point to the Mago valley
where the migrants could keep cattle, it was obviously important

to film there; but after the punishments of Berka it wasn't a trip any of us relished.

The day ended for me and Turton with a scene out of a corny horror movie as we buried our garbage sack by camplight to deter scavenging hyenas. It was a suitable end to a soggy day. And my foot seemed well enough to destroy my alibi for escaping tomorrow's walk.

The hillside was a desolate prospect, a ruined stubble littering the stony red earth. Two men showed us the devastation, pointing out the fat army worms in a hopeless whisper. It was brutally obvious that the Priest's sorghum crop was ruined.

We'd arrived at the place after two exhausting hours with the green slopes of Madadari hanging tantalisingly ahead of us. The Priest's cultivation site was tucked in at the foot of the mountains, a likeable settlement where we were greeted by the cleanest Mursi dog I'd ever seen. A few women sat listlessly outside their huts and a baby was sobbing somewhere. They said the Priest was with his cattle up at Madadari. 'If only he'd been here when the worms came,' a man told us, 'he'd have sent them away.' We filmed the little catastrophe and the bloated caterpillars hanging on the empty sorghum stems, and then we moved on.

We came to the river Banco, a sluggish brown snake coiling through a steep valley. The only way across, it seemed, was via a big bare tree trunk which had been felled to straddle a narrow track. I watched three of our porters skip nimbly along the log carrying our boxes and rucksacks, and then it was my turn. As I crawled up the trunk, unashamedly on all fours, I felt something slip from my belt and I saw my Marks and Spencer's umbrella plop into the water and disappear.

For ten minutes, the tallest available Mursi fished with his feet in the murk without success, stirring the mud and memories of Darchu's rifle hunt. The river was clearly a lot deeper than it looked, and with a final flourish, the man disappeared completely below the surface. After a worrying delay, he burst into view brandishing the muddy Excalibur of my brolly. He'd certainly earned his reward.

We toiled up a hill of shale and I opened the drowned umbrella to dry off, feeling like one of those indomitable Victorian women travellers who marched their parasols across the Dark Continent. Soon I was wishing I had the sedan chair to go with it as the hill became a mountain.

In the early afternoon, we heaved over the top into a high valley with marvellous vistas towards the cattle compounds of Madadari. Blakeley's zoom lens consumed the distance to pull in the circle of huts studded on the lowering backdrop. For the next hour, we aimed at the same destination, moving up the grand swoop of land towards the settlement.

We made camp at last under a solitary tree on a plain buffeted by hot wind. The tent pegs struggled for a grip in a surface like granulated coffee and we flopped on our orange plastic sheet, gaped at by a quartet of naked boys.

We sipped instant soup and looked down the slope over the browsing cattle to the little settlement. I liked being here, enjoying the remoteness of the place, confirmed by the failure of the walkie-talkie to bring in any trace of Mohammed from back in base camp.

I walked down to the settlement with Turton. We found the Priest sitting like a statue inside the doorway of his hut, a tiny white goat nibbling at his rifle strap. He received the gift of Mike's puce shirt and navy blue flared trousers with his usual dignified reserve and returned to gazing at the mountains.

On a soaringly beautiful afternoon, we filmed the Mursi cattle returning to the compounds. Scorched and aching, I scrambled up and down the slope half a dozen times ferrying film magazines and lenses. Back at the tents, I gulped at my water bottle after a torrid half hour in the cattle compounds. I was still preoccupied with recovery when Wason spotted the newcomers.

'D'you know these chaps?' he asked. I turned round, and there was Darchu walking up the slope towards us, with Ulikoro not far behind.

After the hugs and the backslapping, there was the frustration of not being able to ask the hundred questions about what had been happening in their lives over the three years we'd been away. I'd never felt more blocked by the barrier of language or more limited by having to communicate via Turton.

Darchu looked well in the remnants of Mike's 1982 shirt, but he said he was hungry after a poor harvest. He and Ulikoro had heard we were back only four days ago, and they'd set out early yesterday to walk the fifty miles from the Omo. They planned to stay for a couple of weeks, so they'd be able to see our Mago valley preview of television when we showed the two earlier films. Darchu asked after Andy and it felt good meeting old friends on a hillside in the sun.

Ulikoro spotted a tiny silver plane, too high for sound, the first evidence of my world in weeks. Mohammed was still unreachable on the walkie-talkie from our distant base camp.

Against a peach-coloured sky, we filmed the evening return of the cattle. Slender boys pattered between softly clanking goats and a man with a rifle over his shoulder whistled and offered a heroic silhouette. It seemed impossible that we were recording the ending of a way of life.

With Orion sprawled on his side over us and the bright stain of the Milky Way pouring up from the mountains, Turton talked about the tragic delusions of the migrants.

'This is the one place where they're hoping to reconcile the migration with the fact that tsetse flies are far more dangerous in the Mago than back in their traditional grazing lands. The irony is that by moving to this area and putting their cattle at risk, the migrants have done something that's unthinkable from the point of view of traditional Mursi values.'

I could hear our porters gossiping happily in the dark.

'What do they think's going to happen to their cattle here?'

'Well they haven't really accepted the threat to the cattle. They're relying on the Priest's ritual powers to get rid of the tsetse. They also reckon that once they've cleared the trees, the flies will go. But they're relying on something else as well and in the end it'll put the cattle at even more risk. They fancy the anti-sleeping-sickness drugs they can buy illegally in places like Berka will do the trick.'

'What's the problem with them?' Wason asked.

'The thing is, if you're not skilled in giving the inoculations and your doses are too weak, you just build up resistant strains of the parasite. So it looks as though the help they're relying on from the outside world will in fact only speed up the death of their cattle.'

I could hear the faint jingle of the cattle bells drifting up from the compounds. 'So where's it all going?'

'It seems to me the migrants are bound to become different kinds of people, people without cattle. They'll be peasant farmers who've said goodbye to the traditional mobile life of the Mursi.'

I was wakened by the soft drumming of hooves and found the tent surrounded by little goats, brown and white and black and fawn. Then I had blood for breakfast.

It was hard to refuse in the circumstances. We'd gone down to the compounds to begin filming on a calm grey morning with mist bandaging the mountains. Almost immediately, we found four youths hanging on to a frightened-looking black calf. One of the boys stepped back and fired an arrow into the animal's neck from a miniature bow, and the plop as it hit home was followed instantly by a scarlet torrent of blood splashing into a gourd held by a tiny child. Woods and I swapped grimaces as we filmed, but I knew that drawing blood in this way was a harmless routine, no more troubling to the cow than a blood donation, and it would provide a precious addition to the diet of hungry people. We recorded how in seconds, a herdboy stopped the bleeding with a press of his thumb and the calf strolled away unconcerned.

Mike swung round to catch a young man gulping down most of the gourd's frothing contents. It wasn't easy to watch, but he was obviously relishing it. We filmed as the rest of the blood was mixed with milk in a wooden jug to produce a cherry-coloured milkshake. And then Turton delivered his bombshell.

'The bad news is, the rest is for you.'

Blakeley went first and I photographed the vampire streaks at the corners of his mouth. Then there was no escaping my turn. Apprehensive, I tipped up the jug, watched approvingly by half a dozen Mursi. At first it was bland and milky with only the usual tang of the cow's pee that had been used to wash out the container. It wasn't until I'd lowered the jug that I caught the ghoulish aftertaste of blood, like a memory of a bad session at the dentist.

Woods resisted the cultural exchange with quiet conviction. 'No thanks,' he said. 'I did "O" level biology.' He managed not to look too smug when the tropical medicine people back in Liverpool diagnosed that Mike and I contained a choice cocktail of intestinal parasites between us.

We moved on to film a humorous-looking man called

Medarirum. He stood in his compound with his cattle, some of them alarmingly thin. Medarirum had collected evidence of the enemy, wrapped carefully in a leaf. He unfolded it to reveal a store of fat brown tsetse flies.

'Here they are,' he whispered, 'the things that bite the cattle and make them die.'

'If there are so many tsetse, why keep cattle here?' David asked.

'It's my country,' he insisted. 'I've moved here and now it's my country.'

He pointed towards the cultivation sites at Banco.

'Our crop is down there, so we wanted our cattle near. When the children are hungry, we can give them milk to drink. When someone's ill, we can kill a cow and give them soup to get well. I've moved and I mean to grow old here. This has become my home like London is for you.'

He called it Lon-din, and I couldn't conceive how he might imagine it.

'If all your cattle die, is that good?' David asked.

'They won't die. The Priest is powerful.' Medarirum mimed a bite at one of the tsetses. 'He bites the flies like this . . . "Go with the sun to Yal" – that's what he says.' He flung the tsetse away and smiled brilliantly.

The Priest told a bleaker story when we filmed with him in his compound. 'Of course there are tsetse here,' he said, 'but my children are hungry. I was driven here by hunger. It's no place for cattle. Our country's over there, isn't it?' He pointed wearily back towards the distant Omo. 'I was chased here by hunger, to the Mago river. I came to look at this ridge and I decided to put my cows here.'

As the Priest talked, I watched a pair of dung-beetles, shiny green like mirrored sunglasses, struggling to manoeuvre a big ball of cowdung. He looked tired, I thought, under all the dignified reserve. I wondered how it must feel to carry the burden of having legitimised the Mursi exodus to their new home by joining the migration. And after what David had said last night there was more to it than that. The Priest's traditional role was to embody and sustain the values of Mursiness, and he had chosen a course which seemed certain to undermine those values through the loss of the migrants' cattle.

We filmed a young warrior lying on his back with his rifle

across his chest, caressing the neck of a calf. Then around the middle of the day, we walked away from sad, beautiful Madadari and headed for base camp.

I was surprised by the strength of my relief that we weren't, after all, going off to film the Donga fighting. For days, Turton and I had been juggling with the alarming possibility, but now it was finally laid to rest. Slumped in the picnic chairs, flaked yet again after the trek back from Madadari we felt our way to the shared conclusion that it just wasn't on. The vast journey to the place where the stick-duelling was due to take place back in traditional Mursi country seemed likely to involve four days walking in each direction, and we concluded that it was just too great an investment of our remaining time.

I confessed more personal reactions to the diary.

'My relief at not having to summon up the strength for the unimaginable trek is enormous, but it's coloured with regret at missing the essential Mursi spectacle. And, as Turton says, it may be the last chance to get the Donga on film before change warps it. Today's walk back through the heat of the day really blasted us all to our limits and the prospect of doing that for eight successive days was frightening. We're still throbbing with the effort now, six hours and quarts of Mago lemonade later. Thank God my foot survived the test.'

After dinner I watched Mohammed teaching Bedameri to write some new Amharic words. I became aware that someone else was watching with a special attention. Darchu sat close by, following every movement with his eyes, thirsty it seemed for the skill that Bedameri possessed. As so often with Darchu, I was moved by a sense of the man's trapped potential. Then he began to tell Turton about his life since we'd been with him three years ago. It was a story that kept us out of our tents until almost midnight as the insect armada boiled around us.

It seemed that with the money we gave him before we left, Darchu had bought 200 metal bangles in a highland village. He'd carried them across the Omo and into Chachi territory where he sold them for gold, measured out in the bowls of broken torch bulbs. With the gold, he bought cows. Darchu's grand plan, he said, was to swap the cows for a rifle and he'd managed it at last. Now he had only three bullets.

While I'd been driving to work through the Manchester suburbs over the past three years, Darchu's life had been less predictable. He'd found a dead rhino, and his wife had had a miscarriage as well as being attacked and robbed on the way back from Berka market. He told us he'd resisted the Priest's attempts to persuade him to join the migrants in the Mago valley. He'd stay with his elderly mother, he said, at the Omo. In the the harsh light of our hurricane lamp, he looked older than the man in the photograph on my wall at home.

And Darchu had news of how the outside world was reaching out now to touch even Alaka. He'd seen a few adventurous tourists going down the Omo in dinghies, and men were working on a simple ferry to cross the river just north of croc corner. It seemed that the Mago migrants weren't the only ones to be facing great change, and I found it impossible to shut out a sadness that I knew was both sentimental and possessive.

Finally, Darchu told us about the elephants. 'They've gone,' he said, 'across the river and far away into the bush. We don't see them any more.' I fell asleep with my cassette of Joni Mitchell singing about the city and 'the dream's malfunction'.

6

As well as being the first literate Mursi, Bedameri was now their first photo-journalist. He returned at the end of the day, his assignment successfully delivered. He'd taken a crash course in using our Polaroid camera and then gone off to record the devastated sorghum at Banco. Bedameri hoped that the pictures of what the army worms had done might persuade government officials in the highland town of Jinka to send relief grain. We gathered round to look at his pictures while 'Yes Minister' crackled away on the World Service radio. The polaroids were entirely professional, yet another demonstration of how the Mursi were tackling their new life on its own terms.

After three days without rain, we were bombarded by a vintage night of torrential downpour. A smiling man arrived on the dripping site to complain that we weren't looking after his bullrope. As we'd always thought it was our clothesline, we didn't feel too bad about having left it out in the rain and declined the man's offer to keep it dry in his hut from now on.

I counted forty-five lurid bites round my ankles which felt above average for halfway through our time in Mursi country. We seemed to have arrived once again at the quiet centre of the filming after the crowded business of the past days.

I started to read *The Fate of the Earth* about the nuclear holocaust and looked up from the awful recital of technological catastrophe to find a Mursi entranced by our red and white plastic fly-swatter.

Then in the middle of an early-evening rainstorm, everything changed: 'Turton scuttles through the downpour just now and hauls into my tent. A knotted string has arrived from Ulichagi with a message that, after all, the Donga fighting is to be much closer than expected and starts after three nights from now. So suddenly all plans are in reverse as usual, and we're off tomorrow for a giant five day hike. God be with us.'

I felt full of apprehension as the rain bucketed on. It was impossible to refuse the Donga now that it was due to happen closer to the Mago Valley. The spectacle of hundreds of Mursi gathered from the limits of their country for the ceremonial duelling contests in leopardskin armour was irresistible. I'd seen Turton's still photographs of the combatants looking like African Samurai, and his accounts of the Donga were thrilling: 'It's fast and furious and as elaborate as a martial art. The young men say they do it to impress the girls, but it seems more important to take part than to win and they often display their injuries like a badge.'

I'd watched lads larking around with the long duelling poles on the first expedition in 1974 and I remember enjoying the balletic grace of the sparring. But I knew now that the Donga was much more than a scuffle for high-spirited boys. Turton had explained that the big duelling contests seemed to be a vital ingredient in the way the Mursi defined the space they lived in. They see their country as a succession of five territories running in bands down the Omo. The Donga fights are always between unmarried men from different territories, and Turton believed that the ceremonial duelling was the essential means of defining and confirming those boundaries. The analogies with the tribal rivalries of English soccer supporters were tempting. The possibility that the changes we were recording in the Mago Valley might mean this would be the last chance to film a traditional Donga contest was the clincher, especially since the Mursi themselves consider the Donga to be their most unique and characteristic activity. They insisted that none of their neighbours held similar ceremonial duelling events; and their enemies to the south, the Hamar, earned the Mursi's special contempt for their uncivilised way of assessing a young man's prowess – via his killing of a rival.

But even at half the distance we'd rejected earlier, the trek to the Donga was still daunting, something like a hundred miles

209

there and back I reckoned. For those five days, we'd be more isolated and more exposed than ever before in Mursi country, and after the comparative cosiness of our Mago base, it all felt full of risk and uncertainty.

It also meant, of course, almost a week of lonely guard duty over that base camp for Wason and Mohammed. David was obviously disappointed not to be coming on the big adventure, but I tended to agree with Woods' analysis drawn from Long John Silver: 'Them as dies will be the lucky ones.'

It was a wretched beginning. My diary the next morning recorded the farcical nightmare of our attempts at departure:

'6.00 a.m. Still barely light and already preparations for movement outside. It's spotting with rain, damn it.

8.25 a.m. Two hours of scurrying and packing and stuffing and wrapping and we're ready to roll. Now we have a strike. The National Union of Mursi Carriers are holding out for double rates. As we're already paying £20 a man for the round trip, management is determined to hold out.

9.00 a.m. David has told the porters to bugger off if they don't want our money. They have.

9.10 a.m. David ostentatiously begins to unpack his tent, and the crew follow. It's a beautiful morning.

9.45 a.m. Peed on by a colobus monkey from the tree above us is the last straw. Management's will is being tested to the full.

10.25 a.m. David back from riverside negotiations with a possible deal – 50 birrh instead of 40. They asked for 80.

10.35 a.m. Six takers so far, four more needed.

11.00 a.m. Almost repacked, ready for off in the hottest part of the day. Now the camp empties of porters to follow shouts about a captured baboon.

11.25 a.m. Some porters returned, loads being allotted. A dodgy feel about this adventure. I hope it works.

11.50 a.m. Five porters still missing, resigned to lunch in camp. Three and a half hours wasted now.

12.30 p.m. Incredibly salty soup, just the thing to set us up for hours in the sun. Thunder dimly heard.

1.20 p.m. Still stranded in an ecstasy of boredom. Discussing *The Fate of the Earth* we speculate that the Mursi might be the last people left on the planet after a nuclear holocaust. And us at this rate.

2.00 p.m. Under a rumbling, purpling sky, loads are once again doled out. Porters trickle in, but others have left.

2.15 p.m. Teetering for off, full of doubts. Dodgy porters, worrying weather, too late.'

It was three and a half hours later before I managed another diary entry, and then it was only, 'Collapsed on the track, poleaxed.' We were nowhere near the end of the day's walking, but already it was exceeding my darkest predictions. The journey had also been achingly beautiful.

For the first hour, we'd held close to the Mago river, roaring unseen for most of the time behind walls of 12ft grass. Once, we'd stopped alongside rapids where the porters dumped their loads and plunged in, excited and edgy. 'It's the Donga season,' Turton said. 'It always seems to make the men aggressive and hyped up, like a kind of fever.'

They'd needed all their fuel for the next stage, an ordeal of narrow tracks in dense bushbelt, often bent double under the grasping branches. At one place, there were recent hippo prints, and again there was that Tolkien feel of embarking on a huge journey towards unseen dangers.

We'd come out of the forest at last, into a sunlit meadow and another hazard. 'The hot springs are just over there.' Turton pointed towards the innocent looking little river, a continuation of the Banco where I'd dunked my brolly. 'You'll want to keep your boots on as you go across the river. It really is hot under there.'

I remembered this place from David's accounts of the Mursi migration, and how hundreds of exhausted people had stopped here on their exodus in search of cool ground in the Mago Valley.

I wobbled through the fierce little river, struggling to stay upright and very aware that the soles of my boots were heating up alarmingly under the water. It was obscurely disturbing, this alliance of fire and water on a beautiful afternoon.

We'd filed up out of the river valley, climbing through grasslands and on to a stony hillside. For a while, we swapped encouraging chatter, but soon the talking was snuffed out. The slog to a high ridge went on for a long, long time and I couldn't think about anything beyond getting to the top. On the summit at last, a Mursi called Kirinomeri, memorable in his hat like a ruined cricket cap, pointed towards a faint variation in the purple distance. 'That's where we'll be camping tonight,' David translated. I didn't dare to believe he could be right.

For another hour, we'd moved down from the ridge and finally in the late afternoon along the floor of a valley to this merciful halt in the brown dust of what looked like a dried-up river-bed. Now we lay around amongst the parched scrub, just glad not to be moving for a few minutes. Some of the porters went off to look for a water-hole, throwing giant shadows as they came back with the sun behind them.

I risked the question. 'How much further d'you reckon to tonight's camp, David?'

Kirinomeri spoke for a while and made gestures that seemed to suggest alarming distances. 'Well I can't believe he's got it right,' David muttered, 'but he says we've just about come half way.'

He was right. Almost five hours later, I gibbered into the diary: 'Absolutely obliterated, filthy, sticky, wretched. It must have been the longest walk of my life, simply forever and ever. We trudged through the dusk and into the dark, speechless with fatigue, stumbling and gasping over a million boulders, snagging on thorns, arms bleeding, my foot on fire again. We finally stopped in the middle of nowhere at about a quarter to eight. Total blackness, a chaos of rucksacks and half-seen bodies. We sprawl on the earth and moan. An impossible tent-build, scuffling for bits by torchlight, foggy with exhaustion. Then a crisis chat with David in the dark over emergency tea and coffee. Can we go on?'

I'd decided that we had to head back. It seemed inconceivable to take four more days of this and I couldn't imagine how the crew would be in any state to shoot if we ever reached the Donga. I knew they were as exhausted as me now, and I was sure Turton was worried. He was terrific, concerned and entirely willing to turn back if that was the decision. But Blakeley and Woods were made of sterner stuff.

'We've come this far,' Mike said in the darkness, 'and I don't feel like giving up now. I'd really kick myself back in camp for not making the extra effort.'

'If Mike's willing, I'm for going on too,' Woods said, 'though I must be bloody mad.'

In the end, I suppose, it was up to me. The crew's determination moved and revived me. I was still full of doubts and apprehensions, but it seemed we were going on.

I decided to leave my foot till morning. I'd review it at first light and go back with a porter if it looked bad, leaving the crew to press on with David.

I could hear the crew joking with the porters who were doing brilliant mynah-bird imitations of English sounds. Recycled by them, my language sang of pith helmets and privilege and condescension. My torch beam hit the marvellous, live face of Sigi as I fumbled for the tent. Before I lost consciousness, I scrawled 'God this is a tough film.'

It was a night modelled on the storm scene from *King Lear* – cataracts, hurricanoes, oak-cleaving thunderbolts, the lot. A furious wind rattled the tent, but somehow it held out. As the light thickened and the rain drummed on, I lay alongside Turton, my dank shirt smelling like the towel we use to dry the dog after muddy walks at home. Trapped in the tent, I indulged Captain Scott fantasies and studied my foot. It looked better.

'The Mursi are nattering to be away.' Turton kneeled in the mud with me, dismantling the tent. 'They're worried about whether we'll be able to get across the river Usno after all the rain.'

'If they're worried, how should we be feeling?'

Another squall drove seven of us under my umbrella. The rain subsided and we finished packing, hands filthy with mud. Then it was raining steadily again and I sat on a log, sharing my brolly with a smiling Mursi whom Turton knew as 'Sunshine'. Mike took our photo and Sunshine put his hand on my knee. David laughed. 'Sunshine's reputed to be gay,' he said.

We splashed away sometime before nine without waiting for the rain to stop. After about forty minutes, we were scrambling down a steep hillside to the river Usno and I could see why the Mursi had been worried. It must have been half a dozen times wider than the Mago, an angry yellow torrent charged up by the rain. I remembered that this must have been the place David had talked about where a woman was swept away and drowned during his last visit. We all seized on the support of strong Mursi arms and waded into the river.

The water grabbed at me like a living thing and I clung shamelessly to the wiry little Mursi called Murle. Although he was carrying a big rucksack as well as my camera bag and water bottle, he hauled us both across without checking his stride. On the far bank, I gathered my breath on a tree-stump and retrieved a dry pair of socks from Murle's rucksack. It was good to be across, and best not to think how the river might be on the way back.

We came out on to a plain of grass. The rain had turned the earth into an adhesive sponge, and immediately walking was a torment of shrugging off the massive clods of mud that build up on our boots. The rain slackened and then stopped and we walked on, shedding burdens of mud. I caught up with a group of our porters looking at something on the ground and Turton said it was giraffe droppings. A few minutes later, the Mursi halted again. This time, it seemed a couple of them had gone off to shoot an eland, but they were soon back empty-handed.

In the middle of the morning, we slumped at a muddy pool, graced by a flutter of exquisite blue and yellow butterflies. A young Mursi woman, big and humorous, came up and yelled at me. 'She says she'll carry you on her back you look so shattered,' Turton explained.

'Tell her yes please.'

She shrieked with laughter and then said she was Rabithella's daughter. She'd heard we had her father's spirit shut up in our box and her relatives were going to get us at the Donga. She strode off, still chortling.

All I can remember of the rest of the morning are the strange elongated toes of a giraffe printed in the track somewhere, and the walking. I began to revive slowly when we stopped again, shivering in the noon heat under the clammy embrace of my sweat-drenched shirt, and watching blearily as Turton wandered around distributing boiled sweets to the porters. 'I feel like an air hostess,' he admitted.

David's map seemed to suggest we were on the blank space marked 'Plain of Death'. It seemed entirely plausible. We sipped something claiming to be French onion soup while I gaped at powder-blue moths twitching on my water bottle and then I was asleep. I woke and found myself still on the Plain of Death and disinclined to move.

The afternoon was an extended hallucination. At one point

we all flopped fully clothed into a saffron-coloured water hole and stayed for a long time. I recharged for a few minutes and then there was the ordeal by mud.

We walked towards an eternal horizon ruled with demented precision to divide a steely sky from an ocean of grass, waist-high and sickly-looking. There was no earth any more, only a quagmire that never ended, exacting a toll of cloying mud with every step. We squelched forward in a shambling dance of shrugging boots punctuated by thick curses.

When at last I keeled over alongside Blakeley and Woods, we just looked at one another and howled with despairing laughter. Haggard and caked with muck, they looked like cartoon cast-aways. I groped for my diary with a grubby paw.

'4.10 p.m. Absolutely, totally, uniquely knackered. Doubting our sanity. Two hours along a scorching plain coated in un-speakable adhesive mud which makes walking virtually im-possible, stopping every few feet to gouge off huge clods – utterly exhausting labour. David Woods is now the dirtiest human being I have ever seen. He doesn't care and wants to die.'

I scooped up a gobbet of goo and signed the page with loathsome thumb prints. Then I wrote the word 'Mud' along-side. I felt better after that.

For another two and a half hours we sleep-walked along a beautiful ridge between the Elma and Omo Valleys with gor-geous prospects towards the Mursi mountains. It occurred to me distantly that we must be almost back where I'd filmed the ceremonies of 'Spearing the Priest' eleven years before.

We moved down wooded slopes through memories of Eng-lish orchards populated by a herd of grazing zebras. It was a quite perfect evening.

The end of twelve hours of walking on the verge of collapse was a little settlement called Rabwi and a wondering cluster of people moving against a greening sky. I wrote: 'End – golden sunset – drained of everything.'

Groping to build the tents before the darkness, I heard Turton ask a Mursi something and then gasp as though he'd been hit in the stomach. He turned and told me the impossible truth. There was no Donga, no gathering, it was all for nothing. David looked stunned, and I couldn't begin to take it in.

Soon, we crawled into the tents and I tried to face the reality:

'In bed – utterly wasted. All the information on which we've based this crazy journey was wrong. There's no Donga near here tomorrow after all. It's still days away and bloody miles south of here, beyond the reach of our timescale or our shattered frames. The crew are wonderful – willing to accept that's the way things are here and they gave it their best shot. It's been a stunning effort from them, full of commitment and good humour.

Now I really feel like Captain Scott, all those endless miles to be retraced. It's been an extraordinary experience, discovering possibilities I didn't know in myself. Hazy with weariness now, longing for home. Everything else will have to wait till tomorrow.'

'He says you look a lot thinner,' Turton reported. I think Kirinomeri was worried about me. We'd floated through the morning in a fog of fatigue and disbelief, filming a consolation interview with a man who'd moved back here from the Mago to rejoin his cattle. Now it was time to go. I videoed the dismantling of our deluded little campsite and Mike offered an epigram: 'Never have so few done so much for so little.'

The rainstorm seemed to come from nowhere. We were preparing to walk away when the torrent engulfed us. In seconds, the ground was under water and there was nothing to be done but hide. For an hour, we cowered with the porters under my brolly and Turton's orange plastic sheet. Alongside me, I could see four pairs of feet, one with a knotted string round its ankle which had to be Ulichagi. I focussed my frustration on the ankle whose owner's lousy information had led us on this wild Donga chase. Woods was collecting rainwater in a kettle and I pondered the notion that he'd finally flipped. We cackled with misery.

Our unthinkable retreat began in farce, leaping over lakes between islands of grass like contestants in some humiliation gameshow on oriental TV. The scruffy little stream we'd stepped over last evening was now a rushing river, crossable only by a hazardous long-jump. 'The porters say you can't be as old as you look Leslie,' was Turton's encouraging message.

We'd been going a couple of hours when we heard the shot. Immediately, all the porters sat down. It emerged they were convinced that one of their chums had shot an eland and they wanted to stay and eat it. David began to remonstrate with impressive conviction.

After a while, we moved on. The compromise was that a man would head back from wherever we stopped for the night to check out the eland situation. If the news was positive he'd howl like a hyena to signal the success and the rest of the porters would trek back for the banquet. In my weariness, it all seemed quite routine.

At the end of the day, there was a healing sunlight and a beautiful camp in an abandoned settlement overlooking the valley of the Elma river. Somehow, we stirred ourselves to trail off into the bush and film a fine herd of cattle streaming in towards the compounds. In the long evening light, with Mount Mago as a backdrop, bells clanking and herdboys whistling, it was the ultimate vision of the traditional Mursi life the migrants had left behind.

For the third successive night, we crawled into the tents with no possibility of a wash, sticky with the muck of days. Fantasies about lemonade powder and mirages of our palatial Mago base camp shimmered in the dark while lighting flickered all round the horizon, weird and silent.

The porters corpsed with laughter at some inconceivable joke, and the laughter felt uniting, even in this exotic place.

I dreamed of New York bars and chic restaurants and knowing abusive taxi drivers. Then I woke, filthy and itchy, and it was lashing with rain in the half-light.

Four hours into the day, it was still pouring down. My diary preserves the damp smears years later. 'An ecstasy of misery. Crouched in a ruined grass hovel with Turton and five naked Mursi as the rain buckets down again. We have my brolly up, pressing against the roof. A smoky fire stings our eyes. It's utterly wretched.'

It was approaching the middle of the day before we could move out. After ten hours of continuous rain, the landscape was a lake of mud. Under mocking skies, decorated now with in-nocent white fluff, we slopped through hours of sustained vileness, a swinish swill with boots and socks and feet squelching in clinging muck. The plain of mud under a punishing sun was like an ordeal from *Pilgrim's Progress*. Despair walked ahead of me in the form of Turton with his boots round his neck, splashed to his knees. Murle, the little porter who'd sustained me on the way out was now my life support, stopping constantly to offer me my water bottle and a look of concern. At the limits of tolerance, I floundered into a clearing and a miracle.

There was this flowing river and the crew's smiling faces luxuriating in a bed of water. In seconds, I was with them, ravenous for the life-transfusion that sluiced away the sweat of days. Alongside me, David Woods just kept falling in, standing up and falling in. I saw he was still wearing hat and watch.

I washed hair and shirt and socks and boots and wallowed in a forgiveness of water. When I sloshed to the bank, I found a celebration squadron of yellow butterflies parading on my grey socks.

The only surprise, I suppose, was that we got so far before somebody had a real problem. Around five in the afternoon, David Woods quietly announced he was finished. By now, I knew enough about David's boundless commitment to take it very seriously.

More than twenty hours of walking had climaxed at the river Usno, wider and faster than ever now. We fought our way across waist-deep to discover that the other side was another punishment. Woods made it up the vertical track away from the river, but on the top, the discovery of yet more mud was too much. We slowed to a sleep-walk, and the message was hyenaed ahead to the leading porters.

We came up with them in a ravishing green valley. Though they'd obviously wanted to get a lot closer to home, they agreed immediately to make an emergency camp. The porters set about hacking down whole trees, and before we could throw up the tents, the Mursi had built a cosy-looking shelter.

It was an evening of quite unreal beauty, a late white cloud-tower on a weary blue sky over towards the Mago, a delicate paring of new moon on pink beyond the Omo.

With a mug of tea in his hand, Woods began to revive a little. I was very glad we could hope to be safely back at base some time tomorrow. A rain squall drove us into the tents soon after dark and we dined on Dextrosol tablets. As the storm passed, Turton and I were subjected to a lengthy speech through the tent wall from one of the porters about how we should pay them more money. Then the Mursi fire glowed orange and I could hear a man singing one of his cattle songs, grave and perfect.

I was wakened by a strange noise in the darkness. As I struggled for consciousness, I became aware that Turton was doing something with our silver survival bag. It crackled like an amplified chocolate wrapper, and I realised it was hosing with rain again.

'They're going to be drenched out there,' David grunted. 'I thought I'd try and sellotape something together for them.' He zipped open the flap and disappeared into the storm. Minutes later he was back, soaked to the skin, hair plastered to his head.

'I bet they were glad to see you,' I suggested.

'Not really. Somebody just asked me why I'd waited so long.'

I snapped off the torch. In the blackness, David was talking again. 'I feel awful about suggesting this disastrous expedition.'

'Don't be crazy,' I murmured. 'It was just as much my fault. And anyway, neither of us could have expected all this.' I lay awake for a long time, listening to the porters laughing and singing in the downpour.

Come soggy grey morning, I huddled with my diary on a wet rucksack. '8.15 a.m. Nightmarish slow-motion start to the day, all of us punchdrunk and filthy, Turton suffering from yesterday's sunstroke, porters surly and resentful. Last night's money bore is off again on the same theme. He looks extraordinary, wrapped in our silver sheet like a cross between an Aztec god and an oven-ready chicken. Everything moves as if under water.'

An hour and a half later, we were still stuck. The porters were insisting on a promise of double their negotiated pay before they'd move. A tall, raw-boned chap with keys jangling from his ears harangued David for minutes on end, unimpressed by a promise to discuss an increase when we got back to camp. The sun burned through, and we began to measure up the prospects of carrying the vital stuff ourselves. Then, quite suddenly, the porters gathered up the loads and walked off.

Our little procession moved very slowly. We sloshed along mud channels and across flooded grasslands under a sky that seemed full of a huge sun. After a brave start, David Woods looked utterly spent again. At every substantial puddle, he had filled his hat with water and crammed it on to his head so that by mid-morning, he was stumbling along like a drowned man.

Somehow, by early afternoon we were floundering down the slopes towards the Banco river, and the porters were singing as they came towards home territory. After the days out of touch, I reached Wason on the walkie-talkie. 'Happy St George's Day,' he bawled. I ordered buckets of lemonade to be readied.

The hot springs were really difficult this time, the rush of water trying to push us away from helping Mursi hands, the mud almost knee-deep under the surface.

The knowledge that the tangle of forest along the Mago was the last real obstacle put a faint spring in my stride that survived the inevitable slashed and bleeding face. At the Mago rapids, Woods sat mutely in a pool, fully dressed, sucking life from the brown water.

Close to the end now, I let in the fact that I was weary to my guts. Just before three in the afternoon, we limped up the little track that led to home. I fell into a picnic chair and wrote: 'Camp. Bliss beyond describing.'

Wason's trio of polaroid pictures is stuck in my diary. Taken over less than an hour, they capture the speed of our recovery with cartoon-strip vividness. The first picture, taken seconds after we arrived reveals Blakeley, Woods and me: gaunt, haggard, eyes focussed on recent torments. Twenty minutes later, after the transfusion of lemonade and vegetable soup thick enough to stand a spoon up in, we're smiling and relaxed, my arm around Woods' shoulder in a camaraderie of macho survival. The final picture, chinking mugs of brandy, gleaming in fresh shirts and trousers looks like three hell-raisers ready for a wild night on the town.

Heady with relief, I babbled on to the page. 'Sitting in a bath of evening sun, fresh shirt, socks, trousers, shoes, fresh skin it feels. It's still a sensory pleasure not to be walking, not to be filthy, not to be wet. It's quite astonishing how fast the repair system swings into action. As we sit in the picnic chairs and stuff ourselves, I can see my colleagues blossoming back into human beings.'

I knew there was no way we could convey the enormity of the past days. We were all in danger of boring Wason and

Mohammed with our horror yarns, and anyway they had their own story. Only an hour before we got back, Uligidangi had been chasing his brother round the campsite with donga and rifle and David had genuinely feared a murder to greet us. The reason for it all was unclear. Now it was enough to be back in the Mago Hilton with the moon coming up.

We were sitting around happily stupefied after our celebration dinner when I saw Mohammed stiffen.

'Snake!' he shouted.

'Where?' I gagged.

'Under your chair!'

We erupted to the edge of the site and Uligidangi thrashed at a three foot grey squiggle with his donga. In seconds it was dead and he threw it into the bush. It looked very nasty. I'd had enough.

'Donga!' Wason was saying, 'Donga!' I knew I had to be dreaming but why was he shaking me awake on our first morning back?

Feeling for my clothes, I tried to grasp the absurdity of what David was saying. There was a Donga fight a few yards outside our camp. The thing we'd missed after a hundred miles of walking was happening on our doorstep.

7

He looked like an alarming hybrid of gladiator and Samurai and horror film mummy. Furled in coils of cloth round head, neck, torso and forearms and decorated with grey stripes, the man strode through the long grass, hyped-up and whirring with anger like a trapped wasp. As he moved past us, he suddenly thwacked the grass with his donga pole in a ferocious release of rage. There was no sign of his opponent.

Blakeley and Woods had witnessed the beginnings of the dispute during their bathtime in the river the evening before. One of our porters, the chunky man who'd carried the camera tripod to hell and back, was grabbed by the chap who'd been laying claim to our clothes-line, the roguish Arituaholi. The crew had watched the porter walking away from our camp with his pay in his hand being waylaid by Arituaholi, wielding a bush knife and demanding a share of the money. This morning's Donga challenge seemed to be the result.

So it appeared that instead of the ceremonial version we'd walked so far to miss, we now had the real thing within yards of our base. In fact it was almost falling over us. As Dumali, the tripod-carrier stormed around waiting for satisfaction he collided with Mike and for a moment I thought he might bash the camera to pieces.

Meanwhile, there was an action-packed sideshow. A wild-looking man rampaged around with his donga, spoiling for a fight of his own. Soon he was clashing sticks with a skilful young opponent who landed a painful bang on the man's head and sent him running away towards the forest.

Within minutes, the trouble-maker was back, yelling and brawling until he was physically restrained by a couple of laughing chums. 'He's just drunk,' was Turton's analysis.

At last, Arituaholi came loping into the clearing, all smiles and conciliation in someone's second-hand black St Michael underpants. We filmed as the potential violence subsided into talk, and I was intrigued to see how a wiry old man stood between the disputants and became the focus of Arituaholi's abuse. Dumali glowered, Arituaholi smiled and smiled, and it became apparent the duel was off.

Back in camp, Turton talked about the dispute and the donga fight that never was. 'It was really about how these warrior-people manage to damp-down and avoid personal violence. As you saw, the peace was made through the intervention of the old chap.'

'Yes – who was he?'

'Well he's a relative of both the men in the dispute and that's how things are usually settled – through an elaborate network of mediation by relatives. In such a small-scale society, there's almost always a relative around who can calm things down and it's surprising really, considering how aggressive and tough these people are, how seldom quarrels do end in violence.'

Alongside me, Arituaholi was chatting unconcernedly to Darchu. I found myself wondering how long external authority, in the shape of that lowering policeman at Berka, would continue to keep its distance.

In the afternoon, we started the search for an arena to stage our première of television for the Mursi. We'd decided that it would be best to limit that first screening in a couple of days time to an audience of people who had featured in the earlier films. Turton had taken soundings with the Priest and others about the possible distress and disturbance the viewing might produce, and we'd been warned that some people might be upset at the disturbing sight of relatives now dead, walking and talking in our box of spirits.

We settled for a small hollow just outside our camp, hemmed in on all sides by dense undergrowth. The only drawback was that the place had served as one of our latrine areas for the past weeks. Critics of television, it occurred to me, would have enjoyed the ironies.

We were at the Healing Woman's compound when we heard the news. That Donga gathering we'd gone so far to find hadn't happened after all. A Mursi had been killed in the south by a man from a neighbouring tribe, so the whole thing had been called off. 'Our reactions,' I noted in the diary, 'are complex.'

Despite the discovery of a small scorpion under the tripod as were setting up, I'd recovered enough to register that the interview with Nga Lugu seemed good. She sat on a log, spirited and self-confident, mocking David it appeared from time to time. At long last I felt we might have some worthwhile film with women, but I didn't realise how sharp it was until I got Turton's translations.

'We really work hard,' she said, 'cooking porridge, grinding the grain and giving it to the men to eat. They just sit about. What they know about is going off into the bush to hunt and gather.'

David had a message from the liberated kitchens of Cheshire. 'In our country,' he said, 'if the men just sat around all day long, the women would complain.'

'They'd complain?' Nga Lugu looked disbelieving and scornful. 'We don't. We don't mind. They clear the forest. D'you see round here? They've cleared all this. They go into the bush to get honey. If there's no hunger, they stay at home and drink beer.'

David hadn't given up yet. 'When there's no hunger, don't the women still work?'

'Yes, we're the only ones who grind grain. We are the only ones who get water. We build the houses.'

David tried one more thrust for feminism. 'In our country people would say: "Why should women do all the work while men have an easy time?"'

Nga Lugu was contemptuous. 'So you're the ones who work? Really?' She let out a moan of incredulity. 'That's bad,' she said.

'If it's bad, tell me why?'

'A man, a strong man, a warrior, should he work and cook for women? Do you cook for them?'

David assented.

'You cook?' Nga Lugu smiled pityingly, then she asked again, 'You cook?' She gazed with good-humoured regret at this hopeless specimen of white decadence.

It was a relief to have the talk with Nga Lugu on film, even if it had meant a gentle bruising for David. On the way back to camp, lugging a welcome gift of beef on grass thongs, he talked about the regular problems of anthropologists in working with women.

'It seems to be a problem for female anthropologists too, getting information from women. Maybe it's got something to do with the fact that women's strength, their ability to make decisions about their lives, often has to come from an unwillingness to commit themselves and risk male attack. So it's hardly surprising women can be wary of anthropologists and their endless questions.'

There seemed little doubt that the position of the Mursi migrant women was changing rapidly, despite Nga Lugu's support for the traditional division of labour.

'The women are the ones who go most often to Berka market,' David said, 'buying and selling grain. So it's the women who really have the most contact with the outside world and with cash. It's bound to change the relationship between men and women, but I'd be surprised if the men don't try to readjust the balance by taking more of an interest in the cultivation side of things, especially since they won't have their cattle to deal with.'

With only a week now before the helicopter was due, we spent a long evening arranging the first hand-outs. Turton and I were both anxious to try and avoid the pandemonium of previous departures and the only hope seemed to be a policy of gradual distribution. David paid our campsite helpers after a lengthy sellotaping session to make the ragged notes acceptable and the crew passed around soap and empty bottles. Darchu said we were like the rain, bringing out lots of little things.

I decided it was a good moment to make a special presentation. I knew that Murle, my saviour during the awful marathon, had a great interest in my watch. It was a shiny digital job, one of a batch Mike had thoughtfully picked up at his local garage, and Murle had peered at it in fascination every time I collapsed on the track. It seemed it was the pulsing dot marking the seconds which intrigued the Mursi. Turton said they'd concluded there must be a tiny animal inside the watch and the dot was its heartbeat.

Murle looked delighted with the watch, but I soon gave up the impossible struggle of trying to communicate what it was for.

We sat with four of the earliest migrants, the first scouts who'd come to the Mago valley in search of cool ground. There was Arituaholi of the clothes-line and underpants, Kirinomeri still wearing his ruined cricket cap, Miradowa the scourge of the army worms and Ulichagi's half brother Gowa. Turton had gathered them together to talk about how they'd arrived here and how they saw their future.

Arituaholi began. 'I was one of the very first to come here, with Kirinomeri. The rest of the people were back at home. We looked over this place. We said, "We are very hungry. Let us move here." We got hold of a cow and a sheep and drove them here. On the way, we slept at the hot spring, and the next morning we brought them here and sacrificed them. We spread the stomach lining and the blood to purify the land here where we're cultivating. That's how it was.'

Kirinomeri took up the story. 'The people debated. I said, "We are very hungry. This land of ours we call Mara is very hot and dry. If we only get a bit of rain, the crop is destroyed by the sun. Let us move where the clouds are closer to the ground, and when the rain falls, our crop will shoot up and we can eat it. It is cool ground." So the people decided to move here, where there is food.'

As Kirinomeri talked, the other men were prompting him with reminders of the market. They were in no doubt about how crucial the proximity of Berka market and its food supply were in tempting the migrants to come here.

David pursued the more challenging implications of the move. 'I've been thinking that you Mago people will eventually become like the Ari up in the highlands. What do you say to that Kirinomeri?'

'I say that we Mursi are very special people. When you come

back later to visit us again, you'll find that things have turned out well. We will simply go up there and get food when we're hungry, but we'll remain separate. They have their customs, and we have our customs.'

Then Kirinomeri talked about how he'd been recruited in a highland town and flown to Arba Minch to be trained as a militiaman for three months. His instructors had given him the same message we'd heard from the soldier Ulikuri. 'Now you are all the government's people.'

In the afternoon, I sat on a log at the edge of a cultivation site just behind our camp and read a few pages of *Bleak House*.

'Implacable November weather. As much mud in the streets, as if the waters had but newly retired from the face of the earth and it would not be wonderful to meet a Megalosaurus, forty feet long or so, waddling like an elephantine lizard up Holborn Hill. Smoke lowering down from chimney pots, making a soft black drizzle with flakes of soot in it as big as full grown snowflakes – gone into mourning, one might imagine, for the death of the sun.'

While Dickens wallowed in the murk of a grimy London evening, the Mago sparkled behind the sorghum and the mountains were lit with dappled sun. Alongside me, a young brave with chains in his ears chewed on a stick.

Distracted by too much dislocation, I gave up on the book and thought about the epic thesis Turton was developing around the Mursi migration. As he saw it now, the migrants were only the latest wave in a process that had been going on for hundreds of years, involving not only the Mursi, but many other peoples in this part of East Africa. They were all drifting on a huge journey northwards in search of that cool ground. For the Mursi, David suggested, it could be the fact of that journey which was the vital influence.

'Although the Mursi think of themselves as having made a journey to where they are today,' he said, 'it might be more accurate to say a journey has made them, a journey of enormous proportions involving people over many generations which has given rise to many different groups of which the Mursi are just one.'

So our three films had simply recorded some incidents in the story of that journey. The Mursi-Bodi war of the 70s and the Mago migration of the 80s could be seen as different ways of pursuing that same northward drift. The ground I was sitting on had been Bodi territory at the beginning of the century before sleeping sickness forced them to move in pursuit of their part in the bigger design. The new and unpredictable development now of course was that the Mursi's latest move had brought them into regular contact for the first time with the outside world.

I sat for a long time as the river turned violet and a teenage boy strode past thrashing the air with his donga, oblivious of me.

Back in camp, the World Service radio was announcing a programme entitled 'Seventy years of the Girl Guides'.

8

It felt a bit like the final chapter of some Agatha Christie novel, with all the main characters coming back to assemble in the library, and it was just about as improbable. Instead of a library we had our hastily converted latrine area, and the focus of attention wasn't some knowing sleuth but a neat little TV set standing at the end of the clearing on a pile of boxes. Sitting rather bewildered in our picnic chairs were all the stars of our two earlier films: the Priest, Darchu, Ulichagi, Ulikoro, with the Chairman, Nga Jareholi the healer and Nga Lugu to represent the Mago valley cast.

It was a sombre afternoon, gloomy after recent rain. The prospect of unveiling to this audience what we'd been doing here over the years found me more excited and apprehensive than I could remember for any previous screening with hostile journalists or protesting diplomats or dinner-jacketed festival-goers. Not even a preview of a critical film for officials of the Chinese Embassy had bothered me the same way. I set the video rolling and the blue 'Granada' station ident popped on to the screen, a very long way from its Manchester home.

For ten long minutes, they seemed transfixed. Unmoving, eyes locked on the screen, the Mursi looked at themselves eleven years earlier and at a raiding party returning from a shootout with the Bodi. Then the film reached the negotiations with the Bodi elders of Gura, and Ulichagi saw himself again, stranded on enemy territory with our floundering expedition. He pointed and chuckled and it seemed to break the spell for the others.

Soon, there were guffaws of recognition and a background of chatter like the accompaniment to any home movie or neighbour's holiday slides.

The two women giggled over the domestic scenes and Nga Jareholi recognised an old necklace. Seeing his teenage self suckling from a cow's udder, Ulikoro covered his mouth with his hand in embarrassment. Even the Priest deigned a smile.

We circled around filming the scene and its looping ambiguities, for us as well as for the Mursi, left me bewildered. It was impossible even to know whether the flow of images, the succession of close-ups and long-shots and montages, structured according to conventions evolved in distant cities, told any coherent story for them. When it was over, somebody said to Turton, 'You've taken our bodies away.'

We screened 'The Kwegu', panning from Darchu hunting for the rifle in the Omo in 1982 to Darchu laughing incredulously in his picnic chair three years later. The threatening mystery of the spirit box was fading now it seemed, and they were clearly enjoying it. I wondered if Darchu's dramatic account of Mursi domination would embarrass him here, but everyone giggled happily as he talked about the prospect of being bound up and thrown in the river. For some reason, the scenes showing him eating with his family reduced everyone to shrieking heaps of laughter. I felt disoriented, cut adrift from the guidelines for communication I'd taken for granted since I started making films more than twenty years ago.

Afterwards, people got up and stretched and gossiped just like audiences anywhere. They wandered away, and I felt a bit flat.

'So that's it, David. Television reaches one more outpost. I feel like a missionary, only a bit more doubtful about my message.'

We were dismantling our bush theatre in a sticky drizzle, still trying to guess what the Mursi had made of it all. 'I wouldn't worry,' David said. 'I reckon they'll talk about it for ten minutes round their fires tonight and then pass on to more important things.'

For us as well, media introspection was soon overtaken by anxious talk about how we'd get out of here if today's blanket of cloud hung around to prevent the helicopter coming to our rescue in four days' time.

*

I woke from a dream that Turton and I had arrived with a bunch of Mursi in some Danish town called Bugburg, all redbrick gothic, and couldn't get a permit to film.

Outside, I could hear David Woods giving Uligidangi an English lesson. 'Repeat after me, "I am a bloody nuisance." '

It seemed my colleagues were becoming as ragged as I felt, awake now to churning guts and a fresh crop of bites.

Over breakfast, a visitor streaked with white mud insisted we must have some money for him since my mother and father obviously manufactured it.

We passed a grey morning filming Nga Lugu building a new house. She said the mice had made holes in the wall of her old place and she was afraid snakes might follow them. It seemed a good reason to move, we thought.

We watched her stripping off the old thatching, and of course she promptly became 'Mrs Thatcher'. Then she carried the huge bundles across the few yards to where the framework of her new house was taking shape. I thought of my own recent tangle with bridging loans and estate agents, a protracted trauma that had consumed our lives for months on end, and wondered if it might be worth the snakes to be free of all that.

Nga Lugu began to weave together whippy branches for the house frame. She worked, as people so often worked here with an unhurried grace and assurance, singing to herself as she bent and wove and tied. Before the morning was over, the spine for the new house was in place.

On our way back to camp, we came upon the Chairman, acting out scenes from yesterday's television preview for a group of men. They looked as politely bored as I always feel when someone insists on telling me about a film I haven't seen.

I jumped aside just in time to avoid being flattened by a falling tree. Ulikoro's efforts to help clear a space for our main television screening in the riverside forest were impressively thorough, but rather haphazard. In minutes, we had a woodland cinema, furnished with a rustic table to support the television set.

Our audience of yesterday had advised that the films were suitable for general viewing. They suggested only that someone should make a warning introduction, and Ulichagi had agreed to do the honours.

By the time everything was ready there were almost 200 people gathered in the clearing. Darchu and the Chairman, I noticed were in the front row for a second helping. I moved around taking photographs and through the viewfinder it had the domestic order of an English wood – broken sunlight on a carpet of leaves. Without the tidy framing, I was aware again of the heat and the grinding row of crickets and the absurdity of a television set standing in the middle of all this.

Ulichagi rose and made his awkward little speech about how some of the audience might not want to see dead relatives whose spirits were held in our box. On the way to the screening we'd met up with Rabithella's Rambo-scaled son, heading off in the opposite direction to avoid seeing his late father. Even now we had no clear idea of how people might react to the possibility that these white intruders had somehow made contact with the spirit world. But when Ulichagi asked if the films should be seen or not, there was a murmur of consent.

I stood behind the set and watched the faces as the 1974 film began. Once again, there were the minutes of incredulous attention. I spotted a teenage boy kneeling beside Darchu, his eyes lit with astonishment. A woman passing by along the forest track looked in a state of shock. A girl tugged at her cut lip, bemused and disbelieving.

As with yesterday's audience, it was the domestic detail that started the buzz of conversation. And just as before, people were soon pointing and chattering as they identified friends. Ulikoro's teenage snack from his cow brought the house down. When we moved on to 'The Kwegu', so again did Darchu's family meal; he laughed and hid his head in his hands. The penalties of stardom were coming early to Mursi country.

I retreated into the forest for another photograph, framing the cathedral of trees arching over the clearing and the crowd clustered round the glowing box. It was an extraordinary image, somehow embracing my experience of this place. From here, all our weeks and miles, and all the thrills and mishaps were reduced to a bright dot in the greenery.

The Kwegu canoe was launched once again to end the second film and the strange matinée was over. I jabbed the button and the screen died. People stood around for a while, reluctant to leave it seemed.

Turton reported a couple of reactions. One man said, 'What's the point of it? I can't eat it or tie my bull up with it.' Another was more encouraging. 'It's good,' he said, 'because now that our lives are changing, we could use this to teach our children about our history and our traditions.'

On the way back to camp, I took a photograph of Darchu walking through the bush, rifle on one shoulder, television set on the other.

Miradowa marched towards us, chest-deep in his flourishing sorghum. He looked understandably smug. Two weeks after his ritual to drive out the army worm, there was no sign of the things. We filmed as he sucked complacently on a twig.

'Can you see any?' Miradowa asked. 'They were everywhere. When we were here making that fire, we collected masses of worms didn't we? Are there any here now? Where d'you think they've gone?'

'Maybe they went by themselves,' Turton suggested.

'By themselves?' Miradowa smiled pityingly. 'That's what you say.'

It was one of the oddest evenings I can remember. For three hours, as the insects seethed around us, we screened a bizarre triple bill for our helpers.

First, there was that heartbreaking documentary made by Mohammed Idris about Ethiopian famine relief. Watching the appalling images of starvation and death, the Mursi fell silent. They had heard rumours, Turton reported, of a terrible famine somewhere beyond the limits of their country. Seeing the reality now of those living corpses and hearing the cries of starving children seemed somehow to represent for our little audience a shocking confirmation of that government message the ex-soldier Ulikuri had brought home from the wars: 'We are all one country now.'

It came to me that we were offering the Mursi their first television window on the outside world. It was also a first taste of that remorseless diet of information about other people's catastrophes which is so familiar to those of us who live in the world tuned to television. Like the Mursi, we'd had our first sight of the famine which was devastating Ethiopia via television.

233

But for this audience, the suffering they were witnessing was as real as hunger. There was no escape to another channel or the consolations of distance and compassionate detachment.

Darchu commented that the only people who were starving in the world seemed to be the ones with cattle. Seeing a vast refugee camp with hundreds of emergency tents, someone asked if that was London.

Our other offerings were less disturbing. Blakeley had brought a documentary about the Manchester Ship Canal 'to show people a bit about where we come from.' People looked unimpressed. I enjoyed especially the sight of Darchu the canoe expert gazing at a grotty barge as it ploughed through the unspeakable waters of industrial Lancashire.

Finally, impossibly, the crew had brought a documentary about a Wembley Cup Final between Liverpool and Everton. The Mursi watched in obvious perplexity this vision of a place jammed with singing, drunken men in red and blue striped hats, interspersed with other men chasing a white ball.

It made me wonder all over again whether we had any idea of what was really going on in Mursi lives if my own culture could appear so impossibly exotic through their eyes. I remembered what Turton had said a couple of days earlier. 'The longer I go on coming back here, the less sure I am that I understand what's happening.'

The Mursi laughed gleefully as another player was felled by a sliding tackle. Looking at a pubful of Scousers singing "Ere we go, 'ere we go, 'ere we go,' Ulikoro asked where all the cows were in London.

Giant insects crawled across the bright screen, obscuring the strange rituals of the coloured scarves and the pints of beer.

9

I decided to allow myself new bootlaces for the Brideshead dinner. We'd been planning the dotty occasion for days, a farewell banquet modelled on memories of those glittering gatherings in Granada's 'Brideshead Revisited', candle light and silver and brilliant conversation flickering between elegantly attired diners. Well, we tried.

Mike had provided the candelabra, a twig nailed to another twig with three emergency candles stuck in a row. But I couldn't help wondering if Wason had gone over the top with the cardboard bow-ties for everyone including our helpers and his chef's hat made from a bin liner. The cut-up airline napkins were a nice touch, I thought, but the menu was the highlight. Written on a bit of torn carboard box, it was full of wonders.

L'Auberge du Val de Mago

Paté with toast

———

Sardines and celery rolls with
fresh mayonnaise

———

Poulet Ari with rice, mushrooms and onions
in cream sauce 'anthropologist'

———

Surprise

Mints and Dextrosol tablets

Capful of Whisky

Café

The 'surprise' was that there wasn't one.

We took dozens of silly polaroids, and after dinner Turton presented his scarlet snake-gaiters to Arituaholi. He walked off delighted, wearing the gaiters and nothing else.

'Lesalee,' Ulichagi bawled through the doorway of our tent. He'd woken me to ask for a rubber band. It was going to be that sort of day.

Somehow, Turton managed to persuade the scores of bargain-hunters off the site and behind the log we'd dragged across the entrance. By the middle of the day, the familiar shambles of the past month was beginning to resolve into boxes and bags. We pulled down the first canvas awning to find a whole ants' nest inside the pole. The gap brought a curious wrongness into our little universe, a disorder in the shape of things which had anchored our lives.

Wallowing in the river for what I hoped would be the last time, I realised I'd miss the sturdy little Mago which had simply kept us alive during April 1985. A perfect light silvered the water to match my gush of sentiment.

After dinner, Wason and I picked our way to the nightly dance, alongside the place where the helicopter should land tomorrow. The dancers swayed and chanted in the dark, throwing blue shadows under a hot moon. Wason astounded a couple of girls by striking a match to light his pipe. Hands reached out, and voices said 'Lesalee, Lesalee' and I found myself at ease inside it all for a moment. The alarming blur of exoticism that had been my first contact with the Mursi had focussed over the years.

I'd come to know funny Mursi and sour Mursi, boring Mursi and impressive Mursi. And I'd come to understand, perhaps only fully on this latest visit that Turton was of course right: these people weren't living some primitive version of my own life, trapped somehow in a time-warp and offering a glimpse of the Stone Age. Theirs was a complex and coherent alternative existence, still evolving alongside all the other ways of living in the late twentieth century.

Then I realised why the singing sounded oddly familiar tonight. The melody was an eerie replica of that phrase which reached out to the alien space ship at the end of *Close Encounters of The Third Kind*.

In the tent early, I fretted about tomorrow: 'The last of the lasts, the final bag, soaked with sweat, Mogadoned in hope of sleep before tomorrow's uproars. Writing now by a fading yellow torchlight sums up our situation: food almost gone, clothing Mursified, filmstock almost exhausted, time to go home. Now, prayers for a fine tomorrow and a chopper. I don't dare allow the idea of it not happening.'

We were awakened after midnight by a cry in the dark. I realised it must be the poor maimed woman who had crawled into our camp late the previous afternoon. To our horror, we saw that she'd lost a foot, eaten away it seemed by a tropical ulcer. She said she'd crawled on her hands and knees the hour and a half from her settlement. We'd installed the woman in an abandoned hut alongside our camp and given her powerful painkillers. Hearing her cry out now was a wretched confirmation of how little we could do. We raised Turton to give her the mercy of morphine. Soon she was quiet, but I lay awake for a long time.

Before it was fully light, the crew were hauling down their tent and the first claimants had arrived. By breakfast, we had more than fifty visitors. Less than two hours later, our home for the past weeks was stripped to a bare clearing again.

With signal fires burning and our dayglo marker in place,

we waited under a hastily built awning at the landing area. It had been a hectic morning, negotiating the collapse of our whale-sized storage tent and ferrying the dozens of boxes down here. Now Turton sat with a huge pile of hand-outs on the stripped campsite, waiting for the sound of the helicopter before parting with the essentials we'd need if the unthinkable happened and we were stranded.

By midday, I'd decided it was reasonable to be worried. Obviously, there was to be no repeat of the joyously early rescue of 1982, but the prospects of making it back to Addis at all before dark were fading and the skies over the mountains where the helicopter would be coming from looked thunderous. And there seemed no chance now of our relief mission. We'd hoped to persuade the helicopter captain to airlift the Chairman, Bedameri and Ulikuri to the nearest officials in the little town of Jinka so that they could plead for relief grain to compensate for crops destroyed by the army worms. As it became afternoon, the Mursi delegation stood around sadly, considering the days of walking to Jinka. I vented my frustration with the plastic swatter, but the flies seemed contemptuous today.

Two hours later, we were still waiting, and it was raining. Heavy with disappointment, I began to contemplate another night in the Mago valley. The rain passed, and Darchu flipped his sandal to ask the oracle if the helicopter was coming. It said yes, but was vague about when.

On a mockingly lovely evening, we faced reality and began to build a makeshift camp alongside the landing area. It was just after 5 p.m., and at the moment when we'd expected to be luxuriating in the Hilton bar, we were assembling tents and unpacking boxes. Everyone was terribly bright, and sick at heart.

We'd just drawn matchsticks to decide on a rota for all-night guard duty when Darchu said he could hear something. 'I don't believe this,' I said, longing for faith. For endless minutes, we strained to pick up some hint. Then I could see it, and everything went crazy.

The helicopter thrashed over us and circled to check out the landing zone. After that, it was a rush of images. I saw Turton besieged in the middle of a couple of hundred clamouring Mursi, trying to cram some kind of ordered hand-out into seconds. Then the awesome beast was on us, hurling everyone to the grass as it settled. I struggled across for a bawling exchange with the pilot through his open window, stooped under the rotors still slamming over my head.

'You must be quick,' he yelled. 'It's getting dark. We have to overnight in Jinka. I'll take one load now and be back in fifteen minutes for the rest. But you must be ready to go.'

We threw things into the belly and it was gone, plastering us all to the ground again. Somehow, David Woods had gone with it. The light was draining away as we demolished the tents in a delirious panic. Turton was swamped by now, his well-planned distribution collapsed into good-humoured pandemonium.

With the last of the sun, the chopper descended on us again. This time, the gale of its arrival scattered Turton's remaining hand-outs like confetti, pursued by scores of excited Mursi. I struggled to convince the captain that we weren't under siege from the Mursi, but he was really anxious now about beating the darkness over the unmapped mountains. We simply flung the remaining stuff on board, and with the rotors still swishing over us, it felt like one of those scrambled evacuations of a stranded patrol in Vietnam.

Mike filmed the dazed Chinaman as he groped his way through the hatch to join Bedameri and Ulikuri. In the confusion of bodies, I yelled goodbyes to Darchu and Ulikoro and then fell into the helicopter.

Seconds later, we were away, towering up over the Mago, shrinking the Mursi to a litter of tiny white sheets on the grass. It felt even more abrupt than the end of Alaka, flooding me with an impossible mix of regret and relief and joy. Across from me, two of the Mursi pulled on borrowed shirts and trousers. Wason saw a leopard running on a hillside. And then, just seven minutes after leaving the Mago, we were landing and I thought I saw street lights through the window.

We stepped down into a different dimension. On the strip at Jinka there were well-dressed highlanders, uniformed police, an Irish missionary nun and a Landrover. And those really were street lights I'd seen. The Mursi clustered together, looking numbed.

We climbed aboard the Landrover and bumped into the little town. Somebody said we were the first flight to land here in six years and it wasn't hard to believe. Jinka might feel like a metropolis after the Mago valley, but this was still the outer edge of modern Ethiopia and the Morning Star Hotel had a distinctly biblical feel. I wrote by a stub of candle.

'My room's a sort of converted cattle shed with a concrete floor, a worrying-looking double bed and two smashed yellow chairs. Through the hole in the wall that serves as a window, many dogs howl.'

We slumped in the bar of the Morning Star, flattened by too much happening too quickly. On the walls were posters of Finland, and we drank beer off embroidered table cloths with the helicopter crew. Turton returned from finding a place that would accept the Mursi for the night.

In a kind of trance, we walked along dark, rutted streets and across an open space strewn with cowpats. 'They had public executions here until 1970,' Turton said.

Beyond the resting helicopter, watched over now by an armed guard, we came to the Catholic Mission. In the trim bungalow, we were fed on thin biscuits and gin and real coffee by Irish and Tanzanian nuns with the faces of saints. They seemed fascinated by our tales of that other galaxy we'd come from, seven minutes away by helicopter. In the mission bathroom, I turned on a tap and enjoyed the flow of clean water into the wash basin, and I remembered Ulikoro eleven years ago encountering his first bedroom.

Back in my cattle shed at the Morning Star I lay on the troubling bed and decided to try and sleep fully clothed. Tomorrow, it should all be over.

'6.35 a.m. Utterly wasted after a night of endless stunning rain thundering on the tin roof, hours of squalid wakefulness in the uproar, convinced of bedbugs. Now all the cockerels in Ethiopia and a throbbing generator and God knows what in the day.'

Before 8.00 a.m., Turton arrived with the three Mursi and we breakfasted under revolutionary posters on barley grains and black coffee. Afterwards the Mursi stood in the street looking ill at ease, Bedameri transformed in Mohammed's stylish jacket. They knew they were unwelcome visitors in Jinka, watchful of reprisals after recent allegations of Mursi cattle theft.

Mohammed went off to try and find an official who could

discuss grain relief with the Chairman and his delegation. It seemed that the top man was stranded in Arba Minch while Jinka was currently cut off by the collapse of a bridge, swept away in the torrential rainstorms.

Turton introduced me to a pleasant man from the Ethiopian Wild Life Conservation Department who'd been stuck in Jinka for weeks by the floods. David and I had talked a lot over the years about how the plans for Wild Life Conservation and National Parks in the Lower Omo seemed to be in conflict with the Mursi's continued occupation of their own country.

I recalled David's alarming anecdote from the early 70s. He'd met up in Addis with a foreign adviser to the Wildlife Department who had a map on his office wall showing the boundaries of two designated National Parks, the Omo and the Mago. A narrow wedge of territory in between was labelled 'Tama Wildlife Reserve'. Turton had asked the adviser whether he was aware that around 5,000 Mursi were living in this area and if they were excluded from the proposed parks, their basic subsistence would collapse.

'At first he said the area was uninhabited. He'd flown over it plenty of times and seen no "villages". When I'd persuaded him that the Mursi did exist, he said that was OK because the game wardens would need to employ a good deal of local labour.'

David also had a desperate story about how in 1983 at a time of great hunger, he'd heard of a Mursi man forced to parade round the square here in Jinka with buffalo meat slung from his neck because he'd been found by game guards in the Mago valley with a kilo of the dried meat. Afterwards, the man had been taken off to prison with a Mursi woman and two small children. They'd been released after two nights by the administrator responsible for the Mursi who knew how severe the food shortage was in the Mago valley.

I knew how Turton had been angered by incidents like these where the ill-informed demands of conservation took no account of the human inhabitants of the Lower Omo. He was bitterest of all about the possibility that the Mursi might be forced out of their own country to create a park for the entertainment of rich Western tourists, whose own societies, unlike the Mursi, had already plundered and destroyed their natural environment.

David had met compassionate and sensitive Ethiopian officials who were alert to the needs and values of people like the Mursi.

241

For them, the people of the Lower Omo were its chief asset and its most skilful conservationists; and they saw their job as being to introduce vital educaton and health care without destroying that balance or wrecking a way of life.

But with famine raging in Ethiopia, the government was desperately hard-pressed and I wasn't optimistic about prospects for the Chairman's delegation this morning. The worried-looking official in spectacles Mohammed had managed to track down didn't make me feel any more hopeful.

With his boss still stranded by the floods, the man found himself facing three demanding Mursi and a British film crew. He stood nervously in front of our helicopter and listened while the Chairman launched into an articulate and forceful speech, interpreted into the official's Amharic language by Ulikuri.

'Our crop has been finished by the army worm. I've been hit by hunger, so I came here yesterday. If our children die, if they all die, is that good?'

The official listened silently until the Chairman finished with an urgent request for relief grain to be sent. Then he began to speak and I could see the Mursi dejection. I didn't need a translation this time to give me the message. At the end of the official's lengthy response, he shook hands awkwardly with the Mursi and then walked away. Ulikuri turned to me.

'Gara! Ninge!' he said. They were two Mursi words I did know. 'Finished! Nothing!'

The translation only filled in the uncomfortable details. The official insisted that the government had always tried to help the Mursi to leave behind their nomadic lives and settle in one place so that they could receive education and make progress. But then he had hard words for them.

'By refusing to abandon useless customs and by following your cattle's tails, wandering from place to place, you have exposed yourselves to problems. This is because from the beginning, your own behaviour and your way of life and backward customs have burdened you.'

As for the army worm problem, he said they should have reported it earlier and something could have been done. Now, with the roads impassable, there was no way to send relief.

It was a bleak moment to have to say goodbye. Without enough fuel for another landing and take-off in the Mago valley, we could only leave the Mursi delegation to their long walk home. We gave them money and I dashed into the helicopter to retrieve a final pair of trousers for the Chairman. Turton had collected some dried milk from the mission for Ulikuri's undernourished baby.

Then the captain was looking at his watch and it was time to go. We shook hands and the Mursi walked quickly away. Soon, they'd passed into the bush beyond the strip and we couldn't see them any more.

The captain agreed to make a final pass over the Mago Valley before we turned for home. For a few minutes, we circled over a wilderness of unbroken white cloud. There was no evidence of the place we'd known for the past weeks, and no hint of the Mursi.

EPILOGUE

Going Back

David Turton returned to the Mursi and to the Mago Valley
in the summer of 1986. He found a good harvest and prospects of great change.

During the six weeks he was with the migrants, David met
many old friends: Ulichagi, the Priest, Ulikuri, Uligidangi, the
Chairman, Nga Lugu. He saw how they'd cleared new sweeps
of forest to create big new cultivation areas. Standing on a hillside behind the healer's compound, he found himself entirely
surrounded by flourishing sorghum. He heard that the cattle
were gone from Madadari now, driven out by the tsetse challenge. There had been personal tragedies like the death of Ulikuri's young wife and child, shot dead near the river Usno by
raiders from the south. But after the successful harvest with no
sign of the locust plague which had devastated surrounding areas
in Kenya and Sudan, the migrants were more confident and
settled than ever in their new homeland. It was clear that they'd
moved even further from the traditional Mursi ways of mobile
cattle-herding and were more committed than ever to their
new life of settled agriculture.

Turton came with an important visitor. The chief administrator in Arba Minch, responsible for the region including
Mursi country, helicoptered in with David to see for the first
time something of the Mago settlements. It seemed he'd never
been able to find them before, but now they landed at the river
and the official met the Chairman. David found the administrator
compassionate and concerned to improve the migrants' situation

without unnecessarily damaging their way of life. He was impressed that the Mursi had tackled for themselves the crisis of the late 70s through their spontaneous migration and felt that assistance should be focussed on the Mago Valley. A road might soon be made, he said, to connect the Mago with Jinka; he talked about plans for a school and a medical centre.

David also talked to the new game warden for the Mago National Park. He found an encouraging flexibility about the boundaries of wildlife reserves and a recognition that the Mursi should have space to live. The talk of forced removal and resettlement in the highlands seemed to have faded.

The missionaries were in evidence again. After ten years of withdrawal while the Ethiopian revolution gathered force, the Society of International Missionaries were in the area with their roadbuilding and medical outposts and helicopters. Their bibles were less welcome. The government were insisting there should be no preaching or seeking for converts and the focus now was supposed to be on development. Turton tried to talk to the Mursi about the missionaries and their motives, but they were puzzled by the notion of a man who was also a god. They expected that the missionaries would be like other white men, like anthropologists and film-makers, and they wouldn't be giving something for nothing. But they decided that men with helicopters should be rich and the prospect of a medical centre in Mursi country seemed a good bargain for a few strange ideas.

I asked David what he thought the Mursi made now of those three uninvited invasions by the white men with their pointless toys.

'Well, in a way the coming of the film crews has simply confirmed the Mursi's confidence in their own importance. It seems only right to them that powerful people should come from far away to see how they live.'

And it appeared our return visits had been absorbed with the same self-assurance. 'The Mursi like things that recur and become part of a pattern, and the returning of the film team is seen now as an assurance of continuity and rightness.'

At the same time, Turton had the impression that our expeditions had carried a disturbing message. The proud and unconquered Mursi had been compelled to recognise that they might not, after all, be the centre of the world. The white men were awkward and unskilled in all the things that a man should know, but they had very powerful machines like the boxes that allowed them to talk over great distances and they could summon helicopters from the sky. The evidence of unimaginable resources and technologies which we brought with us had inevitably forced the Mursi to review the way they saw themselves.

Turton's news of plans for roads and schools and medical centres was startling. I was also suprised by the ambivalence of my own reaction. If my time with the Mursi has taught me anything, it's been a brisk and sustained lesson in the irrelevance of false sentiment or utopian illusions about noble savagery. I'd learned early that these people would be unimpressed by our post-industrial nostalgia for some soft-edged vision of the simple life. If they felt a six lane expressway through Mursi country would give them a better and easier existence, I had no doubt they'd welcome it. There was, after all, no reason why they should preserve their isolated purity to sustain a private theme-park of unchanging Africa for a visiting television team. I had abundant evidence of how desperately the Mursi needed medical help and I knew that many of them were enthusiastic about the idea of a school. And yet and yet . . .

I've seen too many dismaying precedents, I suppose, for what can happen when an isolated people collide with a more powerful and aggressive culture. Our 'Disappearing World' experience in South America is haunted by the traumatised faces of Indians, after the road has sliced into their part of the rain forest, reducing them to the condition of tramps in the gutters of some squalid frontier town.

I recall a book I was reading at Alaka during the second expedition. It was a devastating account of the results of well-intentioned development and its central theme was: 'When we leave Africa alone, it works.' For a world shrunk by tourism and television and power-politics, I fancy that too is becoming a kind of utopian impossibility. And at least Turton's reports of those official plans sound hopeful. But as I confront that picture of Darchu at home each day, I wonder how it will be for him and for the rest of them.

Of course my encounters with the Mursi have inescapably been part of that process of change and changing expectations. And Turton tells me the Mursi have words for television now: 'Korkoroi wey zuo' – 'the tin box with people moving.'

They asked when I'd be back.

BODI
HANA
River Hana
River Gura
PLAIN OF DEATH
MARA
RIVER OMO
ALAKA
MURSI
RABWI
MOIZOI
MADO
River Mago
RIVER OMO
RIVER OMO